UP THE DOWN

The long business of auditioning began. I had not appreciated how long the process would take, and after I had survived the first round had to decide whether to accept an offer I had received to do a play which might or might not end up in the West End, or to abandon it and carry on with the auditions for *That's Life!* Mercifully I opted for the latter – another of my few good decisions – and began the protracted business of turning up for auditions, interviews and what were called 'observed working sessions', where you were handed a letter from the public and asked to produce an item by the end of the day. My main competition appeared to come from a young man called Simon Bates, and I realized that I lacked the confidence which broadcasting as a disc-jockey had given him. My worst fears were confirmed when, the next day, I got a call from Esther. 'Evil news, I'm afraid,' she said. My heart sank. But it was her little joke. 'If you accept our offer, you'll be working with me for the next few months.'

About the author

Glyn Worsnip was born in 1938 in Highnam, Gloucestershire. He was educated at Monmouth School and St John's College, Oxford. He and his wife now live with their daughter in Glyn's home county, Gloucestershire.

Up the Down Escalator

Glyn Worsnip

CORONET BOOKS
Hodder and Stoughton

For Jo,
to whom I once did not give enough
but of whom I now demand too much.
Her energy, loyalty and determination
have brought us this far.

And for Ellie, who did not deserve any of this.

Copyright © Glyn Worsnip 1990

First published in Great Britain in 1990 by Michael Joseph Ltd

Coronet edition 1991

The right of Glyn Worsnip to be identified as the author of this work has been asserted by him in accordance with the Copyright, Designs and Patents Act 1988.

British Library C.I.P.

Worsnip, Glyn
  Up the down escalator.
  I. Title
  920

  ISBN 0-340-53890-2

Printed and bound in Great Britain for Hodder and Stoughton Paperbacks, a division of Hodder and Stoughton Ltd, Mill Road, Dunton Green, Sevenoaks, Kent TN13 2YA. (Editorial Office: 47 Bedford Square, London WC1B 3DP) by Clays Ltd, St Ives plc.

Contents

I'm told that when I was a little boy aged two or three, I startled my parents by rolling down an up escalator. In adult life I attempted the reverse, figuratively speaking. I almost made it, but then illness dragged me inexorably to the bottom again. This is the story of that journey. It is no fairy-tale.

Acknowledgements

To my friends Libby Spurrier and Sally Hardcastle who persuaded, nay cajoled, me into writing this book and who looked after me while I did so; to Angela and Johnnie Williams, who first wheeled me in a chair; to Dr Anita Harding and all the staff at the National Hospital, Queen Square in London: they did what they could; to Sharon Banoff (*Soundtrack*) and Claire Walmesley (*Horizon*), two fine producers; and to Jenny Dereham, the most sympathetic of editors, who drew the shortest straw.

Prologue

I had known fear, of course. When the blades of the helicopter had edged closer and closer to the cliffs while we achieved some seemingly impossible rescue; when the television cameras rolled prior to some ill-prepared live item; when at the age of seven I toppled out of a tree and impaled myself on an iron spike; when summoned to appear before a sixteen-person committee of the House of Lords to justify filming them for the first time in their natural habitat; yes, I had known fear. But never like this. Always before it had been a matter of enduring the ordeal until it was over and preparing to laugh about it, boast about it, or dramatise it. This time I knew it would never be over; that I would live with fear for the rest of my life.

What brought on that first moment of real fear was a week's stay at the National Hospital For Nervous Diseases in London. Towards the end of August 1987 I had gone there for tests.

As I had slowly undressed I had been watching the other patients. One – a man younger than myself – was bent double and could only just propel himself down the ward. He had equal difficulty making himself understood. Another did not say a word but lay still in bed, and I never discovered whether he heard the occasional and inconsequential chat of his long-suffering visitors. A third tottered about the ward, his speed and movement changing from moment to moment as nature and drugs affected him. A fourth, clearly the ward 'character', was a distorted and contorted wreck of a body, who lived in a wheelchair and derived most pleasure from touching up, and perpetrating ruderies of one sort and another to, the female staff. He could only grunt, and communicated with a small computer on the arm of his wheelchair, with which he tapped out messages.

It was a shock to be in such company, and it put an end to any lingering complacency. Was this my future, staring me in the face? Was this how I would end up? I even started to work out which kind of wheelchair I would prefer.

It had been a good summer, with plenty of work. Perhaps I had relied too heavily on the old theatrical maxim, 'It'll be all right on the night.' But I had found things increasingly difficult to cope with in my private life. When in May I went out for a meal with my friend Rona Christie, not only did I have difficulty writing the cheque – physically, that is – but I had to be supported back to the car. Not drunk, but incapable. It was obvious that a small amount of alcohol had an effect out of all proportion to its size. One evening, tottering across Ealing Common, Rona did what Jo my wife had been doing for some time – she begged me to get a second opinion. She had already mentioned the symptoms (without naming the patient) to Dick Smith, the jovial BBC *Breakfast Time* doctor, who also worked for the *British Medical Journal*. Eventually I rang him, confessed that it was I Rona had spoken of, and accepted his offer of help. He put me in touch with Dr Anita Harding at the National Hospital. She was efficient, neat, personable and about fifteen to twenty years younger than me.

Dr Harding knows as much as anyone about how the cerebellum (the smaller part of the brain) works. Yet even she admits that little is known. She confirmed that what for so long I had been pretending was happening to someone else, was truly happening to me.

'What you've got,' she said, in her matter of fact way, 'is a problem with the cerebellum, which is the balance part of the brain. It operates as a fine-tuner, if you like. It stops you from swaying from side to side. It stops your arm from knocking something over when you reach out for it. This "premature death" of parts of the nervous system, in your case confined to the balance system and the speech, is what we think the problem is.'

'We think!' How could she be sure?

'The same way really that we diagnose any problem in the nervous system. It's a question of weighing up the symptoms. We look at your eyes, get you to touch fingers and noses, hop on one leg and see how you coordinate arms and legs . . .'

It seemed simple enough. But I was to discover that the exact number of people suffering from cerebellar ataxia was not known; that there was no support group; that there was no known cause, no treatment, and no known cure. Nevertheless, although Dr Harding confirmed the diagnosis, she felt that it ought to be possible to do a little more for me than nothing. Hence the visit to the National.

Later, I discovered that my fellow patients did not have cerebellar ataxia, but were a handful of the 1.5 million who at any one time have one of the brain/nerve/muscle-related diseases: muscular dystrophy, motor neurone disease, Parkinson's, stroke, multiple sclerosis, myasthenia gravis, the list is endless. It seems harsh to say so, but the knowledge that, although I might end up in a wheelchair I was unlikely to finish my days as a contorted cabbage, did a little to cheer me up.

CHAPTER 1

Childhood

I bumped along the track towards our cottage. It was a mellow evening, still bright after a warm spring day. The sky was a deep blue. The last of the bluebells nestled at the feet of the banks of fresh cow-parsley which had to be brushed aside to let me in. There were still a few white wood anemones winking their greeting from below. Soon the purple foxglove would be towering over them all. A hare dashed into my path, stopped, turned and cantered away through the hedge and across the field. A charm of chaffinches and a pair of yellowhammers swooped along inches in front of my bonnet, as if leading the way. I stopped the car, tired, but glad to be home. I gazed out over the Wye valley. Through a gap in the hills a little bit of the Severn estuary was visible, glistening at me from a distance. I turned off the car engine and sat for a moment listening to that special mixture of silence and sound you get in the country – a distant dog barking, a tractor, a chain-saw somewhere, I spotted Ellie's pony munching contentedly. The sheep too seemed serene. They were dotted across the fields – brown, black and white, a mixture of pure Manx Loghtans and cross-breeds. Meadow, woodland and hills were spread before me in a pattern of what Jo liked to call 'screens', each a different version of green, each merging into the other like a Japanese print. And yet it was so very English, a part of the country which stands apart, 800 feet up, in the forgotten part of Gloucestershire west of the Severn, edging closely towards Wales and the Wye. I thought for the thousandth time how lucky I had been, despite having spent everything and more, to have made my home here, in an idealized version of the Gloucestershire of my childhood.

Nothing better expressed the 'half-way house' position I have always felt about my life – the mixture of hope and uncertainty, the feeling that, although there is more to be achieved,

4

self-doubt will prevent my being the one who will achieve it — than 'Calton Lees', Highnam, a few miles north-west of Gloucester. That is where I was born. My ageing parents, now over eighty, still live there, although the village has changed and the house, originally named after a favourite spot in Derbyshire, is now a number in a street. It was built in the 1930s, a modern house on a modern estate in an ancient village, and my parents have been its only occupants. In those days it was one of a small spattering of houses built by someone who clearly foresaw that Highnam would one day be a dormitory village for Gloucester. It was in the days before smart folk and incomers took to gentrifying the cottages that had been there for centuries. Not that my parents would have had the money anyway, even if they had had the inclination. My mother, at least, thought the newly built two-and-a-half up, two down, would be an excellent half-way house until my father moved on, or up. He never did. But not due to lack of ability.

From somewhere, my paternal grandmother's children acquired a conspicuous talent for things artistic. My father could certainly draw and paint, and to this day does the most marvellous woodcarvings of animals and birds. His twin sister, too (they claimed to have been so small at birth that they could both be fitted in a three pint jug) was an artist but, unlike my cousin Juliet, I never had the fortune to inherit these abilities. We used to joke that I was world-famous as a child because a portrait of me Juliet had painted had toured the world in an art exhibition. There were other characteristics I somehow failed to inherit: not only can I not draw or carve, but my teeth are full of fillings (my father still has only one filling, and that was done in the war by mistake).

When, after the war, my father entered a national competition to design a whole town, he defeated many firms of architects to win second prize. The entire house was covered in paint and papers, and I got the impression that my mother regarded the whole thing as a waste of time, as well as an inconvenience. Inconvenient it may have been, but waste of time it certainly was not, and I remember being very proud of him. Even then he did not believe in himself enough to leave off being a local government employee, and he remained a Town and Country

Planner all his life. His natural caution (which I think I must have inherited) sometimes went a little too far. A colleague of his once told me that if the boss rang through on the telephone, my father would stand up to take the call!

But lovers of the Cotswolds can be pleased that he looked after their area, and resisted all attempts to build red-brick houses in the middle of Bourton-on-the-Water. He was a stickler for rectitude of some sorts, and always returned even a bottle of sherry sent to him at Christmas by a local builder. Which was why I was so angry when, in a rare moment of fame, he was accused in a *Private Eye* story of taking bribes. His other moment of fame was when the *Guardian* (Manchester, not Dean Forest) ran a story about a rumpus in the Cotswolds due to my father allowing the building of a house in the modern manner. As usual the complainants were incomers to the area, but my father stuck to his view that, as the building could not be seen from any path, road, or house, the owner could have it designed how he pleased.

I will not say he never himself designed anything of import-ance, because the combined public lavatory and bus shelter at Northleach stands as a memorial to his worth. It was opened by local dignitaries in Clochmerlian manner and has brought a good deal of relief to the town, as well as a fair degree of trade to its shopkeepers from passing charabancs.

My mother is very different. If ever the rule which governs the attraction of opposites applied, it did so when my parents met. My father must have been a good-looking young man, and appears to have attracted a variety of admirers. When they first met, my father was in digs in Bakewell. He was courting a more passive, submissive girl. 'Which one is it this weekend,' asked his landlord, 'the lion or the lamb?' I am glad to say he chose the lion.

Although she is a little more bent now in old age, my mother was tall (5ft 8in) and was going grey by the time she was thirty. Born Molly Upton, she was the daughter of a thrice-married out-of-work London cinema pianist or singer. (He was sixty-five when she first met him. Memories are dim.) She was a deter-mined woman with a fierce sense of values and what appeared to be a self-taught code of social mores. I always had the feeling that she was ashamed of her family and was determined to fight her way to a secure position in society, with a decent education and a fixed sense of values. She was liberally inclined, but it sometimes seemed that her liberalism was a triumph of head over heart. She often shocked us with her outspokenness. She would refer to someone, for example, as 'a Glasgow Jewess', which we found embarrassing and intolerable, yet, as far as I am aware, she had never been bitten by a Scotsman nor yet a Jew. It was a childhood fantasy, wrong of course, that she had been with a group that helped smuggle Jews out of Germany before the Second World War. I remember too an occasion on which she claimed that all shop stewards and union trouble-makers were Celts, called Jones or McGahey. (The Robinsons and the Scanlons she ignored.) She was absurdly anti-Welsh, so I often wondered how she allowed me to be called Glyn; it was, in fact, after the Glyn (valley) Ceiriog in North Wales, where my father spent nearly sixty consecutive annual holidays. The thought of him imposing his will on her seemed, by the time I was old enough to notice these things, inconceivable.

Her streak of intolerance is tempered with a great sense of justice. She tells with delight the story of how she went into a Gloucester greengrocer to buy some pears. On the way out she had a sudden thought. 'Excuse me,' she asked, 'but are these pears South African?' The assistant confirmed that it was so. 'Then I'm sorry,' said my mother, 'but I'd rather not have them.' 'Quite right,' said the assistant, 'I quite agree with you. They might have been handled by blacks!'

Mother had been at school at Sydenham and later joined the Civil Service, working for the Ministry of Health. It was the great age of self-education, and she got a place in evening classes at the London School of Economics. One of the lecturers would occasionally take his classes out to concerts, and it is a measure of her proud nature that when someone suggested that she was the reason for this extra-mural conscientiousness, she walked out and never went back.

My parents met, as did all romantic young folk at the time, at a tennis club, in London, but they were married in Bakewell, Derbyshire, since my father was then working in Sheffield. The wedding night was not so romantic. My father spent it alone, at the cinema. My mother had Civil Service exams the next day and had left for London on the train.

When I was born, in 1938, Europe was rumbling towards war. In fact my father was old enough not to be called up for a year or two, and he spent a period with a very rural Home Guard. I have always cherished a story he told me of how this rustic outfit managed to defeat a crack detachment of the Coldstream Guards, who were marching across country giving practice to anyone in their path. They were of course undefeated, and when they got to Gloucester they very quickly mopped up the first two lots of opposition. To deal with the third, Highnam Home Guard, they settled for a flanking movement which involved most of them creeping concealed along the banks of the River Severn. Regrettably their Intelligence Officer had not warned them about the famous Severn Bore, the tidal wave several feet high which rushes upstream at certain times of year and at considerable speed. It chose that moment to do so, and a cheery bunch of the Highnam Home Guard were able to rush down, drag out a dishevelled band of waterlogged Guardsmen and claim victory.

Later my father joined the RAF, so my first memories are of a home life with only my mother there. To me she was strong, supportive, determined, handsome and boundlessly energetic. I suppose it was natural that I should be a 'mother's boy'. I remember her rushing around the garage to tell me she had acquired a banana. It was a brown sticky thing, 'dried' and shaped like a cigar. It was delicious, and I remember when the war was over, and real bananas came back, being ne'er so disappointed. I remember, too, accompanying her to potato picking (we all lent a hand) and to knitting parties where, scrubbed clean and shiny shoed, I would demonstrate my prowess at stretching out my arms to hold a skein of wool while one of the ladies of the village wound up a ball from it. I appear to have been a popular little boy and, although I could never have dreamed I would end up in broadcasting, I was already relishing my public appearances.

When my brother Hugh was born, in 1943, I suppose I was reluctant to share my mother with him, and later as a child I nurtured the fantasy that this very different second son – he was blond, I was dark – was the result of some illicit liaison. Of such fantasies is childhood made.

As luck would have it, the only other boy of my age on the new estate, Malcolm Selway, lived next door, and there quickly developed a well-worn path through a gap in the fence. We were archetypal little boys from families as depicted in the *Radio Times*: a suburban house, a small garden, a *Just William* existence, (though we did not get into scrapes quite so often). We were gregarious and exploratory. There was no crime, no drugs, no danger, and even the war was something that happened elsewhere. The only time a bomb dropped on Highnam was when a German plane, limping home from the South Wales docks, jettisoned its cargo over our woods.

The countryside started at the bottom of our garden. Elm trees (which still existed then) were to be climbed, conker trees to be ravaged and, if we were lucky enough to be invited home by a farm boy, hay lofts to be transformed into dens. We shared open air fried eggs (heaven knows where they got them) with Heinz and Fritz, two German prisoners of war who worked around the estate and were not best pleased with Hitler; we helped Mrs Connolly make cakes; Miss Gunston combined duties as village postman and Father Christmas; and the nearest thing to drama was when Malcolm fell off a wall and broke a leg. And of course in our spare time we listened to the wireless.

I had no inkling that I would ever meet some of the names which looked so glamorous in the *Radio Times*. If anyone had told me I would work with Dick Barton, Special Agent, take the stage with his henchman, Jock, share a microphone with Paul Temple's Steve, or welcome the impersonator Henry Bones to my own chat show, I would have said they were mad. I had no ambition to appear on the wireless, and there was no television in my childhood. I was as conventional as a bar of plain soap.

I do, however, recall one fleeting moment of envy. There was a picture in the *Radio Times* of the smart little boy who played the title role in a very BBC and public school series called *Jennings*. He was about my age and his name was Glyn Dearman (the child actor is now a distinguished BBC drama producer). For years I cherished the thought that it was after all possible for a child called Glyn to be on the wireless. Up until that moment, I had assumed that there was no-one else – certainly no-one of note – called Glyn, and that this name, as opposed to something more conventionally English, was a permanent bar to advancement.

Malcolm did not go to the village school; he went to a posher school in Gloucester. So I was the only ambassador from 'the new estate'. It was at school that I first learned about the British preoccupation with class. I was treated with suspicion by the rest of the school: I had clean shoes and pressed trousers; I spoke differently. I soon learnt the error of my ways. It was not long before I bullied my mother into providing me with a pair of boots so that I could be like the other boys, and not much later that my parents discovered I had one accent for speaking at home and quite another, broad Gloucestershire, for speaking to my schoolmates. I myself was entirely unaware of any difference. It was the first occasion on which a natural talent for mimicry made itself obvious or useful.

Which accent I used for public appearances, when both my mother and my schoolmates were present, is not clear. I can remember to this day, however, the first lines I spoke on a public stage. It was in the village hall, just across the way from the school, and we were representing the seven ages of man. I must have been very young, for I was the last in line and was playing the baby. The lines were brief:

'Baby says "a goo, a goo,
I like bread an' milk, I do."'

I cannot report that I was struck by an immediate desire to make a career of public performance, and my second appearance was more likely to have put me off than to have encouraged any such thoughts. It was again in the village hall (in those days it rejoiced in the name, now abandoned, of 'Council House') and this time the worthies of the village were present. I was playing an owl, and my mother had laboured long and hard to provide me with a suitable mask. It was a triumph, and it was very clear what I was meant to be. Unfortunately, either my mother had forgotten to put any eye-holes in or I was not wearing it properly, for I made a spectacular entrance and exit at one and the same time. I walked, blind, on to the front of the stage, and immediately over the edge into the audience. I took, as they say, no further part in the proceedings. It had been a brief moment of glory and, although it may have revealed a penchant for exhibitionism, did nothing to encourage any desire for a career on the stage.

It seemed a conventional upbringing, and yet in many ways I suppose it was not. My parents did not go to church or vote Conservative. My mother never joined the Women's Institute or the Mothers' Union. My father was demobbed along with everyone else and went back to his job as a town planner. I was never given Beatrix Potter to read, or *Winnie the Pooh*, or *The Wind In The Willows*. Instead I would retire to my tent in the garden and read about Danny of the Dazzlers, Rockfist Rogan (a sort of poor man's Biggles) and Colwyn Dane the Ace 'tec in a comic called *The Champion*, lent by some farm labourer's children I knew and smuggled in. I wanted more than anything else to be accepted by the local community, and touched my forelock to the vicar and the squire with the best of them.

In 1948 three significant events occurred: my brother Patrick (the brains of the family) was born; I went away to boarding school; and the Australian cricket team toured England. I had already become a cricket lover. My mother had regularly taken me to Cheltenham to watch Gloucestershire play, and I had seen the great Wally Hammond. During my last summer at the village school, I had been given a special dispensation to rush home in the lunch hour and listen to the test match commentary, and it was then that I first became aware of how the magic of a single voice at the microphone could enthral millions. The commentator was, of course, John Arlott, and I would wait with some impatience for his turn at the mike. Then, somehow everything took on a deeper significance and he was no longer just describing a cricket match. 'What was the name of that man,' a girlfriend asked much later, 'whose voice sounds like summer?' I knew instantly whom she meant. And then there were the jokes. 'Here come Toshak, bowling to Washbrook; or is it Toshbrook bowling to Washack?' And the *risqué*, subtly stated: as a man doubled up in pain, having been struck between the legs, 'Oh dear, dear, what a place to get hit in your testimonial year!' I was not fully aware of it then, but I had learnt that the best broadcasting is personal, confidential and idiosyncratic.

Patrick was just over ten years younger than me. I was away at school by the time he was born. If I was the prototype, he was the finished article. He too is tall, thin and gangly; he too boarded at Monmouth School; he too went to Oxford – but with more conspicuous success at both. He won the Senior Classical Scholarship of his year, at the college which had turned me down. Unlike me, he did not become a jack of all trades, master of none, never sure at which to concentrate. He went to Oxford determined to be editor of the University magazine, *Isis*, and he was. He took a First in Honour Moderations (Classics) and then determined to finish his degree in Russian and Italian, neither of which language he spoke. He took Firsts in both. Today he is Diplomatic Correspondent for Reuters, the worldwide news agency, jet-setting around the world, from Reykjavik to Rome; yet to Hugh and me he still looks like the school swot, the helpless baby we used to dandle and call Patty Podgkin because he was so fat.

Hugh was the odd one out, yet in his own way is the most admirable of the three. He never went to Monmouth; he never went to university; he disappointed my parents by not taking a safe job in the Weights and Measures Department. Instead, as a youngster, he drove a tractor by day and by night played music, first skiffle, then rock 'n' roll. The band, Tony and the Beatniks, were local celebrities and played with Eric Clapton, Manfred Mann and The Hollies. They retired and made the headlines, saying they were too old at twenty-one, and Hugh rang up the local paper asking for a job as a cub reporter. He got it, and one of his first jobs was covering events at the Gloucester Hippodrome. A group who were bottom of the bill asked him for a mention. They were called The Beatles. They subsequently became quite famous.

I was just ten when I went away to school. I took a trunk, with my name and initials painted on it by my father, a tuck-box and sufficient changes of underwear. We piled into the old Morris 8 and puttered off to Monmouth. It would technically have been possible to be a day boy. The school was only twenty-five miles away, but the travelling would have meant getting up absurdly early and four hours a day on a bus. It was decided I should be a boarder. I was thrilled. I was going to the sort of school I had read about in comics and books. There would be house matches and heroism, rags in the dorm, enduring friendships, japes, cricket and eccentric schoolmasters. It would be a glorious combination of *Goodbye, Mr Chips*, *Greyfriars*, and *The Fifth Form at St Dominics*. As it turned out, there were elements of all those but more besides, not all of it attractive. The balmy days were over.

My education had been a matter of some debate between my parents. My father, ever cautious, had been quite content that I should go to the local county grammar school. My mother, ever ambitious for her children, had found that the cheapest school in the public school yearbook happened to be twenty-five miles away and determined that, with the aid of an available county grant, I should go there. She won the day, I passed the entrance exam and was enrolled in the School House, one of the two boarding houses at Monmouth School. In order to meet the boarding fees, my mother was rigorous in her economies, never went out or spent money on herself, and I shall always be grateful for her determination and her sacrifices. If the Worsnip brothers owe anything, and we owe a great deal, then we owe it to her. She never spent a penny on herself until Patrick was through university, and even after that, particularly after my illness, was especially generous.

''Im did go to college,' said one of the women in the village, by which she meant I had gone on to secondary education, a rare enough achievement. The village was more used to its sons leaving school at thirteen and going straight to work on the land.

It did not work out quite as I had thought, and I had my first lessons in disappointment. I could not wait for my parents to drive away on my first day, but subconsciously I must have been suffering from homesickness, or fear, or both, because almost immediately I took to bed-wetting and suffered humiliation at the hands of my school-fellows because I could not conceal the rubber sheet I had to have, or the embarrassing walk down the dormitory late at night when Matron came in to remind me to relieve myself.

Monmouth School was all that I could have aspired to, but in those post-war days, when it was doing what it could to better itself, there was still an element of the second-rate about it. The list of distinguished 'old boys' was somewhat brief. It was headed by that great Liberal politician and author, Frank Owen (of whom few of us, if any, had heard). It was only after someone noticed that Lord Ezra had been, as Sir Derek Ezra, Chairman of the Coal Board, that much was later made of him. Less was made of Victor Spinnetti, the comic actor, and nothing at all of John Vassal, the spy. After my time Monmouth, which had always excelled at sport, produced Keith Jarret, who scored nineteen points on his first appearance in the Welsh XV at the age of eighteen, and the smallest Minister of Sport on record, the Hon. Colin Moynihan.

The headmaster, who later became Vicar of Stiffkey, used to refer to wrong-doers as 'cads and rotters' and would mutter about 'lack of moral fibre'. There were among the pupils a fair proportion of late comers who had, for one reason or another, been required to leave more distinguished establishments. Among the staff were several who never ceased to remind us that they had taught at schools with names more famous than our own – 'When I was at Blundells . . .' – and, in the days when schoolmastering was still an eccentric's sport, some who would not have been out of place in an Evelyn Waugh novel. There was Mr Evill, our assistant housemaster, whose main pleasure seemed to be taking large amounts of money from boys at the pocket-sized billiard table in the library; Mr Bucknall, who had a nasty habit of picking boys up by the hair above their ears; Mr Purser, whose idea of a fitting punishment for two boys was to place them at opposite ends of the room, bent double, and ask them to charge at each other until their heads crashed in the middle; and 'Foolish Otto', a Polish expatriate art master who was notoriously bad at class discipline and whom pupils would taunt by humming in crescendo through tight lips until the noise was unbearable. This would drive him to distraction and he would charge around the room yelling, in a Polish accent, 'no seenging!' But he could never punish anyone because he could never detect anyone with their mouth open.

I threw myself wholeheartedly into an attempt to be popular, successful and conformist, but never quite made it. I was no longer the star pupil, as I had been at Highnam. For one thing I was a year younger than my form-mates. I was invariably twenty-ninth out of thirty-one in class and had to struggle to keep in the A-stream. My reports were full of 'could do better'. I was much smaller, almost a mascot, and when the older boys took to creeping out at night and meeting girls, I was there, but invariably confined to duties such as keeping 'cave'.

I had my moments. I surprised everybody by coming back first of my house in the junior cross-country. I won my weight at under 5st 7lb in boxing, and two or three years later defeated the dangerous 'Sharky' Bartlett at under 8st 7lb. When I received my house boxing colours that night I felt, at last, part of the team.

I was not. Winning one's weight was all very well, but surviving against bigger and more brutal opposition was more difficult. For many years I was bullied and beaten up by older boys. Looking back on it, the scenario is almost laughably like that of a bad Western. The clock would strike the appropriate hour; the villains would appear in the doorway; my 'friends' would melt into the background, or mysteriously and suddenly find something to do elsewhere, and the one-sided contest would begin. The reason was commonplace enough in schools of that sort. As a youngster I was conventionally pretty, but not ready to substitute for the female sex in accommodating the older boys' awakening sexuality. I had no objection to 'goings on' in principle, but found them distasteful and unpleasant in person. Participation was regarded as a duty of the younger, better-looking boys, like 'fagging', and refusal was seen as disloyalty. In these circumstances I quickly learnt that the spoken word can be more effective than the fist, and took my bruises in the knowledge that I had given as good as I had got, if only verbally. It was a hard lesson, but a good and useful one for someone who would later earn his living as a wordsmith.

My size and youth set me apart from my contemporaries, and so did some of my successes. I discovered early on that I could sing, which led me to the school choir. I had one of those treble voices which slowly sank rather than broke, so I had a long career in the front row of the choir-stalls. Every now and then I would be dragged out, polished up, dressed in a blue cassock and placed in front of the altar to render 'I know that my redeemer liveth', or some other such solo. Since this was met with remarks from the ladies of the parish such as, 'He so obviously means it,' I decided that acting was another of my abilities.

This was confirmed when I took part in the annual Gilbert and Sullivan, which was invariably organised by my house-master, one 'Scratch' Hatton, so-called because of an embarrassing habit he had which was not all to do with hoisting up his trousers. He was an all-rounder – an ex-soldier, a stalwart of the school choir, a sportsman (at cricket he was something of a tonker, an all-or-nothing man) and a naturalist of some note, with a huge collection of butterflies (dead) which we were allowed to gaze at on special occasions. He was another who would remind us that he had seen better things: 'When I was at Cranleigh . . .' He, too, was prone to the odd eccentricity. He would bang on the table during prep and ask, 'Is that YOU talking . . . somebody?' If only 'somebody' had owned up! But he was a fair man, and encouraging.

He would always play the leading male role in the Gilbert and Sullivan, and I would take the soubrette. This was thought to be appropriate because, one year during *The Yeomen of the Guard*, in which I was playing Phoebe, I had suddenly taken it into my head to depart from the script and, during my song to the jailor, 'Were I thy bride', entertained the audience and startled the other players with some improvisation. Mr Hatton decided it was good enough to keep in and, although I could not remember exactly what I had done, thus was a spurious reputation for 'being funny' born. It was a reputation I would have to live up to for the rest of my life.

By now Mr Evill had been replaced by Desmond Vowles (with whom I still keep up a Christmas card correspondence), an English master who shared with a history man, Brian Stevens, the duties of producing the school play. I had some success with Lady Teazle in *A School For Scandal* and Viola in *Twelfth Night*. I was mortified not to be offered the title role in *St Joan*, but it was thought that a St Joan played for laughs would not be quite the thing, and I was left to lick my wounds.

Messrs Vowles and Stevens were very encouraging about my acting, and it was at the suggestion of the former that I first seriously considered it as a profession.

My other claim to fame at Monmouth also came about by accident. Diving. In my second year I learnt to swim and by the end of the summer could just about manage two lengths, paddling frantically like a dog. It is a curious thing, but I could dive almost before I could swim. In order to prove myself 'one of the boys', I had ruined the odd spring or two by showing that it was possible to dive on to a bed from a nearby three-cornered shelf in the dormitory. It was a rather different technique from diving into water, because it involved landing flat in a perfect belly flop, but it must have removed any fear of heights I may have had and given me the confidence to hurl my body into the air and control it.

Be that as it may, I was entered as one of the two School House representatives in the diving competition. The joke at the time was that I was so small that I never made any splash as I entered the water, and was therefore bound to do well. Competing against eighteen-year-olds, I was an incongruous figure. Apart from being so small, I suffered from earache and therefore wore one of my mother's old bathing hats. I remember it to this day: it was light blue, with ear flaps shaped as dolphins. In a long career of allowing myself to look ridiculous, I do not think I bettered that occasion. To everyone's astonishment, not least my own, I came second, and once more had a reputation to keep up which I had acquired quite by chance.

For the next two years, when I was twelve and thirteen, I managed to hold on to second place, and then for three years I won the diving cup outright. In my last year, exhausted by several swimming races, some of which I had won, I came the lowest I had ever been (third) in the competition, but I was the undisputed king of diving and dared to attempt dives which others would not. When the ball from yard cricket went over the wall into the River Wye, it was usually 'Snipsie' who was nominated to fetch it, and everyone would crowd round encouraging me to dive in from the bridge or the jetty.

There was another reward for my diving talent. As perennial champion I was invited to help judge the diving competition of the neighbouring girls' school which was held, along with their swimming championships, in our baths. If the truth be known, I was more interested in seeing certain notorious young ladies in their swimming costumes than in their aquatic abilities, and I gloried in the perk denied to older boys who had something of a reputation (albeit self-made) as lady killers. For once I was envied by the others, and that made up for a lot of humiliation.

Whether on stage or in the water, I was showing and developing individual skills which, though they may have been small, were at least mine own. Yet what I really wanted was submersion in group activities, to be a wearer of one of the chocolate and gold blazers which were sported by members of the first and second XIs and XVs. It was not to be. Although in my penultimate year I was pulled from the 'third' game to 'Bigside' because of absences, and there by sheer chance proved to be the fullback they had been looking for instead of the scrum-half they had not, I was picked but never played for the first XV. The night before the first game, I was practising kicking when I snapped a groin muscle. It was attributed to overuse during swimming, and I never played rugby at school again. The activity in which I had had most sporting success had put paid to the activity for which I would have given up everything else. It was a lesson in 'sod's law' which I have not had cause to learn again until now.

Looking for fellowship and acceptance, I also turned to religion. We had been visited at school by Major Ian Thomas, who was said to have done brave things at Monte Cassino. He was now an evangelical preacher and I, as the estate agents say, was 'ripe for conversion'. For a year or two I underlined sections of my Bible in different coloured crayons, according to meaning, and did my best to lead others to Christ. I had never been christened or confirmed, and opted to be so at the age of fifteen in the school chapel, with two form-mates as godfathers. Whether it was that, or something else, which caused one of them, a hero and a best friend, to turn against me and expel me from his 'gang' I shall never know, but he did. And when this golden boy, top of the A-stream, good at games, Head of School material, was later expelled for fiddling the accounts while on a school camp but given a glowing reference for being a good chap, I began to get an inkling that the world is an unjust place. To those that hath shall be given. I began to doubt whether you could rely on anybody. Even God. The bishop's words at the confirmation had seemed so full of certainty:

'Defend, O Lord, this thy child with thy heavenly
grace, that he may increase in thy spirit more and
more, and finally come to thine everlasting kingdom.'

Cocooned in a pseudo-public school, with a pleasant and
sympathetic chaplain, visits to and from a sincere evangelical
preacher and with all life stretching hopefully before you, it is
possible to believe that you will finally come to the everlasting
kingdom. Certainly I was sincere at the time, but as life has
gone on, revealing more and more gratuitous injustice, it
becomes harder and harder to maintain belief. It is tempting,
for example, to point to my own experience lately and demand,
'Why me?', but I would be on sticky ground, having rejected
God for so long. Yet a vengeful God does not fit the image
either. If you take the millions of stricken innocents, you are left
with the conclusion that God either is not omnipotent or is not a
God of love. You cannot have it both ways, and muttering about
'God moves in a mysterious way', or 'all evil is man-made',
really will not do. In the end I can see no fault in the argument
that God exists, but as an incompetent younger brother who has
been given the world to look after and made a bog-up of it.

At home, to my parents' astonishment, I insisted on going to
church. The choir at that time consisted of me and Ernie
Peachy, a middle-aged farm labourer with a remarkably piercing
treble voice. Whence it came I shall never know, but it was an
early lesson in voice production and taught me that nothing is
impossible if you try. When years later on *Nationwide* I was
asked at very short notice to impersonate Bessie Bunter, I had
cause to remember it. Turning a tall, thin gangling man into a
short, fat, podgy girl is the sort of thing *Nationwide* producers
thought you could do at the drop of a straw boater if you had
an acting background.

Like most villagers, Ernie was very proud and jealous of his
area and he it was, I think, who was sitting with me on the
village green one day when a car drew up and asked directions.
Close by our village were the fields of Newent, which in spring
are a sea of wild daffodils. It was in the days before picking wild
flowers was forbidden, and trippers tended to load their vehicles
up with daffodils, catkins, pussy-willow and anything else they

could find. This was such a car, with herbage protruding from every orifice. The driver screeched to a halt and leaned through the window:

'I say, my man,' he said, 'can I take this road back to Gloucester?'

Ernie regarded the offending vehicle with narrow eyes. 'Thee may as well,' he said grimly, 'thee's taken bloody near everything else!'

Like many boys, I was leading a double life. Like many boys, I did not talk much or confide in my parents about the problems I was having at school. That would have been 'sissy'. At home in the village I continued to lead a charmed existence. Apart from singing in the two-voice choir, I drove tractors and walked behind combine harvesters, I bought bottles of pop from the local baker, I won the booby prize in the WI whist drive and, despite preferring swimming at school, I joined my father in the village cricket team. George Amphlett, sexton and doyen of village cricket life, said that one day I would play for the county, and I could think of nothing better. When my father went out into the Cotswolds for on-site inspections I would go with him, not because I wanted to view the historical delights of Chipping Camden or Stow-on-the-Wold, but because by this time I was heavily into engine numbers, and a trip out would add to my score. My father would drop me off at some quiet spot on the main line and I would happily spend three or four hours there to see as many new engines. Moreton-in-Marsh, Kingham and a little halt called Adlestrop were some of the dropping off points. It always seemed to be sunny, and I was content to commune with the GWR, the hum of the countryside and all the birds of Oxfordshire and Gloucestershire.

At school things were faster moving and altogether less peaceful. Early on, I had been a keen member of the Combined Cadet Force (Army Section). I had taken something called Part One, an examination in basic drills and skills. I had passed with distinction, but afterwards it was discovered that I was too young to have taken the exam, and I was dropped two platoons and told to start again. This is the kind of administrative 'bull' with which I have been impatient ever since, and may explain my subsequent enthusiasm for 'consumerism'. Even at fourteen I resented rule-book insensitivity and I left the Army section almost immediately. I had heard that gliding, and even flying, were possible in the Air Force section, and this seemed a lot more attractive. I managed to avoid wearing the uniform as often as I could think up a plausible excuse and was, as far as I know, the only person to complete three years in the sixth form (an extra year because of my age) without ever achieving any rank whatsoever in the CCF. I was also to be the first pupil to get a commission in the real Air Force.

My mother, who I was aware was regarded as a formidable figure even by the staff, had by then developed a new tactic to encourage her sons. This consisted of running them down, though never publicly. I was too slapdash to be made a prefect, too immature to get a commission, too lazy ever to get to university, and so on. The fact that I did all these things, I have often attributed to bloody-mindedness rather than to any inherent belief that they were a good thing in themselves, although I admit that I was a late developer. I had finally been made a house prefect, out of 'Scratch' Hatton's sheer embarrassment at the fact that I had reached the third year sixth without recognition and that my form-mates were long since school prefects and powers in the land. I had already shared a study with a boy in my class who was not only a school prefect, but Head of House, and had suffered the humiliation of being set lines by my own study-mate. Unfortunately, that Christmas I succeeded in getting a place at Oxford, the only boy to do so. This placed the headmaster in a quandary: I must be made a school prefect in recognition of this, but about seventeen boys were already ahead of me in the pecking order. An awful lot of school prefects were made that year.

No-one could have foreseen such an outcome. I had only spent a third year in the sixth form because of my age, and because of my maths. Or rather lack of it. I have always claimed to have something of a record where maths is concerned. I had been taking the O'level, summer and Christmas, since the age of fourteen. I took it seven times in all, and each time I got a lower mark. When, still sitting in with 3a, 4b and 5c I had, because some others were doing it, sat the Oxford Entrance examination and been lucky enough to get in, a pass in maths became mandatory. In the end my college (St John's) was decent enough to set me the ancient examination which having the O'level excused you from having to take. I travelled up to Oxford for the first time and enjoyed the exquisite theatre of sitting alone in an ancient hall taking an almost medieval examination. I did not enjoy the paper quite so much, especially when I saw that you had to get sixty per cent to pass. I did not do enough questions to achieve sixty per cent and returned to Monmouth with mixed feelings. At least I would not have to go to Oxford. One more stressful event avoided.

Although still at school, I decided on a career in the RAF. I had already had a taste of flying with the RAF section of the CCF, and liked it. I had also been prevented from going on a holiday gliding course by my over-cautious father, who foresaw danger. I was in a rage. It was one of the few times I was really angry with my father, and may have contributed to my decision. If I was in the Air Force as a career, no-one could stop me flying if I chose. I went for tests. I shall never know whether or not, sitting in a mock-up cockpit, I drove my aircraft into the ground. I should not be surprised. But a routine medical examination showed that my eyesight was not twenty-twenty. There would be no flying for me in the Air Force.

Nevertheless I had to do National Service. I decided I would still give the RAF a whirl and, if I liked it with my feet planted firmly on the ground, would sign on. I took a day off school to go up to RAF Uxbridge to see whether I was potential officer material. As (at last) a growing boy, who had never achieved any rank in the Air Force section of the CCF and had only been made a prefect at the last minute, I did not hold out much hope. When, however, I found I knew the answer to important questions such as, 'Who is the King of Iraq?' I thought for a moment I might make it. But when the list of successful candidates was read out, I was not on it. I was almost through the camp gates when a corporal ran up and asked me whether I was Mr Worsnip. I said I was. It seemed I had passed after all – it was just that my name had been omitted from the bottom of the list, in error. Not for the last time, I reflected on the fact that I had scraped through by the skin of my teeth.

That year the school play was to have been produced by another English master called Mr Lancaster and nicknamed (naturally) 'Burt'. His plan was that we should do *The Merchant of Venice*, and that I should play Portia. I dug my heels in and refused, on the grounds that I wanted to leave school having at least played one male part in a play. I pointed out that my voice, if not exactly broken, had sunk low enough for me to have been offered a baritone part in that year's Gilbert and Sullivan, and what was good enough for Gilbert and Sullivan was good enough for Shakespeare. Mr Lancaster was not best pleased and declined to produce a school play at all; instead Brian Stevens produced *Julius Caesar*. I played Mark Antony which was altogether sufficiently butch, the part having recently been played in the film by Marlon Brando.

There was news from Oxford. I had passed my maths exam and could take up my place. I was convinced it was a fiddle, but said nothing. I wanted to do National Service first, being fed up with book learning, and the University was happy to agree. I knew that my mother would be delighted, but keep her pride to herself. I remembered (shall I ever forget?) when news of my passing the college entrance had come. I was in bed, I heard a letter being pushed through the letter box in the hall. I heard my mother pick it up. She saw what it was, bounded up the stairs and thrust it at me. With a show of insouciance, I opened it. It was obviously not a thin rejection slip. I could sense my mother's excitement.

'Well?'

I took my time, 'I've got in.'

She took her time. 'Oh.'

There was a silence. She made for the door. Finally my anger burst through. 'Aren't you pleased?'

She stopped and turned. Pause. 'Well, I'd have preferred Christ Church.'

CHAPTER 2

Joining the Intelligentsia

Cleanliness is next to godliness, and I have long since abandoned godliness. But with cerebellar ataxia, having a bath is not the fun it used to be. It is not possible any more to say, 'I'll just have a quick splash.' It is a laborious business. Climbing in is difficult. Once inside, keeping balance is well-nigh impossible. Whereas before I used to kneel forward on my knees to wash my hair, or my bottom, this manoeuvre can only be achieved with the greatest care. The soap slips out of my hand once every few seconds, instead of every now and again. It is easier if I bath myself by sitting on the back of the bath and pointing the shower-head at myself. I am aware that a new shower will have to be specially built for me in any new house when we move. There will be handles to grasp and pull myself in by. There will be a specially made floor so that I do not have to negotiate any steps. Already, I have watched in amazement as fellow disabled people are hoisted up and then lowered, wheelchair and all, into a swimming pool. The mechanics of the device are simple but effective.

There are obviously tricks for the old dog to learn. For the moment I do the best I can with a non-slip rubber mat recommended by the occupational therapist. Getting out is particularly hard. I cannot dry myself in quick, easy movements, because my lack of balance will not allow it. I have to sit on the floor to rub my feet because I cannot stand on one leg. The whole process takes more like half a day than half an hour and, worst of all, it is so tiring that it is impossible to do anything for some time afterwards.

I was still only seventeen when I joined the RAF in 1956, and I sometimes wondered whether I should see another birthday. There were only two others straight from school, and I was easily the youngest. The rest were graduates. I needed to mature quickly, although even then I asked myself whether some of the more ludicrous 'traditions of the Service', such as the horse play on 'dining in night', meant that I had really entered a grown-up world. We were even instructed in such matters. On one occasion, I was instructed to stand on my chair, face east, and say whether the Russians were coming. When I pointed out that, as the curtains were drawn, it was impossible to see who was coming, this so amused my platoon-mates that I gained a spurious reputation for wit, as well as one for being prepared to stand up against those who used their positions of authority to abuse others. The reply clearly ruined an established routine, which was abandoned for the evening. I was beginning to learn that pomposity was paper-thin, that it was easily deflated and that readiness to resist bullying, with only the poorest use of words, earned a reputation out of all proportion to the effort involved. When I later heard that the officer involved had been court-martialled for theft, I began to feel a trifle sceptical about the concepts of 'honour' and 'officers and gentlemen', which he had done so much to instil into me. These words did not describe that particular man, I thought, and I did not see why they should be drummed into me. Whether it was my youth, or vulnerability, or both, I became the platoon scapegoat. If ever there was a dirty or difficult job, I seemed to get it. If ever there was trouble, I was at the centre of it.

When it was announced that we would be placed in a gas chamber, with masks at the ready and gas feeding into the chamber, to test our sang-froid under pressure, I was the last one to pick up a gasmask. It did not fit. It would not fit, no matter how hard I, or my platoon-mates tried. Meanwhile the gas continued to encroach, and through the glass panel we could see the Flight Sergeant in charge beginning to notice that something was going wrong. He was shouting, 'Get that bloody mask on!' and starting to panic. Eventually, with a superhuman effort, someone forced the mask on and all was well. But it was a close thing. Because I was aware that we were being tested, I had deliberately kept up an outward show of calm, and was mortified to find that I was reported to the Commanding Officer for panicking under pressure. A decision as to my suitability as 'officer material' was deferred.

The Officer Training School was on the Isle of Man, at RAF Jurby. On the whole my sixteen weeks there were fairly bleak. They were capped by time spent under canvas on the northernmost tip of the island, the Point of Ayre. Loitering within tent. Here there was one final exercise, a pretend rescue operation after a bombing raid. I was not too surprised when it was announced that I was to be in charge, and I could see the relief on the strained faces around me.

The staff's role was to obstruct as much as possible and to persuade my platoon-mates to do likewise. One in particular accepted this role with relish and, instead of obeying my orders, used his 'men' to perform irrelevant tasks such as looking for the CO's lighter, which he pretended to have mislaid. Afterwards, I wondered whether I lost marks for failing to control my men, or whether my platoon-mate lost more for allowing himself to be suborned. At any rate, I must have scraped through for, although the decision was delayed, I emerged into a wintry sun as a sprog Pilot Officer. Twenty years later I was presenting a consumer programme called *Help Yourself*. I was due to interview a government minister. When he arrived he rushed over, hand outstretched, and said how good it was to see me again. I recognized my erstwhile 'friend', and reflected on double standards and the suitability of his choice of profession.

There were compensations for the trials of RAF Jurby. On the boat across I had fallen into the company of a young lady. This was a new experience, and when she invited me to visit her home in my spare moments, I felt very grown up. There were also occasional trips to an hotel in Douglas for the Saturday night dance. All the tables were connected by telephone, so that you could ring up anyone you fancied and ask them to dance. Fortunately my phone did not ring and, though I went along with great bravado, I was not forced to reveal that I had never learned to dance.

Although I was now a Pilot Officer, I was not, of course, a pilot. I was not anything, except an officer, and the question had naturally arisen as to what I should do. Here I made one of my better decisions. While at Jurby I had applied to be a Photographic Intelligence Officer. My father had been one during the war, not many years before, and I had a smattering of knowledge as to what they did. My father had brought home some photographs, taken from a great height by a reconnaissance plane, and shown me how it was possible to lay the string of photographs in line and, by use of a 'stereoscope', view them three-dimensionally. In this way, using something called the angle of azimuth of the sun, the known height of the aircraft and the focal length of the camera, you could work out the height of installations, the wingspan of parked aircraft and so on. On the face of it, this did not seem to be a skill for someone who had failed maths O'level seven times, but I found, because I was working with known formulae, that there was not so much pure mathematics involved, and I got through the instruction course without much difficulty.

My father had been part of the section led by Constance Babington Smith, whose book *Evidence In Camera* described, among other things, how the section discovered the doodlebug during the war, and I had read tales of the brave pilots who, with nothing to shoot with but their cameras, had flown over target areas after bombing raids to record the damage. It seemed a good enough second best to flying, and certainly it surprised the powers that be that I applied. I always used to say that they were so surprised that anyone should know about photographic intelligence that they allowed me to go forward on to the instruction course, one of few National Service officers so privileged.

In wartime, photographic intelligence had been a significant component in supplying information at the highest level, and my father used to tell the tale of how they once got it terribly wrong. A crucial bombing raid had occurred, and Winston Churchill wanted to know at once whether it had been successful. The system was that there was something called 'first phase' PI, when the photographs were briefly checked and the answers to the most important questions given. This resulted in a telegram being sent to Whitehall containing the words, 'target completely destroyed.' When the 'second phase' (or more detailed) report was compiled the PIs, as they were known, discovered to their horror that the bombers had mistaken the target completely and destroyed something quite other. Consternation followed. What would the Prime Minister say, when he found he had been misinformed by intelligence sources? Eventually someone had the bright idea of sending another telegram saying merely that, owing to a typing error, the word 'not' had been omitted from the sentence 'target completely destroyed.' In this way was the honour of the Photographic Intelligence Unit preserved.

I was posted to the home of photographic intelligence at Nuneham Park ('a country house, somewhere in England') near Oxford. It was a shambling place. The main work went on in the house, which was surrounded by Nissen huts. There was very much an air of wartime about it, and I was proud to be mixing with men, now grounded, whose medals showed that they had done brave deeds in other theatres. It was here that I first got horribly drunk (being determined to keep up with the many hardliners). It was here that I first handled a pistol specially issued (officers for the use of) during a security exercise, and here that I first saw the blind face of prejudice.

For one officer, as for many others, the war had come at just the wrong time, blighting his youth. He was a New Zealander and a talented concert pianist. He joined up, not waiting to finish his studies, and became the youngest Squadron Leader in the Air Force. He was a handsome man, with the dashing looks of a mustachioed Errol Flynn. By the time the war was over, New Zealand seemed a long way away and he stayed on in the Air Force, the only profession he knew. He drank a lot, and I tried to keep up, glad of such good company. Unlike many, he took his drink well and always appeared at breakfast crisp and efficient, ready for work. He was also gay. Occasionally, when he had had one too many, he would appear in the junior officers' quarters in the middle of the night and plead for more 'conversation', during which he would proposition me. He did not get angry when refused, and would go away into the night, a lonely, dispirited and harmless figure.

One day he was not at breakfast. A batman had made a complaint, and we heard that he was to be court-martialled. It did not seem to worry anyone. There was no compassion, no regret that a friend and drinking companion was gone, no apparent memory of the many double brandies he had generously dispensed, no sense of loss that a man's life was about to be ruined. Instead there were smutty jokes, insouciance, a general feeling that he had got what he deserved and wonder that he had got away with it for so long.

There was an investigation, and someone must have pointed the finger at me, for I was to be an important witness. Luckily, the regulations allowed that a junior officer be accompanied by someone more senior to see fair play, and I was lucky enough to be allocated one of my heroes, Jack Urwin-Mann, DSO, DFC and bar, who had been one of the pilots during the siege of Malta. The investigating officer was evil personified. He took great pleasure in his work and had a knowing, leering, intolerant look which he seemed to want to share with all the witnesses. I was appalled, and decided there and then to lie my head off. I did, but to no avail. We did not see the charged officer again, and heard later that he had been jailed.

I realized then that the law, especially military law, had little to do with justice and nothing to do with compassion. Throughout my life, I have found the gay community to be high-spirited, companionable, witty and generous. I am glad to have had gay friends and, though I may not always have succeeded, have sought to live and let live, on the principle that if there's one thing I cannot tolerate, it is intolerance!

Soon afterwards, Nuneham Park closed down. I was the last officer to leave the station, and as we trundled away in a three-ton truck I reflected that the wartime and immediately post-war atmosphere was gone for ever. The new premises were purpose-built, single-storey, surrounded by a barbed wire fence and stuck in a corner of RAF Brampton, near Huntingdon, at that time the headquarters of the now defunct Technical Training Command.

I could see what a crucial role photographic intelligence had played during the war. But what on earth did it do during peace time? I was soon to find out; especially after I was posted to 'S' (or 'Special') Section. I was an airfields specialist. I could measure the length of a runway, work out how many aircraft it could take and of what kind; I could recognize any aircraft in the world, photographed from 60,000 feet or more. I could tell from the masts what radar and other electronic installations were present, what fuel capacity, what potential. What I did not know, until I joined 'S' section, was that we were keeping a watch on all the Iron Curtain countries, as well as

Russia and China. We evaluated material shot from aircraft travelling through one of the permitted corridors through East Germany to Berlin, as well as photographs shot surreptitiously by agents in the field. This was in the days before satellites made the whole world an open book, when the Americans had developed a high-level reconnaissance plane called the U2 which was highly secret until the world was alerted to its existence by the shooting down of Major Gary Powers by the Russians in 1960. We studied the photographs and reported on the number of fighters (generally MIG-15s) and bombers (Bears and Badgers) at Minsk, Pinsk and Chelyabinsk.

To an eighteen-year-old this was exciting stuff, and I toyed with the idea of not going to university and signing on. Looking back on it from a perspective of illness and insecurity, I sometimes wish I had, for I would have been retired by the time I was forty-three, and living on a pension.

But in those days I was torn. Torn between the excitement of the work, and the absurdities of Service life. With one or two exceptions, the people doing this exciting work were incredibly dull. I was hampered by my own youth and ignorance. At first I saluted everything in sight (only Squadron Leaders and above needed saluting). I often made a fool of myself at the daily flag lowering ceremony; once when I had got myself into the sort of impossible situation that everyone but me was aware of, the Flight Sergeant, enjoying himself hugely, strode over and, while snapping up a smart salute, said under his breath, 'What are you going to do now, sir?' The 'sir' was dripping with heavy irony. I did the only thing possible. 'What would you recommend, Flight?' He told me, and all was well.

I was none too happy that men I played rugby with, and called by their Christian names, had to address me as 'sir' and salute. And when they did not I had to haul them up, in case anyone was watching. I did not enjoy the fact that the meeting times of a new jazz club I had formed could not be promulgated in the daily station orders, on the grounds of being too fatuous; I did not enjoy the surreptitious methods I had to employ to meet the WRAFs I fancied; I did not enjoy the humourless 'bull' of Service life.

But there were moments to savour. I remember learning that

Dirk Bogarde had once been a PI. Out of curiosity, I asked an experienced Junior Technician who had worked with him, what he was like. 'Just like yourself really, sir. Very dull and ordinary.'

I very often found myself Orderly Officer for the day. I suspected that these extra duties were awarded because of my cap, which was an old and wrinkled affair which had belonged to my father. To save money I had commandeered it for my own use, even though it did not quite fit. To remedy this situation, I had stuffed coils of brown paper inside the hat-band. One day the whole station was called out to a special Queen's Birthday Parade, with an inspection by the Air Officer Commander-in-Chief. As luck would have it, I was in charge of a platoon right in front of the Air Officer. The moment came to raise three cheers for the Queen. The drill was that, with the left arm firmly fixed at your left side, you used the right to raise the cap three times as you cheered. Sadly, as the cap was raised for the first time, coils of brown paper descended from the brim and hung down to my feet. I could not move my left arm, so tried to cram the hat back on to my head, coils and all. Naturally I did not succeed, and the end of the ceremony saw one officer, festooned in brown paper, trying urgently to dig a hole in the parade ground in which to hide. I was Orderly Officer for some considerable time after that.

One other absurd incident also involved a hole in the ground. As often happened, junior officers were used for courier duties. If the material was incoming it involved, for example, meeting someone off a plane, avoiding customs and getting the papers back by fast car to JARIC (Joint Air Reconnaissance Intelligence Centre). On the occasion in question, the task was to take some secret papers and deliver them to the Ministry of Defence building in Whitehall. My orders were specific. I should wear civilian clothes, but be sure to have a hat, so that if recognised I could return a salute. I was given a car and driver, but was to be dropped some way from the MOD building, whence I should walk along Victoria Embankment Gardens. Here I would find a hole in the pavement surrounded by hurdles, as if workmen were digging. I should climb over the barrier, descend though a hole in the ground, walk along a passage under the gardens and give the password when I met a military policeman guarding an iron gate. I would now be in the basement of the building. All this I did, though it occurred to me afterwards to wonder, had some Russian spy been lurking on the Embankment, what he would have made of a series of men in flat hats and macs, carrying briefcases, disappearing down a hole in the road. Quite why I could not go in through the front door in Northumberland Avenue I never discovered.

Despite these absurdities and the excitements, I decided that the Service life was not for me. There was too much restriction, too much emphasis on the differences of rank, too much sameness about the everyday routine. There were exceptions. My room-mate, Pilot Officer Don Sullivan, was one. Despite a healthy disregard for anything pompous or unnecessary, he went on to be a career officer and retired as a Group Captain. Once, we clambered on to the roof in the middle of the night for fun (we must have been bored out of our minds), only to see the security guard being called out and equipped with heavy duty torches. We stayed where we were for three hours rather than risk being caught climbing down. Eventually, before dawn, we did, unsure as to whether or not we had been spotted. In the morning, as we contemplated the end of our Service careers, we found they had been searching for a child missing (but happily restored) from the married quarters.

When David Venables was appointed Catering Officer for daring to make a complaint in the 'Complaints' book, (what else was it for?) I wrote a rude message questioning this decision. I was hauled up in front of the Station Commander who finally conceded that there was something faintly illogical about the whole business, and I was let off. I think this was my first successful action on behalf of 'consumers', although I had no idea that I would ever take up cudgels on their behalf. Nor would David again be so indiscreet. He is now Solicitor General, and when I rang him to suggest we meet at a twenty-five year reunion dinner, he sighed with relief. 'I thought you were ringing me about a complaint from the public.'

For variety, I used occasionally to wander over to the old country grange, which was now the headquarters Mess, and drink a half-pint with a small, but perfectly formed young man called Pilot Officer Donald Trelford. Had I known he would end up Editor of the *Observer* I might even have made it a pint, assuming a Pilot Officer's pay of 10/- (50 pence) a day would run to it.

I turned to other unexplored matters. I was all too conscious of my inexperience where girls were concerned, and all too conscious that experience was what I needed. Pat Earey was a local girl from Huntingdon, a blonde, with a tall, fine figure. She was highly intelligent, with a thirst for knowlege which put most of my colleagues to shame. But she did not exactly speak in upper-class tones, and I will never forget introducing her in the Mess to the Commanding Officer's wife. The disdain with which the great lady ignored the proffered handshake said a lot about the manners of the so-called 'officers and gentlemen' class. I took due note.

I was madly in love. I would do anything to reach Pat – beg, borrow and steal lifts, in cars, on bicycles and motor bicycles. I often walked. Once I was caught by the police riding home the few miles from Huntingdon on a bicycle, on the pavement, in the middle of the night, on the wrong side of the road, with no lights. It was the start, and possibly the finest hour, of my acting career. So thick was my accent, so confused my demeanour, that the police never supposed that I was anything other than an aircraftsman second class trying to get back to camp. I stupidly gave a false name, reasoning that the chances of there being more than one Worsnip were minimal. Mercifully they let me off with a warning, and I promised to walk the rest of the way. I do not know what happens (if anything) to officers caught out in a bicycling offence, but I was young enough to imagine the consequences were dire and hoped to avoid the ignominy.

I had mastered the flag-lowering by the time I left, in 1958. I had had enough Orderly Officer's duties in which to do so. Indeed, I was performing that duty on the day before I was due to leave the RAF for ever. But I cannot say I did not have a good send off. The flagpole was situated near to the men's (and the women's) quarters. As the flag came down for the last time under my command, there arose into the Huntingdonshire air such a cacophony of birdsong as to make the unfortunate individual who was hauling the rope waver in his duties. Every bird on the station appeared to be crammed into the WRAF block windows, and making some sound or other. Some were calling, some were whistling and large numbers of them were waving colourful pieces of material not entirely unlike female knickers. I brought the ceremony to a close as soon as I decently dared, and hoped the Station Commander, or some other senior officer, did not happen to be passing by. Not that it would have mattered. After two years' national service, I was leaving in the morning, en route to the city of dreaming spires.

Oxford was not the hazy haven of golden stone and golden youth that I had imagined it to be. It is as noisy as a Chinese fish market, and with about as many bicycles. It teems with intemperate youth going about its raucous business, with dull dons going to give fusty lectures, with shoppers and working wives cramming the high street shops, very few of which are in the High Street. But it is possible to create a story-book existence. All the elements are there: the choristers still sing from Magdalen tower on a misty May Morning; the River Cherwell still glides by; dons still discuss Old High German vowel-sounds in the gorgeous gardens; you still get invited to sherry; you can lie in the Parks and listen to the sound of leather on willow; you can fall in love several times daily; founders still frown down at you from the walls of ancient halls. In that sense, Oxford is timeless. It is now – it was then. Oxford is a game you play, rather than a life you lead.

The President of St John's, W. C. Costin, was wise and kind. He took an affectionate interest in college affairs, and in any undergraduate who drew attention to himself, whether by doing good work or in some other way. He had two vital pieces of advice to pass on which would ensure greater success. One involved bathing. It was his view that no-one should take a bath in the morning – it would weaken you for the rest of the day and prevent your best efforts, whether in work or in sport. At the time, young and vigorous, we regarded such advice as a harmless eccentricity. It has taken thirty years, but W. C. Costin's advice has come home to roost. I think of it often. I can never again take a bath unless I am doing nothing for the rest of the day.

The other bit of advice was more genuinely eccentric. It concerned the taking of tea in the morning. Mr Costin's opinion was that this was a productive habit, to be encouraged. He recommended that everything be prepared, and the lead plugged into the wall, so that when the alarm went off all you needed do was plug the lead into the kettle. But, and here was the vital part, it was important to leave the lead dangling over the edge of some large container, like the marble wash-bowl, lest any electricity escape in the night!

This was how I chose to view Oxford. As some sort of bizarre and colourful interlude in an otherwise mundane existence. Not that I myself would provide the colour, but that I would be given the chance to observe a world of eccentric dons, beautiful buildings, achieving undergraduates and golden girls, like any chance reader of *Brideshead Revisited*. Certainly it was a very different world from the one in which I had spent the last two years.

It took me a little time to realise what Oxford had to offer me. For the first year I was insufferably dull, or so I thought. I did little but play rugby football for the college and work. I was, as a contemporary who kindly wrote to me after my illness, remembered as, 'an efficient, but not outstanding fullback.' Efficient, but not outstanding, was all I hoped to be. St John's, I used to remark, produces first class second rate chaps. It came as a great shock to learn that for my first exams, after two terms, I need study two books of Virgil's *Aeneid* in Latin. It was over five years since I had failed Latin O'level, and I was not sure I was up to it. Nor did I have the guts to try what a brilliant American scholar did. He learned the translation by heart, and also learned to recognize by sight the passage of text from which it came. Unfortunately, on the day of his exam he misread the text and therefore mismatched the passage. The result was a brilliant translation of the wrong piece, and he lost the First to which his other work entitled him. His name was Kark, and for a short while the word 'kark' passed locally into the language, meaning someone who tried it on, who made an extravagant but ultimately futile gesture.

I did not venture much out of college. It was a big enough world, and there was so much to do. I fell in with a group of

Old Merchant Taylors (the school had a link with the college, so there were plenty of them). Rather than put up one of their own, they persuaded me to stand for first year representative on the Junior Common Room Committee. This I did, and to my surprise was elected. Once again an action taken by the sheerest chance set a pattern.

It was also in this first year that I cut my first disc. On Thursdays, I would take an evening off and go along to the Oxford Union debates. I was always impressed by these witty, voluble dinner-jacketed figures, destined to be cabinet ministers, or ambassadors, or famous authors. Peter Jay I remember, smoothly Presidential; and a fiery young hero with red hair and a Gloucestershire accent who would sweep to the despatch box and despatch the previous facile arguments to oblivion. I was to suffer later from his critical pen, but Dennis Potter has always been a favourite. Then there was the President of the Conservative Club, Phillip Whitehead, later to become a Labour MP. Such is opportunism, such their careless confidence.

On this particular occasion, the debate was recorded. The guest speaker was Gerard Hoffnung, whose hilarious story about why a man on a building site asked for a doctor's note became a favourite record, and one I listened to many times in later years in the BBC Archives. I was only in the audience, but my laughter was recorded along with the others' and I was proud to have been there.

At the end of my first year I broke out a little, realising that a little bravado went a long way and that it was possible for the mediocre to have a share in what Oxford had to give. A close friend of mine, who had made his mark as an actor, persuaded me to audition for the University Experimental Theatre Club's forthcoming production of Ben Jonson's *Bartholomew Fair*, which was due to be played in the gardens of the Theatre Royal, Stratford-upon-Avon. There was bound to be something for me, if only a walk on part. In the event, it was put to me that the part of Nightingale, the cutpurse and ballad-singer, was to be played by a young man called Dudley Moore. Unfortunately, since he had been cast it had been agreed that the piece should also be played in the Elizabethan Hall at Leicester, to help raise money for a much-needed theatre in that city. But Dudley had already fixed his holiday. Would I play the part in Leicester, then hand over to Dudley when we reached Stratford? Naturally I agreed. I pretended I could strum a few chords on the guitar; in fact I used the chords I had learnt at home on the ukulele, and made up a tune which would fit. It was a complete con, but it got me the part and the performance at Leicester was adjudged a success. In fact, years later, as a professional, I took part in the final performance at the Phoenix Theatre and so had the dubious distinction of both raising money for the opening, and taking part in the closing, of that particular theatre.

When we were beginning at Stratford, many members of the cast thought it would be unreasonable to deprive me of the part at this late stage, so Dudley, who had by now turned up, was appointed my understudy! But Dudley had the last laugh, as he generally does. He himself played the part originally destined for me, that of the seller of apples and pears, who from time to time wandered through the fairground, dispensing his wares. There were no lines, just one stage direction: words to the effect of 'enter, crying "apples, pears" etc.' With only this to go on, Dudley managed to get a notice in most national newspapers. He wandered through the set eating some of his own fruit and crying, 'apples, apples!' He then looked at the fruit he was eating, did an enormous double take and resumed, crying, 'pears, pears!'

One thing led to another, and I performed in various productions for the Experimental Theatre Club, the Oxford University Dramatic Society, the St John's College Mummers and the specially formed group, the Oxford Theatre Club, which performed on the fringe of the Edinburgh Festival. Indeed, only a couple of years earlier it had been the first and only group to perform on the fringe, which today has grown to become almost as important an event as the festival itself.

In my second year I had gained confidence and really branched out. I continued to play rugby, but the drama was taking over as a spare-time activity. I used to tell my rugby playing friends that I was off to play-practice, and my theatrical friends that I was needed at rugby rehearsal.

I devoted some spare time too – though sadly not enough – to Pat Earey, who spent a good deal of time in Oxford. She still has the letters I wrote during that period, but wisely will not show them to me. She also – much to the amusement of her four sons – has the (probably ghastly) fifties dress I bought her when she accompanied me to a college ball.

I had realized that life at university was one long period of spare time, interrupted by short bursts of frantic work. Most of my essays were compiled with the help of large amounts of black coffee and aspirin, and most of my work done during the vacations, when I used to go and sweat it out in the Gloucester public library. There was far too much to do in Oxford without letting yourself be interrupted by work.

Whether it was the latent actor in me or not, I took an almost perverse pleasure in dressing for the occasion. I would startle my actor friends by appearing in uniform to go and instruct at the Officers' Training Corps, or in blazer and boater for a meeting of the Archery Society on the magnificent St John's College lawns. It is true that I would try and ameliorate the rather strait-laced stalwarts of the Junior Common Room by dressing chappishly in sportscoat and flannels to perform my duties. I could not shave for the occasion, however, and the rugby team were not best pleased at having a fullback who wore sideburns. I even overheard opponents from another college discussing whether I should be allowed to play at all. Increasingly, I became bored with the boorishness of young men one of whose few pleasures seemed to be drinking beer, and after my elegant room in college was desecrated by, among other things, butter-throwing, I decided the whole thing was too childish and vowed to give up rugby during my final year. That was one excuse. Being jumped up and down on by large persons who otherwise played for Scotland was another.

I turned more and more to matters 'artistic'. Under the guidance of a young man called Michael Billington, I took to reviewing theatrical productions for the University newspaper, *Cherwell*. Both commercial and University productions came under my scrutiny, so that one week I was reviewing Bruce Forsyth and John Hanson in *Puss In Boots*, and the next it would be Peter Snow as a Greek god in *Amphitryon 38*. On these I cut my literary teeth, though I do not think they would have been so sharp if I had known that one day I would work with those luminaries and come to appreciate their professionalism.

In my third year I was President of the St John's Junior Common Room. This meant that I represented the undergraduate body at official functions, and also put the undergraduates' views on how the college should be run. I found myself dealing with every problem from how milk cartons in the common room should be opened, to what hours the college should keep. I ran an unsuccessful campaign to get the hours in which women guests were allowed in extended until midnight, and remember having to report back the Senior Dean's final word on the subject, which was that what was not worth doing by 9.30 was not worth doing at all. I cannot imagine what he meant.

When the Queen came to lay the foundation stone for a new college, I was part of the undergraduate group which entertained her to coffee. I remember her being wittier than I had expected. When she arrived she announced in those much imitated Queenly tones, 'Sorry I'm late. The High Sheriff of Oxfordshire fainted over luncheon. Then his wife came out in sympathy. Bodies all over the place!' We were all very nervous, but protocol demanded that none of us could smoke until the Queen either accepted a cigarette or, in declining, gave us permission. For the rest of term I carried the bruise of where the Nawab of Pataudi (captain of cricket that year) kicked me for daring to offer Her Majesty a Piccadilly tipped.

One memorial to my time as President has been overtaken by events. It was unthinkable in my day, but women are now full members of college. If you stay overnight you are inclined to meet them, scantily dressed, on the way to the bathroom, and even though I played my part in their emancipation, there remains the uneasy feeling that something is amiss. Back in 1961, in my final year, St John's was either the first, or among the very first, to allow women to dine in Hall. Wheeling and dealing, I had formed a committee of undergraduates whom I knew were highly thought of by the dons, which I persuaded to write a report recommending that women guests be allowed in on certain nights. Mr Costin, the President of St John's, thought that if it was recommended by such good chaps, it must be all right, so it scraped through. I put up a list inviting guests, and only a few of my cronies signed it. As it happened, I had to go away for a couple of days, and I lived in fear that what I had seen as a progressive move had, in fact, been rejected by the undergraduates themselves. I returned just in time for the dinner, and I and my small gang waited nervously with our lady guests. At the last moment, the doors opened and a huge crowd of undergraduates flooded in, all of them with ladies. For the first time in its history, many hundred of years, the Hall was awash with coloured dresses and full of the sound of female voices. It was an historic moment, and I was only sorry that only three dons were at the High Table to see it.

More than twenty years later, I went to my first reunion dinner. By this time, of course, coloured dresses were a daily normality. I found myself sitting next to a young doctor of philosophy. He asked me about my time at the college and, rather pleased with myself, I quoted the above story. He was not amused. 'Oh, it's your fault,' he said. I asked him what he meant. 'There are women resident in college, now.' I said I did not see what was wrong with that. 'You may not,' he said, looking very glum, 'but I was forced to get married in my second year!'

It was at that same dinner that an old man opposite leaned over and, seeing the card in my place, said, 'I see you are called Worsnip.' I agreed that that was so. 'Do you know a Glyn Worsnip at all?' I said that I probably knew him as well as any man in Christendom. 'He does a lot of broadcasting, you know,' he told the assembled multitudes, 'I know him very well.'

In my third year I took digs in Walton Street with Mrs Messenger, an archetypal figure who had been landlady to generations of 'young gentlemen'. She used to call me 'Wispy Worsnip,' on account of my always looking as if I needed a square meal. Also living there was Giles Havergal, later to become Director of the Glasgow Citizens' Theatre. In those days he was a very Eton, Oxford and Coldstream Guards young man – everything I was most afraid of – but he was very kind to me. I think he perceived my insecurity and did a lot, not only with reviews and my theatrical ventures, but to show me that even those who went to Christ Church, appeared to have been born with silver spoons in their mouths and to succeed at everything with effortless ease, were human beings. He himself was a funny mixture, having this theatrical streak, and we used to do cabaret together at posh gatherings like the Bullingdon Club, which was full of the foxhunting set.

It was at one of these events at which, after an evening making fun of, among others, the Royal family, that an acquaintance came up and said, 'Oh, Glyn, that was frightfully, frightfully funny!' Then, turning to introduce his companion, he went on, 'Do you know Prince William of Gloucester?' I assumed this was some kind of bad joke and all I could think of to say was, 'How nice, I come from Gloucester too.' This was thought to be terribly funny. The Prince said he had hugely enjoyed himself, but all I could do was pray that a hole would appear to swallow me up. Even though I now mixed with an upper-class set (albeit more often than not as a performer), I could not then, and never have, got over the 'Bisto Kid' feeling that I had stumbled into a party at which I did not rightly belong. There seemed to be so much which others took for granted, but which to me was new and exciting. The affair of the avocado was one.

Giles had taken me for lunch at his club. It was a bit crowded and we had to share a table. The man opposite me was delving into a shiny pear-shaped fruit, or vegetable. I asked what it was. He looked surprised at first, then recovered himself. 'This', he said, 'is an avocado pear. It's delicious.' Then he called the waiter, ordered another and passed it across. He told me what to put on it and how to eat it, and watched me enjoy this new delicacy, thus starting a lifelong devotion to the fruit. He could not have been kinder or more tactful. After he had gone I asked Giles who he was. 'Oh, somebody at my college,' he replied. 'Somebody called David Dimbleby.'

As so often in my life, fulfilment came too late. By the time I was confident in my own abilities, it was time to stop. Looking back, I could not have been luckier. I played rugby, I acted in plays, I helped make a film, directed by Gavin Millar and starring Melvyn Bragg, I wrote for the University newspaper, I instructed at the Officers' Training Corps, I was President of the Junior Common Room, I fell in and out of love, I formed enduring friendships, I bicycled hither and yon, and from college to college engaged in one activity or another. I was the envy of many. But I did not know it. Looking back from this chair, hampered now by disease and depression, I realize far too late that I had golden opportunities. Though I have often regretted that I did not specialize, I cannot but admit that Oxford was the happiest time, that it was a kaleidoscope of activity, that I sampled most things that the University had to offer. It was just that I did not realize my good fortune, could not cram enough in, could not succeed at everything.

In my last year, my tutor gave up on me and I was farmed out to one of his more brilliant students. It was my own fault. I was trying to do too much, and not enough of it was work. J. B. Leishman was a brilliant scholar and had written the definitive work on John Donne and a much admired translation of Rilke. No-one could imagine how this eccentric bachelor, who seemed never to move from his armchair in north Oxford, had acquired the experience of life and feeling which burst from these books. Even in death he surprised people. 'He died,' wrote Alan Brien in a poetic tribute, 'falling off an Alp', and it was always hard to reconcile this man of action with the Sherlock Holmes-like figure who shambled through Oxford with loping gait, or on a surprisingly well-oiled bicycle. I will not say that his tutorial life was a dull routine, because his enthusiasm for literature came through even to me, but I got the feeling that one generation of undergraduates was much like another. 'Ah, Worsley,' he would intone on greeting me (he always called me Worsley), 'let's see now, your topic this week has been, "A comparison and contrast between the *Man of Law's Tale*, and the *Pardoner's Tale*"?' 'No sir, my topic this week has been, "The poetry of John Dryden".' 'Ah, yes, I was thinking of you this week, this term, last year.'

In the helter-skelter of life at Oxford, one term was much like another. Increasingly, there was too much to fit in. In what little time I spent in the library I made friends with an enigmatic young man called Brian Wenham, who was, though I could never have guessed it, to play a significant part in my life. Nor could I have foreseen the role a chirpy young undergraduate with whom I used occasionally to perform cabaret, would play. Her name was Esther Rantzen. She was a rotund, talkative girl and had not then assumed the Katie Boyle look she has now. She was the girl next door, the one who cheered you up when your latest love affair went wrong, the enthusiastic younger sister, a somewhat dumpy dark-haired girl always a-brim with ideas for a new cabaret.

She had a bit-part in a musical version of *An Italian Straw Hat* which was directed by Giles Havergal and was considered so successful in Oxford that an impresario, with more money than sense, put it on at the old Lyric, Hammersmith during the vacation between my second and third years. The music was fearfully complicated, as I would have guessed if I had known that the composer, Gordon Crosse, was to become one of the most distinguished of modern composers. When I listen to his work now on Radio 3, I am hard pushed to make head or tail of it. Recently Bryant Marriott, now head of Radio 2 but then an undergraduate drummer, gave me a tape he had made of the show and, listening back, I realized not only just how complicated the music was, but how fragile was my light-baritone voice, and how much I had to learn.

In 1960, flushed with the success of reaching the West End of London before even leaving university, anything was possible. I was playing a sort of Jeeves to the principal role, taken by Jonathan Cecil who is now a successful actor. I had the opening number, which was a flirtatious piece with the maid, played by someone the whole of Oxford would have liked to flirt with, the Zuleika Dobson of her day, Caroline Seebohm. On the opening night I had the idea that I would look more dashing if I had a pencil-thin moustache, like David Niven. Pencil was the right word. With a black make-up crayon I adorned my face, completely forgetting that the song ended with the protagonists enjoying a huge smacker of a kiss. When it came to the moment, I was too occupied with kissing Caroline to think of anything else, and it was only when we parted that I saw to my horror that I had left a perfect black moustache imprinted on her upper lip. The incident got a huge laugh, but not the kind that we would have wanted, and it was only when Caroline came off stage that she realized what a ghastly disservice I had done her. I was mortified, but it was not a mistake I would ever make again.

* * *

Thankfully Caroline forgave me, and it was she and Dudley Moore that I was chatting to at a wine and cheese party when we decided that if there was one organization we would never work for, it was our hosts – the BBC. At that time, in the summer of 1961 during my final days at Oxford, when the BBC was even more of an Oxford and Cambridge graduate club than it is now, it threw a party for the chosen 'glitterati', so that they could 'make their number' with various senior producers and heads of department. I remember wondering why I had been asked, and supposed it was because I had just been working with someone whose mother was a high-flier in the BBC and had helped draw up a list of promising young persons. It was embarrassing to watch our contemporaries engaging in this sort of thing, and we three cringed in a corner while the sycophantic antics took place. As far as I know, none of us three spoke to a single person from the BBC throughout the evening, though we did not forgo the food and drink which our hosts so generously provided.

I had already seen, as I supposed, my last of the BBC when, like many another, I had applied earlier in the summer for a 'general traineeship' with that august organization. I had got through two interviews, but that was as far as it went. So obviously had the interviewer been through the standard routine a million times before, so obviously was the thing timed to a second, so obviously were they looking for organisers rather than doers, so boring was the droning voice of the interviewer, that I disgraced myself by falling asleep while looking out of the window. Of course I was rejected, though not with such glory as my very talented contemporary John Duncan. He was a brilliant young man who had produced the Oxford University Dramatic Society in a gigantic outdoor production of *Tamburlaine the Great* in St John's College gardens, as well as (with Gordon Honeycombe), a spectacular series of Mystery Plays in a nearby chapel. There was no doubting his talent, but his Geordie personality and his Andrew Aguecheek appearance (hair like flax on a distaff) were not exactly what the BBC had in mind. When asked what was the most important headline that week, he is reputed to have replied that the most important headline was unquestionably the news that Newcastle United had beaten

Arsenal 2–1. Though he went on to become a very talented television producer, it was not with the BBC.

One person who did get a general traineeship was my college contemporary, Peter Goodchild. He had the last laugh, for he became Editor of *Horizon*, Head of Science Features and Head of Drama. At the time we could hardly believe it; he appeared to have done only one thing, and that was insignificant enough. It was my proud boast that in every year I was at St John's, we won the University Cup for the best taped 'radio' play. Each year I had a leading part, and various contemporaries wrote or adapted the play. In the first year (1958), Peter Goodchild, a chemistry student whose most noticeable attributes were his staring eyes and check sportscoat, asked if he could help. There was not much he could do with the writing or performance, but he was excellent at arranging people and tape recorders, so he took the credit 'producer'. And credit it clearly was. When, after our Finals in 1961, the St John's College Mummers and guests took a production of *The Merchant of Venice* on tour, Peter was Company Manager, the critic and author John Spurling was Shylock and I was Antonio. One venue was the gardens on Sidmouth Cliffs where we were relieved of our only scenery when the backcloth of black curtains blew over the cliffs and into the sea.

More importantly, on the first matinée the tea to which our small audience of elderly people were doubtless looking expectantly forward had not arrived, and the interval was fast approaching. In the nick of time it turned up and a much relieved Company Manager, wearing a modern dinner jacket, darted forward without thinking on to the greensward and interrupted some amazed 16th-century folk, wearing doublet and hose, with the following un-Shakespearean declamation: 'Ladies and Gentlemen, tea and biscuits will now be served on the lawn, on your left.' Realizing his mistake, he slunk off, eyes popping, to allow the play to continue.

That last year at Oxford was the time of the greatest confidence, and least anxiety, of my life. I made some mistakes. Though I saw a good deal of Pat Earey, accompanying her to my college ball, even getting her into a college play, I was too busy doing other things and she eventually abandoned me. The proprietors of what was to be a new magazine called *Private Eye* suggested I write for them. I declined, thinking it would not last. I lost my bicycle.

Although I started too late, I look back on Oxford with few regrets. And to think I nearly did not go. It was peopled by friendships, many of which are with me still, and whose constancy, despite many and long interruptions, has helped me in my darkest hour.

Only one thing marred that period. My college friend John Eccles, one of the Old Merchant Taylors, a beautiful boy who rescued me from doing too much, who saw through the frenetic aspects of my life, who knew when I was exhausted and who sat me down in his quiet gentle way and restored calm, was killed shortly afterwards in a ghastly car crash. I know that my life would have been better for his friendship. I grieve for him still.

There were others. Cormac Rigby, who thirty years later, after a successful career as a Radio 3 announcer, finally became what he had always really been, a priest and confessor. He lets me stay when I want to, he picks me up and takes me to the theatre and out of myself. He does not say much, unless prompted, but he understands.

Three contrasting girls. Maggie Keswick, excitable and exciting, a beautiful débutante who could have had her pick at Oxford, but who chose me. I was deeply in love, and outrageously flattered. I have seen her rarely since, but when I became ill she wrote me a lovely, caring letter and I was made to feel that our friendship remained in abeyance, ready to be picked up where we left off all those years ago.

Charlotte Holmes, also upper crust but my very best friend, unflappable, cheerful and concerned. Whenever things have been too much I have turned to her and, despite the several tragedies in her life, she has never failed me. As luck would have it, she settled in Bristol and now drives across to advise, chivvy, restore.

The Lady Rosemary Fitzgerald, eccentric Irish aristocrat, daughter of a flying instructor. No-one doubted that Ro would get a First in English. Since then she has had a variety of careers, including that of restaurateur. At last she has become what she always wanted to be – a botanist. We used to share confidences and 2/9d businessmen's lunches at a Chinese restaurant in St Michael's Street.

Although I managed a Second class degree instead of the expected (and deserved) Third, I shall not forget the look on Mr Leishman's face during my final interview. 'If it hadn't been for all those extra-mural activities, this man could have got a First.'

The President, Mr Costin, went further. 'Don't forget the college. It certainly won't forget you.'

It was the greatest compliment I was ever paid. And it was almost true. Thirty years later I was invited to become a member of the High Table at St John's. It is a way of charging you for expensive dinners, but I do not mind. I owe them something.

CHAPTER 3

Theatre

It is amazing how you take things for granted until they are taken away from you. Even if you are not particularly musical, you can sing or whistle along with your friends, or with the radio. You can whistle while you concentrate, you can sing with sheer exuberance at the weather, at a happy prospect, or to cheer yourself up. In these days, when sickness has cast me down, I resent the fact that I cannot whistle or sing in tune. With so much time spent at the wheel, aping the radio was one of my favourite pastimes. Blessed with a passable singing voice, a certain talent for mimicry and an actorish desire to show off (if only to myself), I would one minute be Bing Crosby, the next having a shot at Pavarotti, and finish up being the whole of the London Symphony Orchestra or King Oliver's Dixieland Jazz Band. That is denied me now.

At the moment in my life when I most need cheering up, when, for the first time, I try to shut out thought and dull care and pass the time with simple pleasures, I can no longer hold my head erect or whistle a happy melody.

With the cerebellar syndrome, the fine tuning has gone. So have the fine tunes.

Just as I cannot carry a cup of tea without spilling it, because the muscular control has gone, my vocal chords will not hit the right note or, if by chance they do, will not stay on it.

It is the same with dancing. Jo and others will tell you that I was the world's most uncoordinated dancer, and they are right, but I was exuberant and, though I had little skill, was at least in time. That too has gone. My muscles will no longer do what my brain tells them – I cannot even make a fool of myself with impunity.

The dancing, I can let go; but that they should have taken away my *singing I cannot forgive. The strange thing is that the knowledge that I cannot join in has somehow taken away the pleasure of listening, and I am less inclined to make the effort of switching on the gramophone than I was, and more inclined to turn the radio off. Perhaps it is a sign of depression, but I do not like to be reminded of my infirmity.*

Singing was very much a part of my theatrical days. All four of the shows I was in in the West End were musicals, and though I was not exactly a speciality dancer, I had to do my best in a number of the revues in which I invariably found myself. Occasionally, such is theatrical sod's law, I would find that although I was the only person who could sing and not dance, I was cast in a role which required dancing and no singing.

It was autumn 1961 and the glory days were over. Now the harder business of actually earning my own living faced me. But doing what? I had made only one real attempt to face up to the problem of employment while at university, with the BBC, and that had failed. For a while I pretended that the careless undergraduate days were still in existence. I toured with *The Merchant of Venice*, I went as part of the OTG revue to Edinburgh. But there was no going back to college, no room waiting for me in Walton Street. I had hard decisions to make, and now was the time.

When I could stretch out the university days no longer, I went back to Gloucestershire and thought. Was there anything I had done in my life that I had particularly enjoyed? Yes, appearing on the stage. Was there any possibility of earning a living at it? Possibly, but not probably. I tried to think logically. In the end, I decided that it would be better to give it a go than to sit around in an office wishing I had done so. If it proved impossible, or too difficult, then I could think again. But I would never forgive myself if I did not even give myself a chance. I packed my bag, and, Dick Whittington-like, went up to London to seek fame and fortune.

I shall always be grateful to Henrietta Roberts, who had a house in Worship Street, EC1 and who allowed it to become a sort of home for graduate waifs and strays. We were a mixed bag. There were post-graduate students at the LSE; the editor of

Peace News, a CND publication; me, a Reserve officer in the RAFVR, who would occasionally don a strange blue uniform and go and check up on what the Ruskies were up to; and a delightful girl called Romola who could never quite make up her mind whether to take advantage of her considerable acting talent, or to opt for something professionally safer. She eventually became one of Mrs Thatcher's press officers – though whether that could be regarded as safe is another matter. At all events, they were very generous to a penniless would-be actor, and had a very comfortable sofa.

Thanks to a good friend, Adrian Brine, I had already made my professional début the year before (1960) while still an undergraduate, as a spear carrier in the BBC television production *An Age of Kings*. I learnt a good deal from that brief flirtation with television, and thought myself unbelievably lucky to be working with Noel Johnson (Dick Barton, Special Agent), Jack May (Nelson Gabriel) and Tom Fleming, among many others. One morning, when I had nothing to do, the director Peter Dews blew me up in front of the whole cast for reading a newspaper during rehearsals. 'You are privileged to be working with top-flight actors,' he bawled, 'take advantage of it.' I did not need to be told twice, and I have never again let my attention wander during rehearsal or, later, when directing, allowed others to.

I also learnt how skilful and well-timed television has to be. In those days even Shakespeare was live. Generally, the powers that be did not mind if so prestigious a series overran. But on one occasion we learnt between the dress rehearsal and the live show that the Queen Mother was appearing on the 9 o'clock news, and so no overrun was possible. Such are the BBC's priorities: given a choice between the bard and the Queen Mum, the Queen Mum wins every time. With incredible calm, Peter worked out in a few moments how ten minutes could be cut from just an hour, with the least distress to the actors, and all was well. The episode came out to the second. I knew I could never achieve such a thing, at least not without a major panic.

Down in London the following year, the old-boy network started to operate. Eventually I got my first job in, of all places, Oxford. A friend was working at the Playhouse as assistant to the director Anthony Page, and had a job as assistant stage manager in his gift. I was soon back in the city of dreaming spires, collecting old gas stoves and other household items as props for a revival of *The Caretaker*. It was a very different existence from the one I had known in that city, and I spent a great deal of time explaining to bewildered fellows and friends what I was doing.

My professional stage début came at Christmas 1961. I had stayed on at the Oxford Playhouse, and landed a triple role in *Alice in Wonderland* as well as the assistant stage manager job. I was the Fish Footman, a Playing Card and one of the lobsters who performed the quadrille. As the fish I had to wear some disguise, which made dancing even more difficult than usual, but little was needed for the Playing Card, as I was terribly thin at the time. It was suitable casting for 'Wispy' Worsnip.

The ASM role was, if anything, more testing. Borrowing the relevant props for something as dreamlike as *Alice* proved difficult, and some had to be made. As Oxford's most impractical man, I tried not to panic, but casual requests like the one I received just before I was about to travel home on Christmas Eve had to be complied with. 'Could you rustle up the Madhatter's teapot before you go? Something silver, only about 4 feet in diameter.' It seemed an impossible task, and the shops were all shut. Eventually I found some old chicken wire, bent it to shape, covered it in strips of material and painted it silver. It got by, but I could not help wondering why I had bothered to spend three years getting a degree in English literature. A short course in DIY would have been more appropriate.

My next job, in the spring of 1962, was also as an ASM, at Chesterfield. Here I had more of an acting role, and I much enjoyed playing Frankie Bryant in *Roots*.

One of the members of the company was a young Canadian called Donald Sutherland, fresh from Drama School. He was rivetting to watch – there was no question of reading newspapers while he was rehearsing. Nearly twenty years later, long after he had become a huge Hollywood star, I interviewed him on a film set for *Nationwide* and we recalled how the path from Drama School to superstardom had been by way of the George Stephenson Memorial Hall in Chesterfield.

* * *

My pay had gone up since my days at the Oxford Playhouse, from £6.50 to £8.00 a week, but of course instead of bumming off friends I had to find my own rent. This accounted for £4.50 a week (I had gone for something up market), and I was just able to afford half a pint of beer a day without my money running out. The scaffolding erector I shared a room with expressed amazement that anyone so highly educated should work such long hours for so low a wage, and offered to find me work on the building site. Although it would probably have been more restful, I declined.

I had learnt two valuable lessons at Chesterfield. One was that a provincial audience's taste should not be despised because it is not the same as London's. My landlady, bent over a hot stove, explained that she did not go to the theatre much because they were forever offering the trendy 'kitchen-sink' type of play. 'I get enough of the kitchen sink at home,' she said. 'I like to see plays about lords and ladies.'

The other lesson was the importance of a good 'study' – bothering to get the words right. I was once on stage on a first night when a leading actor stood up behind a desk and announced, 'My name is—.' He then went completely blank and finished, rather lamely, 'yes?' His question was addressed to the prompter. This came about simply because the actual line was, 'I'm Dr Wilson.' When he heard himself start wrongly he promptly 'dried', and ended up doing an impersonation of a man forgetting his own name.

Undoubtedly my moment of triumph came when I brought a play to a close half-way through Act One. We were giving a piece called *Anniversary Waltz*, which hinged on a husband and wife disagreeing about how loud the television should be. The first Act finished with the husband kicking the set, producing a mighty explosion. Half-way through the Act, he asked her to turn it down. She promptly turned it up. The prompter (me) had to give the signal to the electrician at exactly the right moment. Unfortunately, at the moment when the electrician should have been increasing the volume ('go gramophone') my sleeve caught the 'go electrics' switch, and instead he pushed the button to explode the television. The result was that the television blew up about ten minutes too early and made the rest of the Act completely impossible. There was only one thing to do, and that was bring down the curtain, which I did. I can see the director's knuckles now, white with rage, as he worked out what to do next. We would repeat the end of Act One, then go straight on to Act Two, changing the set in two minutes instead of the normal fifteen. Afterwards, when we drank in the bar with the regular patrons, nobody commented at all – except for one old lady at the end who said how much she had enjoyed herself, but supposed she was getting old and had seen too many of those sort of plays: 'Why,' she said, 'there was almost one part where I could have sworn I had heard that dialogue before!' You can fool some of the people, some of the time . . .

That summer, I joined the Royal Shakespeare Company. Well, for a short while. It was a special season at the Arts Theatre in London, and the director was again Anthony Page, so I managed to land a bit part. The play was *Women Beware Women*. We all got equal pay and equal billing. I was still bottom of the bill. If your name is Worsnip you pray for someone called Young or Zoob to be in the company, and lift your name, but it was not to be.

There was plenty to learn. Nicol Williamson was in the company, and so was John Thaw. I was lucky enough to play a serving man to Ernest Milton, who had been one of the great Hamlets of the 1920s. He was an actor of the old school who, with his extravagant arm gestures and sonorous tones, declaimed rather than acted. At one moment, Tony Page was rash enough to suggest that for his big speech he put the goblet he was carrying down on the table. 'Put the goblet down, Anthony?' boomed the old man. 'That smacks to me of realism. I can't be doing with realism.'

Tension was running pretty high at 1 o'clock in the morning when we were doing the technical run. This is the first rehearsal with all costumes and props. A call came over the tannoy demanding Mr Bernard Bresslaw's presence on stage. Silence. The call came again. Nothing. Finally the director himself came on the tannoy. 'Bernard, come down on stage, please. Forget the costume changes, come as you are.' After a minute or two Bernard appeared on the stage – stark naked. 'Well, you said come as I am, and that's how I was.'

Bernard then made his triumphal way back to his dressing room, cheered to the echo by the whole cast. Bearing in mind the size of Bernard, it was a bold gesture, but it certainly had the effect of clearing the tension.

The next engagement brought me my first opportunity of writing for the stage. Once again it was an accident. I was still an ASM, this time with a touring show called *Spoof* that was intended for the West End. It was a vehicle for the great musical comedienne Anna Russell, who could imitate any known type of singer or song, and some that were unknown. The play depended on something called 'Papa's all-purpose speech' which the heroine used to win the day. As the centre-piece of the play it was a pretty poor piece of work and I felt sure I could do better. I worked away in the few hours I had to myself in my humble digs. Actually, the landlady did not think them that humble. She pointed proudly at the bed: 'You'll never guess who slept in that bed last week,' she said. I could not. 'Cliff Richard. You know, with all the Shadows!' I did not like to argue.

My finished version of 'Papa's all-purpose speech' was full of non-sequitur clichés, such as 'with our backs to the wall, we must run the race that lies before us . . .' and Miss Russell was good enough to accept most of it. It did not save the play, and we never reached London, but it was useful practice.

Not that I cared. I was head over heels in love again. There was a wonderfully camp and glamorous juvenile in the cast called Jacqueline Jones, and although she was rather older than me, and certainly had more expensive tastes, to my astonishment she made a dead set at me. Once again I was enormously flattered, and I collected the many front covers on which she then appeared. She had already been a film starlet in Italy and had played one of the leads in Fellini's *La Strada* (under a different name) and although I felt slightly like what is now known as a 'toy boy', I enjoyed being taken round to meet her friends. Meeting people like Lionel and Joyce Blair and Vidal Sassoon made me feel, once more, that I had wandered into a showbiz world in which I did not belong and had no right to be in, but nonetheless was enjoying.

Now came the moment I had been waiting for. In the autumn of 1961 I got my first acting job. I would no longer have to spend my nights dismantling one set and erecting another, and my days begging and borrowing obscure props. I went up to Dundee where a fledgling Hannah Gordon was doing her best to lose a Scottish accent. I remember how, in the arrogance of youth, I thought she was horribly miscast as Eliza Doolittle in *Pygmalion*, and how I ate my words when I saw what a fine job that talented actress made of the part.

The theatre also had an odd-job man, an utterly unsophisticated youth whose manners were uncouth, who normally could not string two words together and, when he did, did so in tones so incomprehensible that he became a laughing stock among the leading players. No-one could doubt his love of the theatre, and when one of the leading players was off sick one night during *Lord Arthur Savile's Crime*, he offered to read the part from the book. The results were embarrassing: mis-reading, mis-pronunciations and the whole performance conducted in a thick Dundee accent which conveyed little of the Italian chiromancer intended by Oscar Wilde. Shortly afterwards he announced his intention of auditioning for the London Academy of Music and Dramatic Art. There was sniggering from the leading players. He did not have a coat to his name, which was Brian Cox, so I lent him a mac and off to London he went. Some time later he appeared in the dressing room with a letter from LAMDA and asked whether he should open it. There was an embarrassed silence. Eventually some of us persuaded him, and to our enormous delight and amazement listened to him read out that he had got in. Three years later Brian was playing Peer Gynt at Birmingham Rep, and shortly afterwards became one of the country's most powerful principal theatrical actors. Nothing further has been heard of the leading actors from Dundee.

I never asked for the mac back.

As luck would have it, I was invited by Piers Haggerd to play in his production of *Henry IV* by Pirandello at the Glasgow Citizens' Theatre. The lead was being taken by Albert Finney, and I jumped at the chance. I was all set to dislike Finney. He had been a member of the RSC when I had been playing in *Bartholomew Fair* at Stratford, and I had taken a shine to deserted wife Jane Wenham, while her husband had been living down the road with another actress. In the event I was once again proved wrong. He was charm itself, gave a great deal, and his compelling performance taught me a lot. He would go out of his way to make sure everything was right for his fellow actors, and was generous with both his praise and his advice.

I was beginning to think I had taken the right decision to become an actor. I knew, of course, that I had joined the theatre because I enjoyed it rather than because I was good at it, and that I was still only at the bottom of the escalator. But I had fitness and energy enough to keep pace, and had no cause to be anything other than content.

I was still in love with Jackie, who was by now starring in a variety show called *It's A Pleasure!* It came to Glasgow while I was there, which was a piece of luck, and we were able to spend some time together. Everywhere I went there were large posters with a picture of Jackie and the legend, '*It's A Pleasure!* WITH JACQUELINE JONES.' I could only concur.

Meanwhile, the Worsnip brothers were hitting the headlines in their various ways. If Molly Worsnip was ever to be proud of her sons, this was the moment. My middle brother, Hugh, was still a popular local rock 'n' roller. But Tony and the Beatniks decided that at twenty-one they would be over the hill, and must play their last concert. My youngest brother, Patrick, was away at camp when the news came through that he had passed fourteen O'levels at the age of fourteen. He had already had an exceptional school career, having bypassed the second form altogether and then taken O'levels in the fourth form instead of the fifth. Newspapers ran several stories within a short time of each other and the local paper, *The Citizen*, ran a piece describing my latest activities.

At that time my mother used to take the laundry by hand into a shop in Gloucester. The story goes that one day she went in and the woman behind the counter said, 'Name?' 'Worsnip.' The woman looked up with interest. ''Ere, are you related to that Glyn Worsnip it said in the paper was acting with Albert Finney?' 'He's my eldest son, actually.' 'Oh, you must be so proud.' Shortly after, my mother called in again. 'Name?' 'Worsnip.' The woman looked up. ''Ere, are you related to that Hugh Worsnip it said in the paper was in Tony and the Beatniks?'

'He's my middle son, actually.' 'Oh, you must be so proud.' My mother went in a third time. 'Name?' 'Worsnip.' The woman looked up with deep suspicion. ''Ere, 'ow many sons 'ave you got?'

After Dundee and Glasgow, I spent 1963 in weekly rep at Oldham. It was hard graft. Sometimes I had to learn thirty pages of a new play overnight, having already done a day's rehearsal and an evening performance. But by the end I had learnt a good deal about economy, and getting on with it. It really was a case, as Noel Coward put it, of 'Speak up, and don't trip over the furniture.'

A good deal of what I learnt came from an Australian actor called Kevin Lindsay. He played 'leading man' roles, and although he was good looking it was felt that his short stature was a bar to his progress. Not that it had stopped Alan Ladd, and Kevin was both taller and a better actor. Still, he had found a niche at Oldham, and seemed happy with his lot. He told me that he had left Australia with his friend Rod Taylor. They had gone their separate ways and Rod had ended up in Hollywood, where he became very big. Kevin used to delight in the story that on one trip back home Rod had called in on Kevin's mum. She asked how he was getting on, and he replied that he had made two films that year, including Hitchcock's *The Birds*. Kevin's mum was horrified. 'Only two jobs this year!' she cried. 'Oh Rodney, I am sorry. If only you had had Kevin's good luck. He's leading man at Oldham, you know, getting twenty pounds a week, regular money!'

In 1964 several things happened: I moved in to a flat with Brian Wenham; I played my first part in the West End; I teamed up with a talented young man called Richard Stilgoe; and I met my future wife.

Although a year ahead of me, Brian had been a good chum at Oxford and he showed it now. He had a regular job as a producer at Associated Rediffusion in Kingsway, and he saw that mine was more precarious. I moved in to his flat in Chalcot Road, NW1, and lived in what for me was some style. For one thing I had a room of my own.

Richard Stilgoe too was at that time still in a regular job, at the advertising agency J. Walter Thompson. He had been sent down from Cambridge for concentrating too hard on his work with the Footlights Revue. We came together because an old Oxford acquaintance, Noel Picarda, asked us both to join him at The Poor Millionaire theatre-restaurant. The theatre-restaurant was the forerunner of today's pub-theatre, and very much in vogue in the 1960s. Noel was doing a review called *Something In The City*, to celebrate the City of London Festival. The fourth member of the team was Susan Hanson, whose first job it was. She later went on to spend many years as a regular in the television series *Crossroads*, and whenever we saw her we used to boast of having 'discovered' her. After *Something In The City* we did one more show with Noel, a James Bond parody called *From Rush-Hour With Love*, full of absurd jokes:

JAMES BOND: I can't get away. The swine has tied my hands together.

BIRDBRAIN JACKSON: I'll get a knife and cut the rope.

JAMES BOND: It's no good. He didn't use rope.

BIRDBRAIN JACKSON: What did he use?

JAMES BOND: Nothing. He just tied my hands together!

Thereafter we did several 'revuesicals' (revues with plots) over the next three or four years, usually parodies of some fashionable book or film, and including *The Carrierbaggers*, *Those Magnificent Men In Their Washing Machines*, (a soap opera), *The Victoria Line*, *Not Bloody Likely* (a sort of *My Fair Lady* in reverse), and *The Cocaine Mutiny*. Richard Stilgoe wrote the songs, I directed and we both wrote the book. The hardest part was the title. We used to say that we spent a week just thinking of the title and only three days writing the whole show.

For each show, we would audition for two other actors, and for the last one we 'discovered' a very tall but talented young actor called Chris Serle. Eleven years later he would, after a varied career, take over from me when I left *That's Life!*

Richard has proved a good friend, being immensely supportive in recent times, and I like to think that I taught him a little of what I had learnt in repertory about performance. Certainly while with us at The Poor Millionaire he turned professional and began putting his many talents to use.

They were heady days. Towards the end of 1964 I auditioned for the part of the chinless wonder, Lord Brocklehurst, in a musical version of *The Admirable Crichton* which Bernard Delfont was putting on at the Shaftesbury Theatre, starring Kenneth More and Millicent Martin. Because I did not need the work (I was already working at The Poor Millionaire) I naturally got the part. It made a change. I had often come away disappointed from an audition, although I had the good fortune invariably to have Dickie Stilgoe playing for me. After that we always did a number from *Our Man Crichton* for luck and, while I sang the main part up on stage, Dickie would throw in Millie Martin's interjections from his position in the orchestra pit. We used to joke that more often than not I would do the audition, and Dickie would land the part!

Kenneth More was, as they say in the theatre, 'tiny blissikins'. He was the least temperamental star I ever worked with. He could not sing for toffee, but carried the part with his immensely likeable personality. With a smile, or a quiet word, or even a party, he would defuse any hyper-tense situation and create an oasis of calm into which he seemed to be able to pull everyone else. Once he was kind enough to draw me aside and offer his advice that I should not let myself get type-cast as a chinless wonder, or I would find myself playing them for the rest of my life. If only that had been true! Still, I was doing well. I found myself rushing from the theatre by taxi every night to start work in *From Rush-Hour With Love*. It was aptly named.

I decided I had taken the right decision. Even if it was luck rather than judgement I had, within three years, got to the point where I was appearing in my own show at The Poor Millionaire, as well as having my name in (albeit small) lights above a West End theatre. I still did not quite believe it, but I was starting to be proud of myself. Never more so than when, one evening, Brian's mum and her friend Gladys came up to see the show. They were affable women from E.10, and thrilled that someone they knew was in a West End show, in a position to offer them tickets, and in a principal's dressing room. When they came round for a drink afterwards, however, much of the talk was of how they had seen Noel Coward in the auditorium. At that moment there was a knock at the door, and Noel Coward himself walked in, looking for an actor in a nearby dressing room. The ladies nearly wet themselves. He was very good. He allowed himself to be lionized and to sign autographs, and was more than charming before proceeding on his way. After that there was no further discussion of *Our Man Crichton*, or my role in it, or anything else much.

On my twenty-sixth birthday (2 September 1964), we opened *From Rush-Hour With Love* at The Poor Millionaire. Three days later I got the best present I had ever had. A friend of Dickie's was having a party. She brought it to the show and invited the cast back afterwards. I spent some time talking to the most glamorous thing I had ever seen. With her deep brown tan I thought at first she was Egyptian, or from somewhere in the Middle East. In fact she came from Streatham, and was an air hostess with BOAC. I quickly discovered that the glamorous exterior concealed an intellect far sharper than mine, a memory more acute and a power of reason more formidable. (Later on I would also discover how easily my friends were deceived by appearances, and how distressed that made her.) She also had a degree in French and German. She had gone straight into the Foreign Office as a translator of secret documents, but had found there was too much Office and not enough Foreign for her taste, and joined BOAC as a way of seeing the world. I was bowled over, and mortified that I was neither wealthy nor in possession of any form of transport. I knew when I was out-classed. I would never see her again.

I had not considered the possibility that she might have been interested in me. She has since always maintained that this was the first and only time that she ever used anybody: she accepted a lift with Noel Picarda, who had a second-hand Jaguar. She dated him until he took her to The Poor Millionaire, where she was able to see me again. I got, with some disbelief, the message.

After that, between trips abroad she was a frequent visitor at Chalcot Road. I could not bear her to be away, let alone half-way across the world. I fretted. The only entries in my diary of the period are in capital letters and underlined. JO FLIES OUT, JO FLIES IN, Hong Kong, Karachi, New York. All very romantic names, but to me they were just names on an indicator board and meant merely a trip on a bus to a crowded terminal at London airport and a gnawing at the stomach until Jo was back safely – and a feeling of insecurity because I would know that she had refused a comfortable lift home to travel on the bus with me.

I had vowed that I would never get married. The uncertainty of an actor's life, the lack of income, the long periods spent away from home made it no sort of a prospect. Jo changed all that. The feeling of incompleteness when she was abroad, the anxiety that unless I did something positive I would lose her, the growing sense that underneath that glamorous and capable exterior there was a little girl that needed protection, all combined to make marriage inevitable, and I asked the question. The answer was an emphatic yes, and for a moment all the doubts disappeared. The London evening papers came and took our picture: 'Air-Stage Romance', they called it.

One evening when Jo was away, I told Brian of our intention. His deadpan features registered no surprise. He sat, unblinking, as if in thought. Eventually he spoke. 'I think this calls for a small whisky.'

Reaction at home was less predictable. I wrote to my parents and, eventually, my mother came up to London. We foregathered at The Poor Millionaire. My fifteen-year-old brother Patrick was there to see fair play. Little was said between the two women. It was hard to tell who was the least at ease.

When mother returned home, on the milk train, my father and brother Hugh were naturally curious. Hugh himself was engaged to a local girl – blonde, pretty, full of common sense, a touch of Gloucestershire. Now my parents were to acquire another daughter-in-law. 'So what was she like?' My mother produced one of her dramatic pauses. Then, demolishing both brides to be in one sentence: 'Well, you couldn't call *her* a country milk-maid.'

We were married exactly a year after we met. Out of deference to Jo's parents, the ceremony took place in a Roman Catholic church, in Bexhill-on-Sea where they then lived. Jo's father, a *Daily Telegraph*-reading self-made man with a house in Spain, was none too happy about his eldest daughter throwing herself away on a ne'er-do-well actor without a proper job, although it has to be said that he was the first to glow with pride when his friends later commented on my radio and television appearances.

Giles Havergal was best man, and Brian Wenham and David Kernan (whom I had got to know well during *Our Man Crichton*), the ushers. My mother did not come. The event was a great relief, if only because it took place at all. As the bride was arriving, one of the priests came up and asked me for the certificate. I had forgotten to pick it up. The priest told me that as it was not a Church of England ceremony, it could not take place. I broke into a cold sweat. All those guests. The bride arriving. Giles slipped away and assured everyone that things were going well. I pleaded, and was taken to see the Registrar. I swore I had ordered and paid for the certificate. He said that if I gave my word, the ceremony could go ahead; we would sort it out afterwards. I took up my place again in the nick of time. The only other mishaps involved the registrar getting the names confused and trying to marry Jo to my father, and Jo's parents not being present to receive their guests. They had been nicked for speeding between the church and the reception.

We honeymooned in San Francisco, Jo was entitled to a ten per cent fare for her and her next-of-kin, and to take her final days as leave. We flew across by BOAC VC-10 and were fêted with champagne cocktails by a friendly crew, more than we could drink. A friendly West Indian carpenter, on his way to Barbados, was pleased to help out, and at the end of the flight another passenger, curious to know why we were being treated like royalty, asked if I was one of The Bachelors. I said no, never again.

Nor did I ever again have a year like 1964. But it was the 1960s; skirts were short and hopes were high. We had got over the shock of Jack Kennedy's murder the year before, and still looked forward to a better and more tolerant world. Everything was to play for, and the thought of sickness, pension, or insurance never crossed my mind.

For the next eight years I plied my trade as a jobbing actor and Jo took a variety of jobs to support us. She worked for the British Council, first in their Accommodation Department, and later as a Programme Organizer. She was assistant to the editor of the political magazine *Socialist Commentary*. Later she went as a mature student to the LSE to read politics, but after a while was obliged to withdraw because of ill-health.

Giles Havergal had now taken over as director of the Palace Theatre, Watford, and I played there several times. Everything from the tallest Feste in the business to Ugly Sister in *Cinderella*. I also played Algernon to David Kernan's Ernest in *The Import-ance Of Being Ernest*, and suffered a déjà vu in several senses when Giles wittily staged my *From Rush-Hour With Love* starring Jacqueline Jones.

In those years (1965–67) I undertook two new ventures. I first performed my own material on radio, having a regular spot on the precursor to *The World At One, This Time Of Day* introduced by Lord Arran. I would stay up all night perfecting the sup-posedly satirical script, scared rigid that the right thoughts would never come my way and that my lack of expertise would be exposed. I was actually glad when the programme came to an end because it meant that I would no longer suffer the kind of cold fear which I now associate with facing up to illness. I did not know my good fortune.

I was much happier appearing in *The Dales* on the BBC Home Service, in which the burden of worrying about Jim now fell on Jessie Matthews. The welcome there was as warm as a tea cosy, scripts were provided and the lady producer still wore a hat to rehearsals. I was only sorry that my stay was short-lived.

I also made my first, and only, feature film, a girlie movie called *I Like Birds*. Here there was no question of wearing hats, or anything else much. I was cast as a gay photographer ('absolutely right' for the part, said the director when I first walked in through the door) and was intrigued to find that it was shot in two versions, the English and the Continental. The difference may be gauged from the following extract:

The boss of a girlie magazine walks on to a photographic set, where a glamorous young lady is scantily clad in nothing but a feather boa. 'Oh,' he says, 'this won't do for our readers!' In the English version he rearranges the boa more decently. In the Continental version he takes it away completely.

In 1966 I had taken over as director of the revue *Four Degrees Over* at the Fortune Theatre, the start of a long association with David Wood and John Gould. Two years later, I directed a touring version of the same revue, and later several more revues, including *Three To One On*, which toured and went to the Edinburgh Festival, and *Postscripts* which played at the Hampstead Theatre Club. It was during the preparation for the opening of one of these shows that the stage electrician came out and said to me, 'I've put a chocolate on your bottom. Would you rather have a strawberry?' It was some time before I cottoned on to the fact that these were technical terms relating to the colours of gel in the lighting. It was one of the hazards of directing that it involved talking to technical experts in their own language. It was a language I had never learnt, and yet another example of how someone with no skill can con their way through life by sounding confident.

Looking back, it might appear that I was always in work. This, however, was far from the case. True, I was working for just more than six months in the year, which was better than average, but a good deal of time was spent out of work, and I am aware that I was not always pleasant to live with. Jo was supportive then, as she is now, but I am conscious that it was not always easy and that our somewhat precarious existence meant that she was never able to train for a proper profession.

We were lucky enough to spend those years living in Jermyn Street. The friend whom we had visited in San Francisco on our honeymoon was away for several years, and passed on his flat to us. The rent and rates came to seven pounds a week in those days, and I remember in one period of acute poverty thinking that if only I could be guaranteed an income of twenty pounds a week, we would be sitting pretty. A quarter of a century later, the thoughts are somewhat similar, but the sum is somewhat different.

Through an introduction of David Kernan's I was able to work, when I could not find theatrical employment, for a Mayfair astrologer called Patric Walker. I acted as a sort of amanuensis and, having done some reading, was soon writing his monthly column for him in the fashionable magazine of the day, *Nova*. It was only a short walk from Jermyn Street to Mayfair, where he had a flat in a house belonging to Cicely Courtneidge and Jack Hulbert, so it was more than convenient. I enjoyed my years with Patric. No-one could have been more cynical than I about astrology's claims, but Patric had an uncanny knack of being right, particularly if an individual's birth-time were known to him and a birth-chart could be drawn up accurately. I have never been able to understand why he was right, but he invariably was and I now treat the whole subject with a great deal more respect.

Patric also had some pleasant friends. Portland Mason was one, and I remember at a birthday party of hers that her father, James, flew in unexpectedly from Vienna where he was filming. Jo and I were for some reason having a discussion on the price of potatoes at Fortnum and Mason. There was a lull in the conversation, and that milk-chocolate James Mason voice was heard to protest with anguish: 'Oh, but you don't buy potatoes at Fortnum and Mason!' The next day we found a huge Fortnum and Mason bag, full of potatoes, propped up against the door of our flat.

Richard Chamberlain was another chum of that time. He was trying hard to lose the Dr Kildare image. He also made sure that he was always seen in public with the most glamorous woman, and Jo was only too glad to occupy the position many women would have given their right arm for, that of Dr Kildare's escort to the theatre and elsewhere. Jo had lost none of her glamour. Indeed, we shall always remember that when she was filming in Shepperton, Elizabeth Taylor was mistaken for Jo by a BOAC pilot.

My period working for Patric came to an end when I joined the cast of *Oliver!* in 1967, and for three years Jo worked for him instead. The show was handily just a few hundred yards across the Circus at the Piccadilly Theatre, in the eighth and final year of its first run. I was playing Mr Sowerberry, the undertaker, and was also understudying the part of Fagin. Indeed, I played Fagin several times in the next year, including on the last day. I very nearly played it on my first day, too. I was asked to stand by, as there was some disagreement over the star's contract. I was not sure then that I could manage it, not having had any kind of rehearsal, but to my great relief the need did not arise. Fagin at that time was to be played by the original Mr Sowerberry, Barry Humphries, in the days before he became Edna Everage, superstar. Marti Webb was playing Nancy, and my apprentice was played by a rather spotty and unprepossessing youth called Phillip Collins, who later made something of a hit in the pop world.

Oliver! was enormous fun to be in, if energetic, and I thought the outsider's view of people in the theatre was summed up when I returned, exhausted, to the flat in Jermyn Street. 'Why are you so tired?' said Jo. 'After all, acting is only walking about and talking!' We were not rich, we were not particularly successful, but we felt very 'West End'. The escalator was still running, but we had no trouble keeping pace, and the company was better than we had ever bargained for.

After its London run, *Oliver!* was due to open in Japan and I was asked to go with it. Here I ran up against the actor's perennial dilemma: to go, or not to go; to be in work and disrupt family life, or to stay at home and risk being out of work. I did not always get it right, but on this occasion I think I did. I declined, saying that I thought I had done enough to be offered the part of Fagin, which was vacant. The management did not agree, and I stayed in London. But the fact is, had I been offered the part, I would still have put my career above my private life, and left Jo to cope alone. I do not remember such decisions with pride.

It was a bizarre life. On the one hand we were nonchalantly entertaining the 'stars' – as Jo said, it is amazing what you can do with a bit of rolled breast of lamb; on the other we were poor as church mice and wondering where my next job was coming from. To this day, I wear a suit that Richard Chamberlain had had made for himself but was too small.

Towards the end of 1968, we lost our flat in Jermyn Street because it was discovered not to comply with fire regulations. In an ill-considered move, we took a large house in Teddington. It had a flat downstairs which was used by Jo's parents, who had little sympathy with our lifestyle. We stayed there until 1971, when we eventually moved into a small flat on our own at Hampton Wick. The 'West End' days were over: people were less inclined to visit us in the suburbs, and the business of catching the train every day did a lot to restore our sense of reality. So did unemployment, although here I was lucky.

Being out of work as an actor is probably more stressful than being in work, and I was always very firm about admitting it.

People would ask knowingly if I were 'resting'; I would always say, 'No, I'm out of work.' There is an assumption about 'resting' that working in the theatre is not a serious business, and that you are taking it easy. It is like those people who, when you are working eighteen hours out of twenty-four as an actor in rep, say, 'Yes, but what do you do during the day?' In fact, the periods spent out of work are considerably more stressful than periods in work. Being turned down for work two or three times a week does not do a lot for morale, or for home life either. That is why working first for Patric and then, after 1969, for Geoffrey Plumbly, was a blessing.

Geoffrey Plumbly was an eccentric, easygoing, pipe-smoking ex-Army officer who had invented a sort of postcode system, to assist large firms marshal their deliveries. He had the good sense always to employ actors who were out of work, not only because they were cheap and intelligent, but because they were well spoken on the telephone. A good deal of time was spent making excuses to clients, and a smooth telephone manner was essential. Geoffrey Plumbly was incredibly loyal to his staff, and once you had worked there, he would always take you back whenever the theatre did not want you. He had Dickensian premises near Charing Cross, but the lack of cleaning and the carpetless, dust-covered floors, were nothing new to the actors, who were deeply grateful that, by hook or by crook, Geoffrey Plumbly managed to stay in business.

Between periods of unemployment, I was to be in two more West End musicals. During 1971 and 1972 I spent eighteen months playing the lecherous Friar in the long-running *Canterbury Tales* at the Phoenix Theatre, and the following year I landed a large dual role (father and son) in John Hanson's *Smilin' Through*. It was through *Canterbury Tales* that I found my agent, Jeanne Griffiths, who represented another member of the cast and sought me out. I left the show because, once again, there was no prospect of advancement, despite the fact that by the end I had taken on no less than seven understudy roles, and had at one time or another played most of them. I think I was probably miscast as the Miller and the Host, lacking both age and corpulence, but I had always enjoyed character parts which required a good deal of make-up, rather than 'juvenile' parts which did not. Indeed, not to put too fine a point on it, I was, with one or two exceptions, the world's worst juvenile. I took on so many understudies because I was bored with the routine of giving the same performance every night. It is true that every audience is different, and that keeps you on your toes as far as pace and comic 'business' are concerned, but it is much more exciting if you are also hyped up by playing an unfamiliar role.

There are other ways of being kept on your toes. Working with Frankie Howerd is one. Someone had remembered my performance as Lord Brocklehurst in *Our Man Crichton*, and I was once cast as Frankie's silly-ass son in an adaptation by Galton and Simpson of de Obaldia's satirical Western, *The Wind In The Sassefras Trees*. One evening, we realized that the great stand up comic, who had little experience of ensemble playing, had cut from the beginning to the end of the last Act. Since most of the plot was explained in that section, and since it was my big scene, I improvised some line like: 'But surely, father, you'd like me to tell you . . .' Frankie stopped dead, and then said: 'Oh, all right, bore the audience, bore them rigid!' The play never reached the West End, so maybe I did just that.

After an extensive tour, *Smilin' Through* did reach the West End, but sadly lasted only a month, until the owners wanted their theatre back to put on another show. I have always thought, such is his appeal to the old ladies, that John Hanson should be provided free as a social service. Certainly there is no question that *Smilin' Through* would have run had the Women's Institutes had time to galvanize themselves into arranging coach parties and the like; we had gone down a treat in the provinces and there was no reason why we should not in London. But plays are not always withdrawn because there is no hope of their making money. Sometimes the impresario thinks there is more chance of making more money with something else. *Smilin' Through* was a victim of this system, and I felt sorry for John as this was his own *magnum opus*, and he had set his heart on it being a success.

Three things I remember in particular about *Smilin' Through*. First, the ending, where our hero and his bride ascend triumphantly to heaven amid a swelling chorus and against a background of moving clouds set in a brilliant blue sky. One night the lighting got reversed and instead of blue we got red, giving the impression that the pair were disappearing into hell. A fate, some said, that they richly deserved.

Second was the way that, by a curious chance, John invariably managed raucously to clear his throat throughout my tender love scene prior to his entrance.

Third was a moment during rehearsal, when we were practising that scene for the first time with John's poignant music underscoring it. I was the First World War hero explaining to the heroine that I could not marry her owing to the fact that vital bits had been shot off me by the wicked Germans. When we got to the end of the scene, John explained that we had not spent long enough over it and that there was still some of his music left. Thinking it would raise a smile, I said, 'Don't worry John, it'll be longer when the laughs are there!' For a fraction of a second I did not realize my joke had misfired, until I heard John protesting, 'No, no, there mustn't be any laughs, this is a serious scene.'

I was to do two more musicals, both out of town. The first was *My Fair Lady* at the Opera House in Harrogate. When my agent came to see the show she happened to sit next to an American woman who had toured the world to see every production of the musical. In her opinion, I was the best Freddie Eynsford-Hill she had seen, and the only one who had treated 'On The Street Where You Live' not as a romantic ballad, but as the outpouring of frustrated puppy love by an immature fop. Even I was pleased with the result, and realized that in my mid-thirties I was at last old enough and experienced enough successfully to play a juvenile.

I was not, however, old enough to avoid falling in love. At Harrogate I fell heavily for a beautiful singer called Jane, and our days were spent exploring the Yorkshire castles and other beauty spots, and walking in a landscape as magical and other-worldly as Nutwood. The reality at home was that Jo was badly ill with a pelvic inflammatory illness and, actor that I was, like Ernest Milton, I could not 'be doing with reality'. Not that there was anything unreal about Jane. She was probably the most down to earth person I had ever met, and we agreed to confine our affair to Harrogate. Sadly we could not and did not.

It went on all summer, until eventually I was found out. Having to choose, I chose Jo, and was at length forgiven, but I derived no credit from the affair and it was the first time that I consciously inflicted hurt on anyone. Living in a world of make-believe, you do not escape reality.

In 1973 Jo and I made a decision. Work was getting sparse, so it was decided I should simply take whatever work was offered and see where it led. On this principle, I went first to Leicester where, as I remember saying, I had the title role in *Much Ado About Nothing* – About Nothing! After that we closed the old Phoenix Theatre in the bus station, which fifteen years earlier I had raised money to build, with a musical called *Happy As A Sandbag* and the company moved on to sumptuous new premises in the Haymarket. I went back to Plumbly's and shortly afterwards accepted two contrasting parts at the Alexandra Theatre in Birmingham. One was Miles Gloriosus in the musical *A Funny Thing Happened On The Way To The Forum* which called for a great hulk of a braggart soldier. I could sing the part all right, and I could wear padding, but there was nothing I could do about my bare legs, and the lines, 'Look at the size of my thighs, Like a mighty machine,' used to bring the house down for quite the wrong reasons.

The second play was *The National Health*, in which I played a drunken wayfarer. I shall not forget it because one night there occurred one of those pieces of serendipity which make the magic of the theatre even more magical. It was a quiet balcony scene, at dusk, in which I was chewing the cud with another hard case in the hospital. Suddenly a beautiful tortoise-shell butterfly got caught in the beam of the spotlight, and stayed with us for some considerable time. We improvised a whole scene around this butterfly until it went away. The audience was still and the only sound was people backstage rushing downstairs thinking that because they could hear unfamiliar dialogue they were 'off' and had missed their cue. It seemed the most natural thing in the world, and when it was finished we simply went back to the scripted dialogue. How well it fitted was summed up afterwards, when a member of the audience asked, 'How did you work that butterfly?'

I stayed on for two more plays which finished the season at

Birmingham. The last was that hardy perennial, *The Ghost Train*. I do not know how I had survived so many seasons in rep without ever having played in it, but I had, and I much enjoyed it. I did not know it then, but it was to be my last appearance on the stage.

Geoffrey Plumbly was proud of his 'old boys'. He suggested I get in touch with a recent ex-employee who had finally gone to the BBC as a drama producer. He was a former child-actor and his name was Glyn Dearman. It seemed inconceivable. I thought back to that photograph in the *Radio Times*. Reality was catching up with my childhood fantasies; two worlds which had seemed a million miles apart had almost caught up with each other. It was possible for a boy from a Gloucestershire village to appear on the wireless. Or even the television.

It was October 1973. At Plumbly's the phone rang.

'It's your agent.'

News of more disasters? 'Put her on.'

A click. Then, 'Hello. The BBC are doing a new show which needs versatile presenters. Would you like to audition?'

'Who's in it and what's it called?'

'Esther Rantzen, and *That's Life!*'

CHAPTER 4

That's Life!

Antidisestablishmentarianism.
Llanfairpwllgwyngyllgogerychwyrndrobwllllantysiliogogogoch.
Floccinaucinihilipilification.
Whenever there was a complicated word, or set of words, an incomprehensible place-name, or an example of indecipherable bureaucratic or technical jargon, I would be assigned to read it. My acting training had taught me to master words, and the clearer and quicker I could be, the more po-faced, the bigger the laugh. Now I can not only not negotiate the complicated words, I cannot even manage the simple ones. I have trouble saying my own name. An explanation as to who I am is frequently met with incomprehension down the phone, and I am recognized more often by my lack of clarity than by my clarity. Gone are the days when I could bring comprehension to the incomprehensible, when I could clarify the unclear, when I was That's Life!'*s king of gobbledegook.*

'What's it like working with Esther Rantzen?' If I have been asked it once, I have been asked it a thousand times.

Over the years, I developed a single adjective to answer the question, one that covered all eventualities. The word was 'challenging'.

Like most big stars, Esther divides her audience: some love her, some loathe her. To many she can do no wrong; to a few, everything she does is wrong.

Sometimes the question is asked out of genuine curiosity; sometimes it is asked provocatively. The answer, of course, depends. It depends on what kind of a mood she is in. It depends on whether things have gone well or badly. It depends on whether she has been working too hard. The same rules apply to her as to anyone else. But she is a larger than life figure. The extremes of her moods are more extreme. Because she is more articulate, she can be more devastating; because she is more powerful, she can be more effective. Because so many depend on her, she can be intensely kind. Because she is cleverer, she can eliminate doubt and uncertainty. Because she is more determined, she can cut through red tape. Because her position is so secure, her success so unquestionable, her self-confidence so apparently unassailable, she can be both superbly supportive and devastatingly destructive. She brings out the best in you, she brings out the worst. Yet I would be prepared to swear that she is not always aware of what the effect of her actions will be. I say her 'apparent' confidence because I am not convinced that confidence in self is the same as confidence in power or success. I think there are times when she knows she is wrong, but it would be too damaging to her pride to admit it.

It would be idle to pretend she was not stimulating to work for. She is a first rate producer, even if she is, as my fellow presenter Kieran would say, a hard taskperson. When I was convinced an item was about the iniquities of airline freight handling, Esther would see that it was about disappearing elephants' feet. When Kieran said that he was convinced that a mortgage broker was a con-man but that we could never run the story because we did not have enough proof, Esther read the research and picked out the relevant details. We ran the item, and as a result the Consumer Credit Act was tightened. She is perceptive, tough, charming and determined, and it does not do to get on the wrong side of her.

In the early days, one of the ways in which she laid down her power base was through her present husband, Desmond Wilcox. He is the sort of likeable maverick the BBC could do with more of, and he was head of the department which produced *That's Life!*, General Features (Television). Intensely loyal to the programmes and people he cares about, he will fight to the death to protect them.

As Head of Department, it was Desmond's normal responsibility to read every script, every commentary, every billing for *Radio Times* that came out of his department. However, his burgeoning relationship with Esther sometimes made things difficult for the rest of the *That's Life!* team. If at any time there was a disagreement about the script, Esther would merely say, 'Let's see what HGF (TEL) thinks about it', and wander off down the corridor. Scripts which we had thought to be final on Friday night would occasionally be changed (often for the better, sometimes not) by the time we arrived for rehearsal on Saturday. Desmond, who often appeared on the set on programme day, was understandably interested in the success of the programme. The decisions that were taken were often very courageous and, in order to nail a 'baddie', we would take risks which other programmes would not.

It was a brilliant formula: vulgar jokes, valuable research, performing animals, persistent pursuit of the unacceptable. It was the first 'consumer' programme of its kind. It brought an awareness of their rights and a determination to fight for them to an audience which did not necessarily read *Which?* or the *Guardian*. It restored the fast-dwindling notion that 'the customer is always right', and was prepared to take on the complacent, the well-established and con-men large and small. People went to jail, companies folded, legislation was changed.

Sixteen years later, the programme is still hugely popular. The same mis-shapen carrots, the same talented pets, the same jokes, the same cons, sometimes even the same con-men. The show is not as taut as it once was. When I was on it we rarely spent more than six minutes on an item, and therefore were able to cram more in. But the formula still works and, although television audiences are not as large as once they were, it is still among the most popular of programmes. It did not in principle appeal to the intellectually snobbish, though as one of them once explained to me, it was 'the sort of programme you don't turn on, but if it's on you don't turn it off'. I took some pleasure in the fact that many of its twenty million audience would not have admitted that they were watching.

Back in 1973, I had a decision to make. I was working at Plumbly's when the BBC decided, unusually for them, to throw the whole thing open and audition for presenters among whoever offered themselves. They advertised in the journalistic press, and I am told that over a thousand people applied. These were whittled down and the long business of auditioning began. I had not appreciated how long the process would take, and after I had survived the first round had to decide whether to accept an offer I had received to do a play which might or might not end up in the West End, or to abandon it and carry on with the auditions for *That's Life!* Mercifully I opted for the latter – another of my few good decisions – and began the protracted business of turning up for auditions, interviews and what were called 'observed working sessions', where you were handed a letter from the public and asked to produce an item by the end of the day. Eventually we were down to eight, and we all competed with each other in a 'pilot' programme, with a genuine audience to test reaction. My main competition appeared to come from a young man called Simon Bates, and I realized that I lacked the confidence which broadcasting as a disc-jockey had given him. My worst fears were confirmed when, the next day, I got a call from Esther. 'Evil news, I'm afraid,' she said. My heart sank. But it was her little joke. 'If you accept our offer, you'll be working with me for the next few months.'

I was eager to accept, and the BBC Contracts Department was soon on to me. They could offer me a researcher's fee of £60 a week, plus all of £5 for appearing. My agent was not very happy about the £5, and it was certainly not the figure that had been mentioned by the editor of the programme. In the event, with much reluctance, the BBC settled on £100 all in, and it seemed like a fortune. Like most people when they first get a job there, I would have been prepared to work for anything. Only later did I discover that the BBC is well aware of this, and treats its employees accordingly.

In January 1974 I gave up smoking. Despite our poverty, and because I was a nervy person, I had been smoking about forty a day for fifteen years. I knew that this new venture would up my consumption, if only out of sheer cold fear, and one week before I went to work for the BBC I quit smoking altogether. I have not had a cigarette since.

From the start the tone was set. At a pre-season lunch we met those members of the team we had yet to meet, and we all outlined some of the research we had already done. I was working on a story about how a Mr Pratt had bought some waterless saucepans after an exaggerated spiel from a Mr Fidler, and I remember Cyril Fletcher saying that with stories like that on the programme who needed jokes?

Cyril was destined to be one of the popular successes of the programme, with his odd odes, misprints and malapropisms. I could remember reading of his exploits in a comic called *Radio Fun* some twenty years earlier, and I still could hardly believe that I was actually working with the same person. I was never quite certain about his persona on the programme, being by nature keener on the raised eyebrow school of humour than on the wicked lewd leer which figured so heavily in his repertoire, but he was kindness itself to Kieran and myself, and unstinting in his praise and encouragement. His wisdom and experience taught us a lot about tolerance and temperament, especially when the going was tough. We were inclined to ignore persistent rumours that the original idea had been to ask Ronald Fletcher to give the inter-item readings in his suave straight-man manner, but that the BBC, with greater serendipity than miscalculation, had booked Cyril by mistake.

However arrived at, the chemistry worked. The team of Rantzen, Prendiville and Worsnip proved popular, and it was not long before the programme reached the top of the charts. A huge correspondence was generated and it became obvious that the stories which hit the screen were only the tip of the iceberg. The letters were selected, from among the thousands that came in, by a very small team – Esther, Kieran and myself, four or five researchers and two or three secretaries. We tried to read everything, and it was very hard work. Inevitably mistakes were made. Our first task was to make sure the writer was neither a liar nor a loony. We quickly learnt to spot them. Letters with long sentences underlined three times in green ink tended to be from the latter. Some were either 'bum or boring' and were quickly rejected. Nothing was regarded as 'too hot to handle'. Indeed, the programme quickly gained a reputation for being fearless. It became obvious, too, that besides the stories which lent themselves to humorous or dramatic treatment, there was a mass of the more mundane; that the British public, though sometimes painfully gullible, was persistently being swindled; and that there was plenty of room for more consumerism on other programmes and other channels. The newspapers, too, somewhat belatedly, took up the cudgels and soon the freedom to fool the public, whether by business or bureaucracy, was being questioned everywhere.

The team worked hard and played hard. And it was a team. Presenter or secretary, film director or researcher, we spent the vast majority of time in each other's company. We discussed items, and each other, together. We ate together. We misbehaved together. We moaned about, or praised, Esther together. Always we talked about her. There was a fierce programme loyalty. Most of us were doing our respective jobs for the first time. Kieran Prendiville had been a journalist on a Lancashire local paper and later came to London and worked as a researcher in television – indeed in the very department in which he was to find fame! He was able to help me with journalism, just as I could help him with performance. Ian Sharp, who later directed *Who Dares Wins* and other feature films, cut his teeth on 'Heap of the Week' for *That's Life!* Every week we would find new ways of destroying some particularly useless item of consumer goods. Sometimes we would dress it up as a Western, sometimes a gangster film, always a suitable pastiche. Colin Cameron, now head of the BBC's Documentary and Features Department, learnt his trade filming dogs that answered the telephone and grand prix motormower racing. Pat Houlihan, now boss of the *Holiday Programme* got women's gymnastic classes to dance with umbrellas in rain (created especially by the Special Effects Department). Dozens of the BBC's best producers spent their time organizing people who could play tunes on their teeth or produce music from a watering can. As well as that, they had to be able to pursue con-men who were selling pups to honest punters; they had to wrestle with company law and lawyers; they had to be sure enough of their facts to make certain that innocent people did not go to jail. For all the misprints and bad puns, the mis-shapen tomatoes and *double entendres*, the stories that people remembered were of the old lady who was swindled out of her savings, or the family who lost their home.

It was a hard school, but a good one. It was all encompassing. Rarely did we have time to go to the theatre, cinema, a cricket or football match. More often, we would end up at one of the restaurants we had adopted, such as the Greek 'Kleftiko' in Shepherds Bush, endlessly discussing the programme or Esther's latest demands. That she was a first class producer (although, like the rest of us, doing the job for the first time) no-one denied. Whether her goals were always achievable was a matter of constant debate, but she certainly stretched us to the limit, and by doing so brought out the best in us.

When she was in a bad mood she could be very trying. She appeared not to be able to make a distinction between professional disagreement and personal attack. She expected blind loyalty and was personally hurt when there was a difference of opinion. On one occasion, when such a difference had occurred, she rapped on the table, knowing that everyone would pay attention. I was the target, and she announced, 'Considering the difference in our relative positions, Glyn, it's amazing to think that you are in fact older than I am.' I bit back some remark about how, when she was eighteen and hard-pressed, she had been glad to copy out my essays. A wounded Esther was a dangerous thing, and to be avoided at almost any cost. At such moments it was better to swallow the pill, but it was hard not to wonder at the change in the jolly, tubby, short-dark-haired young girl next door of fifteen years before. Yet she had the skill of regenerating devotion in an instant, her tenderness towards her own children was touching, she was a superb hostess and, above all, a seeker after professional excellence in both herself and others. Some have questioned her motives, some have found her unerring popular touch distasteful, but no-one can deny that she has put her 'showbiz' talents to superb use, particularly in the area of child care, and when she finally becomes a Dame or a Lady I, for one, will applaud.

Kieran and I quickly became the victims of our own success. With one third of the nation watching, it became impossible to do undercover work or to stake out 'baddies', for fear of being recognized. It became impossible, too, to convince viewers that we did not simply wander in at the weekend, read the words off the autocue and collect a large sum of money. Part of the programme's success, I have always believed, was that much of the reading, research and telephoning was done by the presenters themselves. It meant that by the end of the week we tended to know a story intimately, and thus deliver it with that much more authority.

The effect of all this on myself was a curious one. Although I never really believed I would do so, I was nearing the top of the escalator. I was, because of the programme, among the most viewed presenters on television. I could not go to a restaurant or appear in public without being recognized. Life for my friends and family tended to consist of waiting around while I was accosted by fans. Although I often resented the intrusion, I felt that I owed a debt of gratitude to the fans. They were the people who made the programme, by providing both the material and the viewers, and I always tried to reply to those who wrote to me. As time went by it got harder, I had several offers of marriage, and one woman wrote in to say that she wished only to share a bath with me. I was reduced to giving the standard reply, thanking them for their interest in the programme.

There was a good deal of correspondence about the punchline we developed, and I invariably delivered. This was, 'Unless, of course, you know different . . .' Many people wrote in to say that this was an incorrect use of the language, and the phrase should be, 'Unless, of course, you know differently.' No amount of saying that 'different' was being used as an adjective governing a noun which was absent but understood, would convince them, and I resorted in the end to making the point by suggesting that next time they chose a different colour writing paper, perhaps bluely instead of whitely! It would be silly to say I did not enjoy the fame, I did, but I always felt that there had been some mistake and that one day it would end. I never guessed how.

For the first time at home we did not have to worry about money. We did not have a lot but it was regular and enough. I grew fatter in the face. I put on a couple of stone, partly because I had taken up drinking in place of smoking, partly, as one of my friends satirically remarked, because I could now afford lunch.

After the first season of *That's Life!*, in 1974, it became obvious that we had a success on our hands. The BBC offered me a two-year contract, and undertook to find me things to do in the six months of the year when the programme was not on the air. After years of insecurity this seemed like forever, and Jo and I thought about moving. It had always been an ambition of mine to return to Gloucestershire, and Jo had always longed for fresh air, open spaces and country living. With the two-year contract in front of us, we threw caution to the winds and bought a house at Clearwell in the Forest of Dean. It was, as they say, 'ripe for development', and we borrowed a caravan while the work was done, parked it in the garden and lived in it during the winter of 1974–75.

It was a hard but happy time, a new beginning. I was destined once more to become a country person and Jo, who had spent some formative years in Ireland during the war, was never happier than when cultivating her garden. She learnt quickly by trial and error, and soon even the villagers were popping their heads over the wall to see what she was up to. She was by no means conventional in her approach, but definitely effective. We would have crops at unusual times – times which the local people did not believe possible. Soon we not only managed to keep ourselves in vegetables, but were able to sell some of the produce, and by doing so introduce the locals to untried delicacies such as Hamburg Parsley (a kind of nutty white carrot), and Good King Henry (a spinach-type plant, also known as Fat Hen).

At the start we had a garden but no house, but by the first week in June 1975 we were ready to move in. It was not going to be a palace, but it was habitable. I was still frantically busy with *That's Life!*, and one Tuesday drove up to London for the week's work. Jo decided not to move in until I came back after the weekend. On the Wednesday morning she called me. The house had burnt to the ground during the night. The alarm had been raised by a neighbour who happened to be going to the bathroom at 1 o'clock in the morning. The kitchen was on fire. In the ten minutes it took the fire brigade to reach the scene, the whole house was in flames and uncontrollable. During a long night, Jo had sat on the hillside in her nightie and, with much of the village, watched while the first home of our own was destroyed.

We never discovered the cause. There was much talk of arson, and the possibility that I had upset someone through the programme. I was inclined to discount this theory, on the grounds that if someone had wanted to teach me a lesson they would not have been able to resist telling me, but certainly it was a reminder of how vulnerable we were. Kieran once happened to mention on the programme that he had been threatened. There was an almost immediate phone-call: was he one of the Prendivilles from Kerry? He was. That being so, he need not worry about any threats. The caller and some of his larger pals would visit the offender, and there would be nothing else to fear! Kieran did not hear another word on the subject.

Jo, as always, reacted well in a crisis, handling many of the arrangements that had to be made. I went into shock, and to emphasize how all-encompassing television was, especially to the inexperienced, I will always recall walking in the morning after the fire muttering that it was a bit embarrassing, but my house had burnt down, and could I have a couple of days off? The reply was 'yes', provided I stay and finish off an item that was needed for that week's programme. I had not yet learnt the lesson that 'it's only television' – but later I would.

It took exactly a year to rebuild the house – The White House, as it was known. In the interim we managed to rent a cottage nearby, complete with damp and death-watch beetle, and I often wondered what viewers would think if they knew the conditions that one of their better-known presenters was living in. Curiously, the episode had one good side effect. Those who had regarded us as trendy television people from London, and therefore separate, realized that we were ordinary human beings like everyone else, and just as vulnerable. Occasionally, people would tramp up the garden path, knock on the door and assume I could do something about their three piece suite. Or trippers would bring a picnic to the adjacent hillside and eat it while gazing over into our garden, which was very boring. The fire, and the knowledge that I was born and bred in west Gloucestershire, made me human and did more for our acceptance by the community than anything else. It was extremely pleasant to be treated as a human being rather than a television personality, and made life at home much more attractive. Now that I am ill, and live several miles away, the village has not forgotten me, or that I spent more than ten happy years there.

They were full years. I never really decided whether I was a country boy or a London television person. I tried to be both, and did not really succeed at either. I did not stay in London and mix with the right people at the weekend, go to the right parties, make myself indispensable; nor did I devote enough time and energy to Jo, to my daughter (when she arrived, miraculously, a blessing late in life) or to my little patch of Gloucestershire.

Jo was pregnant during the long hot summer of 1976. That she was at all was, according to some doctors, inconceivable – if that is the right word. After exhaustive and embarrassing tests on both of us, we had been told that the possibility of having a child should be discounted. We were both thirty-seven and, if we had wanted children, should have sought help sooner. Jo was, as usual, determined to defy the accepted mythology, and when she announced cheerfully that she was pregnant, surprised us all.

It was a happy time. I was successful; Jo was content cultivating her garden and looking forward to motherhood. The only thing she missed was permanently stimulating company. 'There are a limited number of things you can say about Princess Anne's baby,' she would say, or, 'You know what I miss? . . . Jews.' Every now and then, a friend would arrive from London and the need would be fulfilled.

It was sweated labour in 1976, and Jo had problems. Nourishment was not getting through to the baby. Jo went into hospital. It took some weeks, but they sorted it out. Then pre-eclamptic toxemia developed. She stayed in. By November *That's Life!* was between seasons and I was guesting as a film-reporter for *Nationwide* (which I continued doing until 1978). On the evening of 24 November I was sitting in their office preparing for the following day's filming. The phone rang. It was the sister at Gloucester Royal Hospital. Would I ring the consultant at home? That sounded ominous. I did so. He told me that he was in a dilemma; unless he performed a Caesarean section in the next twenty-four hours Jo might not live; but on the other hand, if he did, the baby might not yet be strong enough to sustain life

– he would have to decide. I had no doubts. If there was any choice, the decision must be in favour of Jo. We could try for another baby. The consultant was not so sure about that, but he agreed that there was no question but that Jo should come first. 'What are you doing tomorrow?' he asked. 'Making a film about the inadequacies of the National Health Service,' I replied, truthfully. There was hollow laughter at the other end. 'Ring me tomorrow,' he said.

I looked up, shaken. Tomorrow's editor of the day, Andrew Taussig, had heard my end of the conversation. He did not hesitate. 'If there's any problem, go!' he said. I rang the film director, Alan Ravenscroft. He agreed. 'We'll find a way round it,' he said. 'Remember, it's only television!' I went out to supper with Esther and Desmond. When I got back to my lodgings, at about 11.30, Norma Shepherd, my colleague, friend and landlady, was waiting up. 'They won't tell me anything,' she said, 'but they've been ringing all evening. Will you go to Gloucester at once? They're operating about now.'

It was the longest, coldest, most frightening two-and-a-half hours of my life. I had no means of communicating with the hospital. I had to keep my eyes, if not my thoughts, on the dark road. I did not know who would be alive when I got there, who would be dead. It could be either, or both. I told myself a thousand times that it was going to be all right, that the hospital service could do almost anything nowadays. I thought again of whether I had done the wrong thing in not taking the advice of those who had advocated private care in London. I knew that the answer to all my questions would be written all over the face of the receptionist as soon as I gave my name.

As it happened, there was no receptionist when I arrived. It was 2.30 in the morning. The hospital was bleak and Kafka-esque. The corridors were dimly lit and empty. I did not know where to go. Jo had been taken from the maternity ward she had been in. Eventually I found a solitary nurse, quietly knitting. She pointed me towards the emergency theatre. There I found some more nurses gathered round a desk. They were whispering. I explained who I was, and was taken to a nearby room. There, at last, I found Jo, tubes protruding from every orifice. She was being monitored every five minutes, but she was at least alive.

The nurse waved me to silence until she was ready. Eventually she explained in a whisper that Jo had not woken since the operation, but that, all being well, she would survive. The unspoken question must have been written all over my face, for she stopped short and said, 'Has no-one told you?' My heart sank. 'You have a daughter. She's being treated as an emergency at the moment, but she's alive and well and more than three pounds.' I rocked with relief.

Eventually I found her. It meant donning a cloak and mask, and in her glass case she looked for all the world like Sir Alec Douglas-Home, with rubber bands for arms and legs. But she was alive, and certainly kicking.

I sat with Jo for most of the rest of the night, and the one time she regained semi-consciousness I told her the news. 'Of course,' she murmured, smiled and went back to sleep.

Five weeks later she came home, and so did Elinor. The baby was five pounds and had never been in a temperature of less than eighty degrees. It was New Year's Eve, the snow was thick and icy and I had to choose a roundabout method of getting up into the Forest. We made it without incident, but then the central heating chose to break down. I spent part of the night of Jo's and the baby's return humping electric fires from the attic, and part with the central heating stove in bits and pieces on the floor. It was not the most romantic of homecomings, and hardly the way to spend New Year's Eve, but it was better than it might so easily have been.

Apart from visits by friends, the two worlds of television and the Forest of Dean rarely coincided. One occasion when they did was when The White House unwittingly provided the programme with material. My agent had sent me a postcard, correctly addressed, to 'The White House, Clearwell, Nr Coleford, Glos.' Someone at the Post Office obviously read only the first line, for the card was sent to America and delivered to their White House. Fortunately, as I liked to pretend, President Carter knew who I was and scribbled 'try England' on it. The card came back and eventually, five months later, was delivered at the right address. I was glad to have got it, for the message read, 'Please ring me urgently!'

I opened village fêtes and persuaded other good friends such as Cyril Fletcher and Richard Stilgoe to do the same. Even Esther sent a deputy. We were treated with commendable good sense by the local population, which was always much more sanguine about television personalities than the fête organizers. On one occasion, the important announcement was made that Mr Glyn Worsnip of *That's Life!* was about to declare the fête open (as if people were not already more interested in bargains on the stalls). A woman burst in, rushed eagerly up to the stage, took one look at me and said loudly, 'Oh my God! I hoped it would be the other one!' It did not do to take one's status as a television personality too seriously. I was always reminded of some good advice about television dispensed by James Hogg of *Nationwide*: 'Do it seriously, but don't *take* it seriously.'

Among many successes on *That's Life!* we had few real failures. One was when we tried to make a record of it. By its nature the programme dealt, as Esther used to say, with 'real people, in real situations.' Therein lay its drama. The record could not and did not. Without the important ballast of up to the minute drama, the songs and jokes were exposed for what they were; fillers, amusing, but essentially trivial. For many weeks I received statements from the record company listing the profits as £0.00. In the end I got a statement declaring that I owed them money!

Another failure was the item that never got broadcast, despite several attempts to persuade the then editor, John Morrell. We had received a cutting from a local London paper. There was a photograph of a contented group who had just enjoyed a Chinese meal at a new restaurant; underneath we were told that the restaurant was owned by a Mr Chong Sen, who came from the Fu-kien province and specialized in food from that region. Then came the punchline: 'Said Mr Kenneth Lo, the well-known gourmet, "Mr Chong is the finest Fu-kien chef in London!"'

It was surprising how often the stories wrote themselves. Not only did the people involved manage frequently to have names which suitably matched the content (an antiques dealer called Robin Bastard, a dentist called A. Fang, but the story would provide its own punchline.

One example was when a viewer wrote in to complain of Post Office inefficiency. They had cut off her telephone for non-payment, when the bill had in fact been paid. I rang the Post Office and said it was grossly unfair that, owing to their own inefficiency, our viewer was quite unable to use her phone. A spokesman called me back and apologized. 'You're quite right,' he said. 'The bill has been paid. This must be sorted out. I'll give her a ring right away.'

On another occasion, someone wrote to us whose car had been badly damaged when a herd of escaping bullocks had leapt over a fence on to it. The problem was, who should he claim against – the owner of the bullocks, the firm that was taking them to market and from whom they had escaped, or the owner of the field from which they had jumped? It turned out that, under a special order, he could sue them all and the judge would decide which was the guilty party. This was known, believe it or not, as Bullock's Order, after a Mr Bullock, and it meant that when the judge enquired under which order the request was being made, Counsel could justifiably reply, 'Bullock's, m'lud.'

Another correspondent objected to an advertisement in the London *Evening Standard* for computer operators overseas. The *Standard* had taken it upon itself to specify that applicants should be male only, which our correspondent felt was against the law. I rang the *Standard* and asked to speak to the Classified Ads Manager. I was told the Manager was busy, but that I would be rung back. Eventually a man came on the line and, in a rather pompous old-fashioned manner, insisted that there was no way the *Standard* would condone sending women abroad to work. Nameless things might happen to them – they might be carried off into the white slave trade, for example. The *Standard* had to protect such people. I thanked him and then, just as a check, asked if he were the Classified Ads manager. 'No,' he said, 'but I'm speaking for her.'

Bureaucracy was a favourite target. We frequently blew up the Gas Board, shocked the Electricity Board and dampened the spirits of the Water Board. If there was scummy water on hand I would be pushed in it; if there were rotten eggs about, they would be broken over my head. The more po-faced I was, the better – it was funnier that way. We did not only discomfort ourselves. We parked an old hill farmer in a dentist's chair on a cold mountainside and checked which of various new dentures would best allow him to carry on whistling his dog. It made an hilarious film, but we all suffered for it.

We were often hoist with our own petard. I talked to a solicitor accused of over-charging; he sent me a bill for the time he had spent being 'consulted' on the telephone. The Law Society upheld his right to do so.

A hairdresser we admonished for completely ruining a customer's hair put up a sign in his window saying, 'as advertised on TV!'

We pretty soon learned that the professional bodies – those representing lawyers, doctors, builders, policemen, customs and excise men – were far harder nuts to crack than the unions or the small shopkeeper, and we began almost to feel sorry for the petty criminal who did not have the resources or the strength of the bigger companies. We found that there was more cynicism about consumer rights among the larger firms, and a huge hole in the Companies Act which enabled those who were convicted of fraud to keep their ill-gotten gains and simply start up another fraudulent business under a different name.

Whenever I was asked to speak to a women's club, I would invariably begin by saying, 'As you probably know, I spend a good deal of my time dealing with corrupt solicitors, bent policemen, shady business men and inefficient bureaucrats. What a pleasure it is to come here today and meet their wives.' This was greeted with hollow laughter.

Looking back, we were never knowingly cruel to either humans or animals, though sometimes we sailed pretty close to the wind. But it has to be said that we were game for anything if it was of help to the programme. I did my first animal film with a parrot on my shoulder. Throughout the day it excreted down my back, so that at the end I could walk away while its owner could remark wistfully, 'What the eye doesn't see, the heart doesn't grieve over.' It was a valuable first lesson in television: watch your back.

I went to Lancashire to interview a dog who could count, and to Lincolnshire to meet a crow who rejected any beer but real ale. It took some time, but in the end the bird turned up trumps, we got an added bonus of a shot of it visiting the 'gents' and, to our delight, it could only walk home at the end of the day.

Of course we had our disasters. A cat which was reputed to be able to predict the weather by the way it waved its tail simply could not, or would not, despite the best efforts of our Special Effects Department, who brought sun lamps, tropical foliage, snowstorm effects and hosepipes. It also went missing for three or four hours during filming, though whether this was because it disliked my interviewing technique, or simply did not want any publicity, it never revealed. It was a measure of our dedication that we did not dare return to base with a mission unaccomplished, so we shot a film about a cat who *could not* predict the weather; it was a measure of Esther's skill that she could see how to do it and still get laughs.

I spent some time fondling an alligator in a basement flat in Surbiton, where it lived with a retired colonel and several reptilian companions. 'Perfectly harmless,' said its fond owner, 'I often show it to schoolchildren.' Half-way through filming, he went to put it away and came back covered in blood. 'Excuse me just a moment,' he said, 'but I think I'd better nip down to the hospital. The alligator's just bitten a hole in my arm.'

One evening after work (did it ever stop?), we travelled down to Swindon to listen in on a con-man selling his dubious wares to a client who had asked him to call round. It was hard to get permission for secret filming and recording, but the Office of Fair Trading, which was always kept informed of our proceedings, backed our request to the Director General of the BBC and, as it was a nationwide fraud, permission was granted. We were due to spring out on the rogue at the vital moment, and elaborate arrangements were made for us – director, reporter and four-man camera crew – to be hidden in cupboards and other orifices. We waited in hiding for several hours. At last there was a knock at the door. We were at the ready, queasy with tension, when the client opened the door. A small boy scout stood outside and timidly asked for a bob-a-job. He was the only caller that evening and we went home empty-handed.

Successes were many. None more so than the almost weekly appearance of a wonderful old lady called Annie Mizen. She endeared herself to millions in our regular '*vox pops*', or street interviews. We first discovered her when I was offering passersby one glass of pomagne and another of champagne and asking if they could tell the difference. Annie claimed never to drink, but kept returning to the champagne to make sure. The result was hilarious, and thereafter not only was she a regular feature of the programme, but she Irene Handled any interviewer with consummate skill. Many viewers thought Annie's regular appearances were set up, but that was not the case. We just happened to film street interviews on Mondays in the North End Road, and she was constantly passing on her way to a regular hospital appointment. Whenever we spotted her, we knew our item was safe. Later, Annie was asked to Esther's regular parties and though there were some doubts expressed as to her ability to cope with such smart folk, all such worries were confounded and she was never anything but perfectly at ease.

On the more serious side, nothing gave us greater pleasure than seeing the law amended as a result of our investigations and, though we were sometimes over confident, sometimes too self-important, I like to think that we played our part at a time when consumerism had few enough champions. Certainly nothing gave me greater pleasure than the moment when a government spokesman said, 'It grieves me to say so, but I think you're on to something here.' The result was a Royal Pardon for a woman who had been convicted and fined in her absence on a road-tax payment charge. She knew nothing about it and was startled to be arrested for non-payment of a fine she did not know had been levied against her. It came as no surprise to learn that there was no machinery for court officials to admit they had made a mistake. The then Home Secretary, Roy Jenkins, was thus forced to authorize the Royal Pardon.

We had particular help from the Consumers' Association, notably from their legal officer David Tench, from a small but skilful team, particularly of researchers, and of course from Esther herself. There is no question but that at times we were exasperated with her. She could be over-demanding and less than understanding, but she was a marvellous hostess and a permanent stimulus. The five seasons I spent on *That's Life!*, from 1974 to 1978, were fulfilling and famous years and I would not have missed them.

* * *

Leaving was a stressful business. Both Kieran and I felt that we did not want to live and die with one programme. We were starting to repeat ourselves, both in terms of research and in performance. The battle against milking the audience and self-congratulation had been fought and lost. I was always in favour of a good vulgar joke, never vulgarity for vulgarity's sake. We had acquired a confidence which perhaps was misplaced but which nevertheless was there. We had successfully guested on other programmes. We were nearing the top of the escalator, and did not think that a sidestep would drag us down. We felt that a change of programme would do no harm, although the chance of being as well exposed was minimal. There were many who wondered why we were prepared to give up a programme which had made us so well known, or perhaps notorious, and who questioned our decision to leave. There were some who said it was because they would not pay us enough, or because we could not get on with Esther. Neither was the case, although Esther's feeling that she had been let down sometimes manifested itself in the sort of ill-humour which made us wonder whether we had not taken the right decision.

Yet Esther has been nothing but supportive since my illness was announced. When in the district, she has actually come to see me at home. She has also telephoned. In recent times, no-one can say but that she has been anything but scrupulous in her concern. She has never spoken anything but good of me to the press, has never proffered anything but praise for my efforts since the disease struck and has always been most co-operative on the several occasions when I have, for one reason or another, needed to interview her. Nevertheless I could not help remembering her remark about our relative positions when I saw that, in one newspaper report on my illness, I was described in the headlines only as 'Esther's Pal'. It reminded me of an appearance we once made on *Start the Week*, when the best Richard Baker could do to describe Kieran and me was as 'Esther's adjuncts'. Satellites though we may have been, we could not have had a more conspicuous planet to orbit.

Me aged five.

An early success as Tessa in *The Gondoliers*.

Pilot Officer Worsnip, wearing my father's old cap, 1957.

An 'air-stage romance'. Jo and I announced our engagement in March 1965.

An actor laddie, posing for publicity, 1973.

Above Kieran Prendeville, Esther Rantzen and me in *That's Life!* 1978 (BBC)

Left 'Vox pop' interviews were a feature of the perogramme. (BBC)

Below Kieran and me. 1978.

The great
lawn-mower
Grand Prix;
Kieran and I
took part with
Cyril Fletcher
dressed as a
Hell's Angel
for the
occasion.
(BBC)

The *That's
Life!* team.
(BBC)

Jo and me with Ellie, aged twenty-one months, at The White House, 1978.

Five characters from *Pigeonhole*, on *Nationwide*, 1979.

Reconnoitering the rock in *Rescue Flight*, 1981.

Meeting Princess Anne at the Institute of Neurology, London, April 1989.

Jo, Ellie and me, Christmas 1990. (Dean Forest Studios)

CHAPTER 5

Television and Radio

It is not more than 300 yards to the shops from my digs. That is about as much as I can manage now. I walk with a stick, but I have not yet learnt how to let it help me. I have to gaze at the pavement while I am moving, or I topple over. My head is permanently bent. I try to tell myself that I am not missing much in Shepherds Bush. There are few bushes and no shepherds. But there are things to look at: people, sunshine, blossom, traffic, shop windows. To do so I have to stop and position myself. Adopt a pose. At home in Gloucestershire it is worse. The ever-beautiful surroundings demand attention. I cannot walk up the drive and look around me. My eyes are fixed on the ground, looking for obstacles. My natural sense of balance has gone. At night I cannot move without switching on the light. In the morning I cannot leap out of bed, even if I wanted to. I have to be able to see where I am going. If it is dark I cannot move, cannot feel my way. When I am driving, I must keep my eyes firmly fixed on the road. I cannot look to right or left in case the car veers. I am getting close to having to give up driving.

I know what it is like to be old and infirm. It is twenty-five years too early, but I have that insight. I know what it is like to have to go slowly and painfully. I know what it is like when every step hurts and may result in a fall. I know what it is like to hold up the queue in the supermarket; to delay the bus; to stand, incapable, on the pavement edge. It was not like that until I was forty-eight. During my days in radio and television I had rude good health. I never went into a hospital except to report on it. I took on anything and everything, however dangerous; insured, or uninsured. I was confident in my fitness. I had no cause to doubt my physical ability. I travelled here, there and everywhere, fast.

* * *

I clung for dear life to the diver as we swung slowly on the winch nearer and nearer to the rock. It was in the middle of the sea, about eighty feet high and eighteen inches across at the top. No-one could possibly have been stranded on it, unless dropped by a helicopter, but it was a graphic illustration of how people get themselves into seemingly impossible situations and have to be saved by the Search and Rescue services, of which the Royal Navy helicopters are the most dramatic arm.

We had practised the manoeuvre once or twice, in full gear, including helmet, and I had gripped the top of the rock precariously while the aircraft had swung away and the cameraman, Paul Berriff, had practised shots. The idea was to make as dramatic an opening as possible to our series illustrating the rescue work of 771 Squadron at the Royal Naval Air Station at Culdrose in Cornwall.

Now this was the real thing. I was dressed only in shirt and shorts, and was carrying on my back the NAGRA sound equipment so that I could do a piece to camera while the supposedly rescuing diver was swinging towards me. As we descended, inch by inch, a cormorant landed on the rock, shat and regurgitated its lunch. There was nothing else for it but to continue, and I settled on the sticky, slippy mess. The diver swung away and I edged into position, keeping the sound equipment concealed from the camera. On a given signal, I started my piece and the diver descended again from the helicopter to 'rescue' me. He fixed a strop round the base of my back and, as I clung gratefully to him, we were whisked off the rock and upwards into the safety of the helicopter.

I did not do anything quite as dangerous again in that series ('One of *Nationwide*'s greatest hits,' said the London *Evening Standard*). I was used as fodder by the crews, and spent a lot of time being dropped into moving lifeboats for the entertainment of holiday-makers grouped round various Cornish harbours. I was in my mid-forties, about twenty years older than the crews who were flying me.

It was the first time a film crew (in this case just Paul and myself) had ever been allowed to fly on genuine missions with a rescue squadron, and throughout 1981 we returned several times, flying twenty-two in all. It was enough to do a full portrait of their work, and what started as a series for *Nationwide* ended as *Rescue Flight*, a full-blown documentary which was repeated three times.

After the first showing I got a call from the Department of Trade and Industry, which funded the service. Some big-wigs, including the Chief Coastguard, had failed to see the programme, and could there be a special viewing? I made the necessary arrangements and laid on some coffee. I was glad I did, given the august company. When it was over I was congratulated on showing something that portrayed British effort in a good light. 'But tell me,' said one member of the party, 'I've had some experience of these things, and you got into some pretty hairy situations there. Was there really no bad language from the helicopter crew?' I assured him there certainly had been, but that the *Nationwide* editor had insisted it be cut out. 'But this is filming real life, and death, situations!' I assured him that that point had been vehemently made, but to no avail. 'Well I think that's ****** disgusting!' said Norman Tebbit. It was not the last time he was to disagree with BBC policy.

That's Life! was the perfect grounding for the hotch-potch of television and radio that was to occupy my attention between 1978 and 1984. During 1976 and 1977 I was working on *Nationwide* when *That's Life!* was not on the air. John Gau was the editor, and he was not best pleased to have a 'personality' from *That's Life!* foisted on him. After the first season, however, he was good enough to change his mind and say I would be welcome back at any time – and if by any chance I ever wanted to leave *That's Life!*. . .

I learned my trade as a general film reporter on *Nationwide* in those years, and I could not have liked it more. I reported on everything from Dutch Elm disease to the making of Perry Como's Christmas Special. I now had two strings to my bow, and that was very valuable. My first film for *Nationwide* was, however, almost my last. The subject was a bird sanctuary in Oxfordshire. The day after we filmed it we were off again, and so were not there for the editing. I managed to watch the programme and, to my chagrin, the film was not on it. I naturally assumed it had not been considered good enough and determined to do better. In fact (as I learned later) an interview had overrun and there had not been time for the film; it would be run the following night. In the meantime, out of interest, I asked to see it the following day. To my horror, there was a ghastly error, in fact several. At one point in the film I had listed the birds in the sanctuary's care. Where I spoke of a magpie there appeared a sparrow; when I wrote lyrically about Sammy the sparrow, there appeared a ferocious-looking buzzard; when I spoke of the buzzard, there appeared an orange-eyed owl, and so on. The pictures were out of synchronization with the sound. I pointed this out, and remarked drily that I supposed even a film-editor could tell the difference between a sparrow and a buzzard. The chief film-editor, a wonderful man called Bill Billett with whom most of the female staff (and some of the others) were in love, had the great skill of always appearing calm when all around were panicking. He was very sympathic, but pointed out that there must have been a mistake in the paperwork we always prepared giving the film-editor our instructions, as these were always followed to the T. He took me through the film bit by bit, showing great patience with a new and anxious reporter. Eventually we discovered the mistake. The assistant camera person had put the same shot number on the clapperboard twice, and thereafter every shot was out by one. The mistakes were hastily rectified and the film shown, as promised, that evening. Once again, I had escaped by the skin of my teeth. It was the first of many services performed for me over the years by the unflappable Bill Billett, and one of innumerable for Lime Grove.

I soon discovered several things. First, that the film-makers were never recognized as much as the presenters who introduced them. Everyone knew who Frank Bough was, but far fewer recognized the talents of a James Hogg or a Luke Casey, however often they appeared on the programme. Indeed, a film by one of those worthies would often elicit a response from the viewer, but the letter would begin, 'Dear Mr Bough,' or 'Dear Miss Lawley'. The presenters, too, had an unfortunate habit of patronizing the reporter by saying, 'We sent So-and-So down to . . .' or, 'Our So-and-So went to . . .' I learnt this lesson the hard way. After I had sat around for three days to discover how the programme worked, the net effect was to make the presenters very uncomfortable – whose job is *he* after? Even presenters (or 'autocue readers' as Bernard Falk disparagingly dubbed them) are absurdly insecure. The editor then sent me to watch a film being made. When we arrived on location I found myself being greeted by the residents as the well-known personality from *That's Life!*, and everyone assumed I would be asking the questions. I had to explain that someone far more skilled than I was the actual reporter, and that this was *Nationwide*. It was embarrassing for all of us and, after I had had a word with John Gau, it was not a mistake we made again.

Second, I found that every person, every family, was far more individual, far more interesting than at first you might suppose. Whether it was an amateur back-garden boat-builder in darkest Leicestershire, or the man who had covered his entire house and garden with sea-shells from the beach at Clacton, we would be there, cameras at the ready. It was a standing joke among *Nationwide* reporters that, if in doubt, it was possible to begin any such film with the words, 'This may *look* like an ordinary suburban garden shed, but behind these locked doors John Smith is doing something out of the ordinary . . .' John Smith would turn out to be tending his champion orchids, or running the most authentic model railway in the country, or building a spacecraft out of old sardine tins. There was also an all-purpose ending to any more serious film: 'What happens next, we may never know. But one thing is certain, for the Jones family life will never be the same again . . .'

Third, just as the *Nationwide* reporter was an expert for five minutes on every known subject, so he or she was a friend of the famous for as long as it took to interview them. Some had the skill of making you feel that you had known them all your life, some that you were just another interviewer, and it was surprising how often the bigger the star, the more often they did everything they could to put you at your ease. Into this category came the American singer, Perry Como. Despite the efforts of his 'minders', he insisted on being interviewed at the end of a long day's filming. I asked him how, now that he was what we in Britain would define as an 'old age pensioner', he managed to keep the voice so mellifluous. He paused for a moment, then said, 'Well, Glyn. I drink a lot.'

This use of the reporter's first name was particularly gratifying, and more common among American than British interviewees. Not only had they taken the trouble to find out your name, but by dropping it into the conversation from time to time they gave the viewer the feeling that their representative was well known to the star guest and likely to be getting a more revealing interview than someone else.

It was a kind thing to do, but never so rewarding as when it happened naturally. As all-round reporters we had, perforce, to cover the seamier and more tragic side of life, as well as the more entertaining. One such occasion was the Penlee lifeboat disaster of December 1981. The lifeboat had perished with all hands on the Cornish rocks, while trying to rescue a freighter in distress. The village of Mousehole had lost the cream of its manhood in one blow, and the old enemy, the sea, now looking so innocently calm and blue, had claimed more victims. It was no place for an intrusive press to be, but I knew that if I did not go, someone else would. Such is the public thirst for information, particularly of the more prurient kind.

I first heard of the disaster on the 7 o'clock morning news. It was a Sunday and I was at home. Within minutes, the cameraman Paul Berriff was on the telephone from Belfast: should we go? *Nationwide* would surely want an item. I rang Roger Bolton, the *Nationwide* editor, at home. He had not heard the news, but would like an item for tomorrow night's programme, a reflective piece along the lines of 'the tragic village the day after.' It was the middle of winter and there was some doubt as to whether we could get there in time. I was snowbound in Gloucestershire, Paul in Belfast. But we did know the territory, and were known to the rescue services from our time in Cornwall making *Rescue Flight*. It was agreed that a local crew should be put on stand-by in case Paul could not get an aeroplane, and in fact he never made it.

I set out at once by car. I had a tough time getting out of Gloucestershire, but fortunately the weather improved as I proceeded south-west and I was in Penzance four hours later, at about 12.30. In the meantime, a researcher (an unaccustomed luxury) had been sent from Plymouth to do some preliminary setting up. Here I was lucky. She was Rene Wyndham, in the days before she became a reporter in her own right for Television South West, but she had some bad news for me. No local film-crew would work with us. They were in dispute with one of the *Nationwide* editors of the day, and would do nothing until it was resolved. We tried to buy a drink for my old friend John Walmesley, the Plymouth reporter, but were told apologetically that it was more than his job was worth to be seen talking to us.

We were stymied. The item had to be transmitted the following day and we had no crew. I phoned in and explained the situation. A crew and two film-editors would be sent from London, but would not arrive until the following day, some twenty-four hours after the decision to transmit the item had been taken. We did what we could. Luckily Rene had her radio sound equipment with her and so we spent the afternoon and evening recording everything with that – the memorial service, the mayor's appeal, the sound of the waves – in the hope that we would get some matching pictures in the morning. It was the only time I embarked on a film without a camera, and it was no fun. We also begged some of the people we would like to interview to make themselves available in the morning, and luckily they agreed. At first, understandably enough, none of the relatives would talk, and we began the distasteful business of trying to convince them to do so. By nightfall, none had agreed.

The crew arrived mid-morning the following day. We had about two hours. While I did some interviews and got some shots I had had particularly in mind, Rene had some luck. She persuaded one of the bereaved parents to talk about his son and the rest of the lifeboatmen. It is always a difficult question for reporters, whether or not to intrude. But the fact is that more is done for the appeals and charities, more understanding is gained by the viewer about the risky work and the bravery involved, and about what the families have to go through – even at the best of times – if the words come from someone involved rather than from a half-baked reporter. It is also infinitely more moving.

We were fortunate to get the only interview with a member of a bereaved family, and it made the film. I was never more flattered than when the bereaved father called me by my first name throughout the interview. In a curious way he had wanted to talk and I, who had so often been in his home, was the friend he chose.

We finished at lunchtime, and set out immediately, instructing the crew to get a few more shots and then follow us. I drove at eighty miles an hour along the dangerous road between Penzance and Plymouth, with the valiant Rene being sick in the passenger seat. She played me the interviews and I selected the material to use. I dictated the commentary and she wrote everything down. Eventually we reached Plymouth and started on the final version, handing over what film had already been shot to the technicians for processing. Unfortunately, the cameraman had underexposed the film and the corrective measures would add an hour and a half to the processing time. Fortunately, the film-editors that London sent were Mike Davidson and Adrienne Walsh, two of the best and fastest in Lime Grove. Mike had already proved himself as a fine director but, in the way the BBC has, had not been 'made up' and was back at his old trade of film-editing. I was never more glad to see him, and when the pair eventually had some film to work on they did a fast, furious and efficient job. But it was a close run thing: I made the studio (in a borrowed jacket) with about five seconds to spare. There had been no time to record the commentary, and I read it live while the film ran, hoping it would fit. It did, just. I made just one fluff, but otherwise got through it without a mistake. We had fooled them again, and not been rumbled. I was sick with tiredness when it was all over, and vowed never to try such a thing again. Today I would welcome the chance.

Another sad film I made concerned a woman who was given six months to live. She determined that, in that time, she would raise enough money to provide breast-screening equipment at her local hospital, which had none. I joined the committee, and in the end we raised about £80,000 and installed the machinery. As if there was not enough tragedy in her life, we discovered that although the equipment could be put in place, it could not be used because there was not enough extra money to pay for staff. It was a salutary lesson. The film, however, was made while the money was being raised, and contained a strong element of hope. It concerned the school attended by her children, and how it organized a marathon run for pupils, well-wishers and parents: we filmed the marathon, and the bittersweet message was emphasized when, even as we were running, the rumour spread like wildfire that the wife of the master in charge had died overnight – of cancer. It proved to be true, and once again your reporter was put in an impossible dilemma: record the facts as they happened and be accused of exploitation, or ignore them and fail to tell such an effective story, as well as endure the accusation of lying by omission. I chose the former. I am aware that a chance happening made 'better television', and that the accusation of exploitation could be made, but I have always believed that, although television slots must be filled, it is the reporter's duty to do so as effectively as possible, using all the facts at their disposal, in the hope that the point will be made as tellingly as maybe. No one is forced to take part in a film, and their willingness to do so signifies their wish to see an effective result.

When, some time later, Edna Healey was interviewed on television, she cited that film as being an example of the moving and the useful, as well as being typical of the reasons why the late lamented *Nationwide* was so watchable.

Those were the moments when I felt that, albeit by luck, I had slid into the right profession.

Sometimes film-making was harder work than the viewer might suppose. While in Cornwall making *Rescue Flight*, I had been tipped off that Viv Bellamy, who owned Land's End Airport, was building a First World War aeroplane, but was in deep financial trouble. The original buyer had dropped out. The craft was a one-and-a-half strutter bomber, and Viv was working from the original plans drawn up by Sir Thomas Sopwith. Over the next six months, as the plane advanced from a beautiful wooden skeleton to a complete canvas-covered article, I visited it from time to time whenever I was in that part of the world. Viv's only hope of saving his money, nearly £40,000, was a sale to the RAF Museum at Hendon, there being no examples of that particular plane still extant. But to secure the sale the plane would have to fly, and the question was, would it?

Winter was approaching, and Viv was worried that conditions would not be suitable for a test flight over the rocky Cornish cliffs. The plane was ready, but the skies were not. Several attempts had to be called off, and we got some excellent footage of a disappointed elderly pilot looking at a horizontal windsock while the aircraft itself shook in the wind, as if in trepidation. Finally, Viv announced to me over the telephone that he could wait no longer – he would fly in the morning, come hell or high wind. This was all very well, but in 1981 there was no way of getting from London to Land's End in that time, even by driving all night. The *Nationwide* offices were closed, there was no chance of going through the formalities of getting a crew there. It seemed that my chances of ever finishing the film I had spent so much time on were scuppered.

Suddenly, I had a brainwave. I knew that Tony Harold of the RAF Museum had to be present. How was he getting there? I began the long process of looking up in the telephone directories all the A. Harolds in and around London. Eventually I struck lucky. He was flying down in the morning in a four-seater and could give me a lift. I rang Graham Edgar, a superb freelance camerman I knew in Bristol. He was willing to leave at the crack of dawn, without authorization, to try and make Land's End by mid-morning.

The following day I was in the office by 8.30. 'Where are you going today?' asked Janice, the mother-hen of *Nationwide* and authorizer of all things. 'Land's End, filming with Graham Edgar,' I replied truthfully. Janice gave a tolerant smile. 'Yes, dear,' she said.

At 10 o'clock I was at White Waltham Aerodrome near Maidenhead, and a couple of hours later we were touching down at Land's End. We were just in time. Viv was wheeling the little plane out, and the weather was turning nasty. The first question was whether the engine, which had been in a crate in France for forty years, would work. After a few splutters it did, and we breathed a sigh of relief. Viv climbed aboard, wearing his usual blazer and flannels, plus an old leather flying helmet – the English eccentric *par excellence*. He then felt as his pioneer forebears must have felt when they took off into the unknown for the first time. A cheer went up as the little craft got airborne and headed out over the sea. Viv completed a circuit and then turned back to the airport. The landing was a trifle bumpy, but as Viv said afterwards, he was more interested in getting it down than in executing a perfect landing. As he taxied up to the airport buildings, the rain swept over the cliffs. He had completed the flight, to the satisfaction of the man from the RAF Museum, in the nick of time, and we had finished the film. The money was saved, I did a quick interview, and then ran for the Cessna which was waiting to take me and Tony Harold back to London.

At 5 o'clock I was back in the office. 'Where have you been?' said Janice. 'Filming. Land's End.' She gave one of her tolerant smiles. Just one of Glyn's little jokes.

No matter how many films with serious overtones I made, the reputation for being a humorist prevailed. But I did not only make flippant films. Long before, thankfully, Esther took up the cause of Ben Hardwick, I made a film about liver disease in children. I made films in Northern and Southern Ireland; I interviewed film stars and politicians, working men and successful women; I spent nine months negotiating with the House of Lords to make the first film-series behind the scenes at the Palace of Westminster. But I always believed that a touch of humour, even in the most ponderous of topics, led to greater understanding, and I approached everything with a certain scepticism – what I liked to call the 'raised eyebrow' school of reporting. My view was that the audience preferred their reporter to approach any subject with an element of doubt – that one should always have the feeling that he did not believe everything he was told – and not to allow the interviewee to get away with it. If humour helped that cause, so be it. There was humour in everything, no matter how seriously people took themselves, or how weighty the topic.

Two stories make the point. I was filming in Northern Ireland with my friends Jane Drabble and Paul Berriff. At that time my daughter was about three, and we were becoming worried about her speech. She did not speak in English, but had her own language. Thus, 'Ky daddy ba day, no tea gargen,' meant 'it's raining', being literally interpreted as, 'the sky is daddy's car [grey] today, so there'll be no tea in the garden.' She had a habit of identifying all colours by their similarity to people's cars. Thus, 'Liddly daddy ba,' meant 'Lucy's daddy's car' – i.e.

white. While I was in Ireland I promised to find some white stones ('liddly daddy ba tones') to add to her collection. These I found on a beach and we dumped them in the otherwise empty boot of the car. When we returned to the Europa Hotel in Belfast, we were naturally searched by a zealous security man. He took the keys to the boot and came back very suspicious.

'Would you mind telling me what those objects are in the boot of your car?'

Jane sprang into action. 'Oh those,' she said, 'those are liddly daddy ba tones.'

The security man snapped to attention and saluted. 'Oh that's all right then, madam,' he said. 'You can pass inside.'

The other occasion was at the House of Lords. We had an unexpected chance to interview the erstwhile radio doctor, Lord (Charles) Hill, who had been Chairman of both the BBC and ITV. He was robing up at the time, putting on his red dressing gown, prior to introducing a new peer. Then he saw me.

'Oh, no,' he said, poking me in the stomach with his pipe, 'I know you! You'll make us look ridiculous and extremely silly!'

'Oh, no I won't, Lord Hill,' I protested, 'I'll allow you to do that for yourselves!'

He took it in good humour and granted us the interview. They were both courteous and helpful in the House of Lords (unlike another place I could mention) and I like to believe the official who said of the series that it was, 'valuable pioneering work . . . which contributed in no small measure to the eventual televising of parliament.'

During 1982, I was lucky enough to be given time off *Nationwide*, having been chosen to report on *The Paras*, directed by Bill Jones. It was the year of the Falklands War and *The Paras* proved to be the most popular series ever made by the Current Affairs Department. Thirteen million people watched its first run, eight million its summer repeat. We followed a platoon through its six-month training from raw recruit to polished soldier, saw it reduced by two-thirds as soldier after soldier dropped out (and not all of them from an aeroplane) and finally went with them on their first proper mission. The question of course was, would they go to the Falklands as replacements? In the event, they missed that dubious distinction by a few days and went instead to Northern Ireland, where the threat of death was no less real.

It would be untrue to say that we did everything the recruits had to do, because we were fortunate enough to be able to live in pubs and hotels, but when they ran, we ran; when they 'tabbed' (force-marched) to the top of a mountain in Wales, we were there to greet them; when they dug themselves into trenches in the middle of the night, we were watching. By the end of their six-month training we had a healthy respect for each other, and they had learned to treat us as part of the scenery.

Yet the series (it was seven weekly half-hour programmes) very nearly did not happen. At the outset, an over-zealous civilian Public Relations Officer, fresh from Northern Ireland and full of self-importance, tried to tell us that we could only do the series provided we never talked to any of the recruits! Naturally, we could not agree, and it was only when we produced a letter from a senior officer sanctioning the venture, that we were able to proceed. We finally came to an arrangement whereby we could film the course, warts and all, provided we concentrated only on those recruits who gave their agreement. Of more than forty, only two preferred not to speak to us, both Irishmen, both of whom left the course early and one of whom proved to be an IRA plant.

Only once was there a hiccough. This occurred when the colonel in charge of training reneged on a deal made by his Commanding Officer. On the whole, we were treated with considerable kindness and hospitality by the Parachute Regiment, and it was only sad that we had to stop filming because one officer did not keep the regiment's promise. The agreement had been that we could film anything, but the officer in charge of training refused to allow us access when one of the recruits was on a charge. This was the unfortunate Private Cunningham, who had suffered every ignominy the Army could throw at him, but who somehow managed to survive. For a while he became the best-known Private in the British Army, as he staggered from one tribulation to another, and very popular to boot. We were naturally very upset when we were not allowed to film his most dangerous hour, namely the second time he was up on a charge. Fortunately he survived, and we returned to filming after some renegotiation – and when Private Cunningham's trousers split from crutch to ankle on his passing out parade, we were there to record it. It could not have been better for the series if it had been fiction.

The tensest moments came when we showed what we had filmed to the regimental brass. We retained full editorial control, but had agreed that they should be allowed to make their comments. They were not best pleased with our coverage of life in Northern Ireland, particularly with the footage of 'bloody Sunday', but they could not fault us as to matters of fact.

The most explosive moment came when we showed footage of a particularly cocky officer lecturing the recruits. After he had had a go at the film-crew, he turned his attention to the regiment's General, General Sir Anthony Farrer-Hockley. 'If you are on guard-duty,' he yelled, 'and you see the General's car coming, remember the words of Captain Mainwaring in *Dad's Army*: "Don't panic!" Demand to see the bloody General's pass, and don't let him in without it!'

General Sir Anthony (known as 'Farrer the Para') was present at the viewing. When we reached that moment he turned to his aide, face as black as thunder. 'The fool! The bloody fool! Who is that man?' We held our breath. 'Doesn't he know it was Corporal Jones who said "Don't panic!"''

The *Nationwide* years, from 1976 to 1983, were the halcyon days. I was never officially a presenter, but I presented the programme many times. It was an endearing programme, as much for its faults as for its virtues. It had a curious way of going wrong just at the worst possible moment. I remember when Sue Lawley introduced the programme in total darkness. As she said, 'Good evening,' the studio was immediately plunged into blackness. She did not bat an eyelid but continued, 'and if someone will put on the lights we will start *Nationwide*, which tonight . . .' Someone obliged and the programme went on as planned. Sue was often involved in cock-ups of one sort and another, although it was never her fault. Once, through the miracle of television, she introduced an item while apparently sitting on her own shoulder, and once she was talking away when a stage-hand walked into shot behind her. He was gaily going about his business when he glanced up at one of the monitor screens and saw that he was being watched by ten million people. Very slowly and gingerly, he edged his way off, as if making no noise would render him invisible. The audience was enchanted, but Sue continued unabashed.

There was a tremendous amount to learn from the professionalism of presenters such as Sue Lawley and Frank Bough, and for sheer expertise they are worth every penny of the considerable amount they get paid. Once, Frank and Sue kept the show running for five or six minutes by improvising a discussion about gardening, and once when an item had 'gone down', Frank called back an interviewee who had been in the local, first half of the programme, and interviewed her again on some quite different topic.

I shall never forget the time when the jovial Hugh Scully, at the end of an interview with Liza Minnelli, finished by saying, 'Judy Garland, thank you very much.' Quick as a flash, Liza replied, 'I'll tell her when I see her,' while Hugh held his head in his hands in mortification. There was an occasion, too, when Hugh was about to interview someone on medieval armour. A display was ranged in front of the guest's chair, but when someone was brought in Hugh was busy preparing his notes and signalled them to sit down. The guest inspected the medieval display with interest. Only with a few seconds to go was the guest whisked away by a floor manager to another chair in front of another presenter, to give an excellent interview on gynaecology, or some such topic. Afterwards, Hugh apologized on behalf of the programme for the mistake. 'Oh, that's all right,' said the guest. 'I assumed that it was an initiative test. If I did well on medieval armour, I would get to speak on gynaecology!'

Another star of the show was the delightful Bob Wellings, a man completely unspoiled by television. He was caught smoking by an accusatory film-camera during the programme's 'Give up with *Nationwide*' campaign, but the only occasion on which his impeccable manners slipped was when he once conducted an interview on uniform. One of the extras in uniform, a formidable-looking fat lady, waited until Bob was level with her then keeled over in a dead faint in front of him. After a quick apologetic word to viewers about how long the extras had been kept waiting, Bob took a gigantic step over the body and continued the interview as if nothing had happened. It would not have been so funny if he were not normally so suave.

Overall, it was a happy ship and the presenters pleasant enough people to work with. Despite the fact that he was nicknamed 'Grumpy', Michael Barratt was always very kind to me, as were the other regular presenters, including Valerie Singleton, John Stapleton (the only man who continually upstaged himself with the loudness of his ties), Richard Kershaw and Sue Cook, who became a close friend.

I made my own contribution to *Nationwide* boo-boos on more than one occasion. Once, I was doing a two-pronged interview with fishermen in Birmingham and Manchester. The information I had been fed by the researcher (now a good friend and in a senior position in television), was, first that bait had gone up to a pound a pound and was therefore beyond the purse of the average angler and, second, that owing to the bad winter there were not enough fish anyway. Unfortunately, the picture up in front of me was of Birmingham, whereas my first question went to Manchester. I could hear the answer, but it was quite clearly not coming from the man pictured in front of me, who was still visibly fiddling with his fishing tackle. The director's voice in my ear-piece told me that I had got the wrong city. When we had sorted it out we started again. I put it to angler one that the price of bait was too high. This he denied vehemently. I cursed the researcher and moved across country to angler two. 'In any case,' I said, 'there aren't enough fish to go round.' 'Completely untrue,' said angler two, 'who told you that?' I was flabbergasted as well as scuppered, and also felt like telling him. I concluded there was nowhere else to go with the item and quickly wound it up and handed over three minutes earlier than expected to a somewhat surprised Hugh Scully. Had I been more experienced, like Frank or Sue, I should undoubtedly have kept going for the right amount of time by discussing the price of cod or something, but I was not, and I did not. The whole incident summed up the speed at which research for magazine programmes has to be done. One short-cut is to accept as gospel anything that is printed in the newspapers. This is an error. Newspapers are notoriously unreliable (this was a case in point), so it is always worth checking the story, and what your interviewees are going to say, before lumbering some unfortunate presenter.

For some reason, I acquired a reputation for saying something unexpected when introducing the next item or presenter. When the apparently unflappable Desmond Lineham, who used to present the *Nationwide* Sports round-up, learnt that I was introducing him he used to beg me not to say anything unexpected to which he had to reply. The other method was to ignore it completely. When the nation was about to discover who shot JR in *Dallas*, it was an event of such national importance that we did an item on it. The burden was that there were seven different versions ready in Television Centre 'and,' as I remarked in my hand-over, 'as to which is the right one, that is not yet known to anyone in the BBC, however important. Not even Richard Kershaw.' This sally was, with lofty disdain, completely ignored, and Richard continued with the next item as if nothing had been said.

When John Travolta came into the studio to be interviewed about his new release, *Grease*, there was great excitement. Bob Wellings was due to talk to him, and I was the other presenter on the show that evening. After a typically witty and lugubrious introduction, we were astonished to find that Travolta was an even slower speaker than Bob and the interview, though only six minutes, appeared to take sixteen. It ended with an extract from the film in which Travolta, all flashing thighs and waving arms, danced his socks off. The extract ended and the camera was on me. I said, 'John Travolta. Well, at least he dances quickly.' I heard an intake of breath from the editor over my ear-piece, and it was some time before I presented *Nationwide* again.

It was surprising how often the decision as to who was to present a programme was taken at the last minute. On one occasion, I had just finished a complicated recording and was still in 'make-up', when an editor rushed in and explained that there had been some confusion over the rota. Would I present *Nationwide* in about an hour's time? I was exhausted, but said I would, checking quickly to see if I had the right clothes. If you had anything to do with filming or reporting, it was as well always to be wearing a suit – you never knew when you might be unexpectedly called upon to interview a cabinet minister. Less than a minute later, a producer from *Tonight* popped his head round the door: Val Singleton was stuck at the airport in Iran and could I present *Tonight* tonight? I said I did not mind if *Nationwide* did not. They did not. There was just one thing: one of the items needed to be pre-recorded in about half an hour because the interviewee was not available later in the evening. I just had time to drive frantically back to my digs, grab another change of clothes, record the item and turn up at *Nationwide* with minutes to spare. There was no time to prepare the questions for the interviews, but somehow I scraped by and then went to the *Tonight* offices and started writing the script for that evening's programme. I cannot remember much about it, except that John Cleese and Michael Palin did their hilarious best to sabotage a live interview, and that one question I asked the jazz singer, Marion Montgomery, landed me in trouble. She was due to appear in a Richard Rodney Bennett concert the following evening at the Festival Hall. It was my job to elicit this information in as subtle a way as I could. The somewhat puritan editor did not approve of my methods. I said, 'Marion, a question I've always wanted to ask you. What are you doing tomorrow night?' This produced a flirtatious response: 'Oh, isn't he lovely? Well, as a matter of fact . . .' I was not asked to deputize again. I still claim it was the only time the same presenter has introduced two different programmes within three hours of each other, on the same channel, on the same evening. This time it was BBC1 itself that had scraped by, by the skin of its teeth.

I was never a really good presenter. I was inclined to let the heart rule the head, to get too upset and in a muddle if things went wrong, to see the opportunity for an off-the-cuff remark when I would have served myself and my fellow presenters better if I had stuck to the script. It was a difficult enough business without adding complications. But sometimes circumstances were not on the presenter's side. Early on in my *Nationwide* days, I conducted a complete interview with a racing car parked on my foot. I had my eyes fixed on the camera as I walked across the studio giving the introduction. Someone had thought it would be fun if the interviewee drove the car in at the same time. They did, without perceiving the result, and I was too naïve and frightened to ask them to move. I had a bruised foot for weeks afterwards.

The final insult came one evening when Richard Kershaw and I were presenting. Richard is a testy but likeable fellow, with years of experience. But even this did not save him on this occasion. For some reason the autocue, on which we relied for those items, such as the news, which were read 'sight unseen', went wrong. Suddenly, in the middle of the programme, it became misaligned, so that the last word of every line was missing. It meant we had to make up the missing words. They were guessable in some items, but not in others, for example the routine news. What we saw, for example was:

Today, after an accident in
a car, which was coloured c
was burnt out. The driver a
escaped with very little i
She was immediately taken t
where she is now making a s
recovery.

The problem was, what to put in the gaps, and I have no doubt that a certain amount of hesitancy crossed our faces while we decided. Should we, for example, try:

Today, after an accident in Tooting,
a car, which was coloured cerise
was burnt out. The driver, a Mrs Snodgrass,
escaped with very little injury.
She was immediately taken to hospital
where she is now making a satisfactory
recovery.

You can see the problem. What if the relevant words had been: Tottenham, crimson, Mrs Wentworth, injury, her home and slow. The possibilities were endless.

At the review board, where senior management discuss the week's programmes, it was observed that Richard and I did not handle autocue very well. 'Ah,' said the Head of Current Affairs (who, needless to say, did not know the circumstances), 'but you cannot expect the A-team *every* day.'

I never made the A-team.

*   *   *

When not filming or presenting, I was doing my own thing. In the autumn of 1978 I took over as presenter of the 'Pigeonhole' slot from my good friend and erstwhile colleague, Richard Stilgoe. This was a sort of weekly 'letters on the air' spot, which Richard had made his own by using the Colour Separation Overlay (CSO) technique – a device whereby you could project several images of, say, yourself on to the same background. This background was provided by the technicians' gallery and was quite invisible to the presenter. Everything in the studio, except what was to be projected, had to be of a uniform colour (usually blue), in order to make all except the background invisible to the camera. Thus if, by mistake, you wore a blue tie, it would disappear and the background would show through. CSO is a common enough technique nowadays, but twelve years ago Richard Stilgoe and 'Pigeonhole' did a lot of valuable pioneering work.

I was at my wits' end trying to imagine how I could equal Richard's trick of having half a dozen images of himself appear on screen at the same time. Once again, my acting came to the rescue. I hit on the notion of making all the images different by disguising myself as half a dozen different characters. By recording six times, by clever timing and by making sure I was in different positions in the background, I could pretend that I was six different people, all of whom could talk to each other in any combination.

Thus was invented Wilson Pryng (anagram of Glyn Worsnip), a Clouseau-like reporter (complete with mac, moustache, pork pie hat, and notebook), who helped me with many an investigation but who invariably put his foot in it. Wilson engendered quite a correspondence. Many viewers clearly believed he was a real character, despite the fact that (through the wonders of CSO) he reported 'live' from such places as the top of Mount Everest and the atolls in the South Sea Isles. All that was needed was a colour transparency of any given location (without objects which were obviously moving, such as buses) and Wilson could report from there. I spent many hours writing Wilson's letters for him, although I confess to having been a little deflated when I heard that a friend's bank manager had described me as, 'that silly fellow who talks to himself on television'.

I also built up a repertory company of 'baddies', all played by me, who would reproduce the answers I got to viewers' enquiries from various businesses and bureaucracies. Chief among these was a sharp-suited smoothie called A. Spokesman. It was amazing how often he turned up. The group also included a PR woman, and once they all sang a song together.

Nationwide ended in 1983. No-one has ever given a satisfactory explanation as to why this popular show was taken off. Edna Healey and seven or eight million others enjoyed it, and I have no doubt it will soon be 'invented' again. It was replaced by a poor man's version of the same thing, called *60 Minutes*. This had all the technical faults, but none of the charm which Michael Barratt, Sue Lawley, Frank Bough, Bob Wellings, Sue Cook and Hugh Scully had brought to *Nationwide*. On one occasion Desmond Wilcox announced that there was to be an item about the worst and most unpleasant criminal in Britain; behind him was flashed up a picture of Leon Brittan, then Home Secretary. Even this boo-boo did not save the programme, which lasted one season before it, too, was taken off. Brian Wenham, by now Director of Programmes (Television), said it had a 'design fault' – whatever that may mean.

At first I did not work for *60 Minutes*. The editor, David Lloyd, had said he was trying out a new programme, on which he would not employ me under any circumstances. After a disastrous while, he rang me. 'Would you make some films for the programme?'

'I can think of eleven good reasons why I shouldn't work for the programme, quite apart from having seen it.'

There was a silence. David said there had been some improvements and then added that he supposed I had heard that he had said he would not have me or anyone who had had a high profile on *Nationwide* on his programme.

'You mean like Bernard Falk, Bob Wellings, Nick Woolley and Luke Casey?'

'Touché . . . Would you at least come and see me?' David is an affable fellow, and a good editor. He had been given (perhaps on purpose) an impossible brief. I said I would.

The net result was that I was offered my pick of the films and some work abroad. Eight of the thirteen films I made were in foreign countries. I kept up the variety: one was about some hairless cats claimed as a new breed by a pair of Parisians (soon debunked by a member of the British Cat Fancy from Glossop); another was a profile of the European Parliament in Strasburg (a cross between the House of Lords and an international airport). At home I went on a sailing barge race from London to East Anglia and met Billy Graham – though not in the same film! I had a thoroughly enjoyable time on *60 Minutes* and was mortified when it was taken off.

When *60 Minutes* finished I went to *Breakfast Time*, where David Lloyd had taken over as editor. *Breakfast Time* still ran colourful and popular features and, as well as general reporting and film-making, I did a Friday morning spot called 'Worsnip's Week', a humorous review of the most absurd stories in the week's press. This enabled me to poke fun, not only at the news itself, but at the way the press treated it. All very enjoyable.

In the autumn of 1984, there occurred an event which shook the nation: the Brighton bombing. Since the days of *Nationwide*, I had attended all the party conferences, compiling a regular Diary. This was now part of *Breakfast Time*'s output. I used snippets from the day's coverage, out-takes and off-cuts from the films that were made, suitable still photographs and specially shot incidents and interviews of my own invention. It was hard work, and I was often at it from dawn until well into the night, prowling in search of suitable material. I was not best pleased when in 1985, when I was covering what was to be my last Labour Party conference, Peter Pagnamenta, newly-appointed Head of Current Affairs, came down to visit the troops and, seeing me, said, 'Oh, I suppose you are just doing your funny five minutes, are you?' Apart from the fact that I had conducted the main political interview of the day (with Eric Hammond of the EEPTU), which Peter had not got up early enough to watch, I resented the implication that it is somehow easier to be funny than to be serious. It is much harder, particularly if, as I always tried to do, you use a funny moment to make a genuine political point.

Whatever the management may have thought, it was hard going, particularly as all the conferences came in turn and two nights a week were spent editing the tapes. I was always fearful lest I should not have completed the Diary by the time of transmission in the morning. I only failed once: we were editing the Diary when at 3 o'clock in the morning there came an almighty explosion from the Grand Hotel next door. What followed is history, but we dropped the Diary immediately and I spent the next ten hours, four of which were live on the specially extended *Breakfast Time*, interviewing survivors, officials and cabinet ministers.

At one point, thanks to my producers Sarah Ramsden and Sarah Nathan, I got an 'exclusive' interview with the Deputy Prime Minister, Lord Whitelaw. A forest of microphones and tape recorders appeared over my shoulder as I did this, and I felt as if I was interviewing him for the whole world. Somehow the depth of responsibility carried me through safely, but I still shudder when I think of interviewing such an important man on such a momentous occasion. All the interviews that morning were completely off the cuff, and I thank heaven that the adrenalin flowed as it did. The Whitelaw interview was recorded simultaneously in London, and I was amused to see that there they stopped what they were doing and, with a short introduction from Selina Scott, ran it immediately, while the editor in Brighton was still spooling it through to see whether it was worth running at all!

Owing to somebody's foresight, all the families of those on the programme had been telephoned and reassured that their loved ones were safe – with one exception. As I was permanently on the screen it was not thought necessary. When at 8.30 a.m. Jo discovered from a friend that there had been an explosion, she rang the programme saying that she had rung my hotel who had said I had been out all night. 'Yes, he's been editing,' said whoever took the call, 'but he's been on the screen all morning!' The idea that there was anyone who did not watch breakfast television clearly amazed them. Jo said afterwards that she was worried not so much that I had been blown up, as that I had been sleeping with a Tory!

The most reassuring thing to me was that I was chosen for the job. I may not have been the best at any particular skill (apart perhaps from being amusing), but my colleagues at least believed that I could be switched from comic diarist to serious reporter when an emergency arose. That was good enough for me.

It was typical of the BBC that they did not tell me when the programme was nominated for a British Academy of Film and Television Arts award, and even more incongruously typical that I should have been the reporter *Breakfast Time* sent to cover the award ceremony. I arrived to find my own face on the screen and that one of my interviews had been chosen to represent the programme.

The following two years, 1985 and 1986, were not so carefree. For one thing, in March 1985 I received something I had not been expecting from the BBC: the sack. For many years I had been on a rolling contract. When one year came to an end, the contract would be renewed for another year, and so on. Now, although the BBC was prepared to honour our contracts until the beginning of 1986, we were peremptorily told that this would be our last contract. From now on, if we were to be employed by the BBC at all, it would be on a programme to programme basis. David Lomax, Philip Tibenham, Nick Woolley, Luke Casey, Bob Wellings and I had, between us, put in more than 112 years of service to the BBC, and some of us had risked life and limb on their behalf. We became known as the 'Lime Grove Six' and our removal caused a brief strike at the BBC. I found my picture, for the first time in my life, on the front page of *The Times*, not for what I had achieved, but for what I had failed to do – have my contract renewed.

The reason why the BBC's best and most experienced reporters should be given the heave-ho was not clear. One theory was, in the words of a senior manager, 'that we should show Mrs Thatcher that we are prepared to put blood on the carpet'. Perhaps the real reason was that it was costing the BBC much more money to continue employing six experienced, senior reporters, than it would to take on six eager young rookies in their place.

Whatever the reason, the affair was very badly handled. Those who did the deed – Bill Cotton, Managing Director of Television, and Brian Wenham, Director of Programmes – refused to see the individuals concerned. Instead they asked Peter Pagnamenta to do it. It was our biased impression that Pagnamenta was promoted to management simply to do other people's dirty work. He too refused, and insisted on the editors of the relevant programmes doing the job. This was very embarrassing for David Lloyd, editor of *Breakfast Time*. He apologetically handed over the brown envelope containing the offensive letter. Only a week or two earlier he had assured me that, despite any rumours I might have heard, I was not on the list of those who would be sacked. As my editor, he would have been consulted. He had not been.

In that two weeks I had contracted to purchase a new house, beautifully set above the Wye Valley. It cost us everything we had and more but, assured of continuity of income, I had gone ahead. It was a small cottage, but with land enough to house the flock of sixty or so sheep out of which Jo was planning an interest and an income. In the four years we have been there, she has built up a flock of rare-breed Manx Loghtan sheep, learned to look after it, taught herself to shear and spin and generally set herself up as proprietor of a small cottage industry. It is the sorriest part of this whole sad affair that the sheep and the house have had to be sold.

Peter Pagnamenta was a pathetic creature. He could not even project his personality across a room – nor did he bother to try. When I eventually secured an interview with him he said that, although he agreed with it, he had simply been given a list of names. He said that I was on it because I had too high a profile in Current Affairs, and was doing too much; within a few seconds he was maintaining that I only appeared once a week and was doing too little. The poor man clearly did not know what to say next. We felt he had libelled us when he was quoted in the *Guardian* as saying that, given the names on the list, no-one could say that the standard of journalism had suffered.

He also said that I could not expect to get work in Lime Grove or in the Documentary Features Department (which produces much of my kind of work from BBC Kensington House), 'otherwise the BBC would look silly'. I remarked that the BBC looked silly already, that this was a clear attempt to prevent me from earning an income, which I suspected was against the law and which made me very angry.

Eventually, I got an interview with my erstwhile friend, Brian Wenham, who had written the sacking letter. He suggested we have lunch together, and said he would send his car for me. The car came and the driver explained that we were going across to Television Centre to pick up Brian. When he got in, we still did not move off and Brian announced that a friend would be joining us. To my astonishment, Bill Cotton clambered in. His first remark was charming: 'If you think that my coming means you are ever going to get a contract with the BBC again, you are mistaken.' I felt I had nothing to lose. I said, 'I can hardly imagine that you would do anything that would benefit the BBC, its viewers, or its employees.'

It was not a relaxed lunch, Both Bill and Brian tried to make me say how badly *Breakfast Time* was doing under David Lloyd, and claimed to have had nothing to do with the sacking. I refuted both claims. Eventually I made Bill Cotton agree that, although he might take away my long-term contract, Peter Pagnamenta had no right to tell individual editors not to employ me on a one-off basis. He said he would have a word, although whether or not he ever did I never found out. Certainly, individual editors like David Lloyd continued to use me, and I was grateful for that. As for Peter Pagnamenta, once he had done his dirty work he was relieved of his personnel duties and returned to what he was best at, which was making programmes.

While I was serving out my notice in 1985, I was chosen to make *The Best Bargain in Britain*, a film about the BBC which showed viewers what an efficient, cost-effective organization it was. The licence fee was safe in their hands, or so the story ran. I was in a quandary: on the one hand I believed in the BBC and public service broadcasting; on the other I had cause to believe that they did not always treat their employees well. I made the film, but the irony of a film in which the cost-effectiveness of the BBC was proved by sacking the reporter who made it, was not lost on the diarists in the heavier dailies.

I had a good time on *Breakfast Time*. After arriving at London Airport at 6 o'clock in the morning to do a live broadcast, I flew on Concorde to New York and made a film about the trip. I did not mention the slight hitch. We landed perfectly at JFK airport and drew to a halt at the end of the runway – then the entire hydraulics system failed. Eventually we were towed in, but it had taken as long to get from the end of the runway to the airport buildings as it had to cross the Atlantic! I met the pilot on the way out and he wondered whether I need mention the incident in my report. I happened to remind him that we had been denied permission to film on the flight deck while airborne. 'Ah,' said the pilot, 'I've been thinking about that. I think it may now be possible . . .' With such deals are successful films made.

Because I wanted to do a piece to camera with Concorde taking off in the background, we spent the afternoon in a Nissen hut at JFK, while the British borrowed a spare part from Air France and repaired the aircraft. Our plans to spend the afternoon looking round New York went adrift, and we eventually got to bed at 5.30 a.m. London time. We were up four hours later to catch the morning flight back to London.

I was delighted to read later in the national press that '*Breakfast Time* is better in almost every respect . . . and the brew is improved by brisk idiosyncratic films like Glyn Worsnip's.' It made all the hard work worthwhile. I had obviously not been rumbled yet.

Nowadays, I think constantly of all that hard work and the long hours I was able to put in, only three years ago. Like the time I broke the world record for the time taken by a fee-paying passenger to cross the Channel. It was a stunt, of course, but nevertheless I did it. The method was a power boat, and we leapt from wave to crashing wave for forty-five minutes. There was no safety harness and no insurance; I simply had to hold on, with a female reporter from the *Daily Mail* holding on to me. We made it, but arrived in Dover sick, tired and plum-coloured, with bruising from crutch to ankle from where we had been sitting astride a metal canopy. There were no seats on the boat.

Perhaps the essence of those halcyon years can best be summed up by an incident which occurred early in my days on *Nationwide*. The director, Peter Bate, and I had been sent to Scotland. Troops from the Castle in Edinburgh were laying on a special version of the Tattoo for patients in the grounds of the Princess Margaret Rose Hospital. We were to make a film about it. We travelled up overnight and filmed all the next day. We were too late to book a sleeper, and had to catch the milk train back to London. There was no restaurant and no refreshment car. We arrived next morning dirty, dishevelled and dog-tired. We knew that we had at least another thirteen hours to go, because the film had to be ready for that evening. At seven o'clock in the morning we staggered into the station buffet for some breakfast. Sitting at the plastic table we stared mournfully down at two cold, hard, fried eggs. They stared balefully back at us. Peter lifted his head.

'You know what I like about working in television?' he said.

'No. What?'

'It's the glamour.'

CHAPTER 6

Onset

*I did not see it coming. It was towards the end of the day, dusk. I slowed
to a standstill, looked in my mirror to check that the lights behind me were
far enough away to allow me to turn across the road and into the parking
space in front of the hotel. They were. I edged forward about a foot. It
was enough. A dark car had come round the corner, I saw no lights. In
that terrible moment I heard the impact and watched, in a deathly calm, as
the driver fought magnificently with the controls. Somehow he remained
upright – but not before he smashed into a parked car, destroying it. Relief
that no-one was hurt was replaced by the indignity of having to go into a
crowded restaurant and ask, 'Will the owner of car number . . .?'
Everyone agreed that the smash was the result of lack of judgement rather
than lack of control, but I have sometimes wondered. Certainly nothing
seemed to go right from then on.*

*I had always suspected that I would get my come-uppance. The good
things in life, such as BBC contracts, do not last for ever. I had had a
good run in theatre and television – radio as well – but I had never quite
been able to believe my good luck, never quite managed to realize why I
had slipped by without someone noticing that I had no real ability, never
quite, as my friends put it, learnt to believe in my own talent. I always
thought of myself as a Bisto Kid among giants.*

*Insecurity is, of course, a trait shared by performers from Terry Wogan
downwards, and I always remember a rehearsal for a Yorkshire Television
situation comedy series starring the late Roy Kinnear. Half-way through
the morning, I was standing by Roy when he turned and whispered into my
ear, 'Well, we've got through to coffee break, and they haven't rumbled us
yet!' Perhaps it was the fear of being 'rumbled' that kept me going –
through the long years of life in the theatre, when the enjoyment was*

matched only by the obscurity; and then during the less obscure, but frenetic, days of television and radio.

It was a conceit of my youth that I would one day end up as drama critic of a well-known newspaper. Thinking precociousness was de rigueur, *I remember daring to declare this likelihood to my first College Examination Board at Oxford. They failed me, of course. I remember thinking that that was how you were repaid if you were bolder than you should be – made claims you could not substantiate. I never again overstated my ability.*

Yet had I not, by the sheerest luck, done far better than a mere critic? Can I not look back and, through blind good fortune, rewrite Shaw's famous dictum about teachers? Those who can, do; those who cannot, criticise? Even in the theatre did I not work alongside Albert Finney, Donald Sutherland, Barry Humphries, Marti Webb, John Thaw and Kenneth More; write material for Anna Russell and Richard Stilgoe; sing with John Hanson and Millicent Martin; direct Moira Lister and Leslie Crowther, make 'em laugh with Barbara Windsor and Frankie Howerd? And in broadcasting did I not sit with Esther Rantzen, Frank Bough, Michael Barratt, David Dimbleby, Selina Scott, Sue Lawley and Robin Day? Did Paul Eddington and Sir Michael Hordern and Claire Rayner, and Henry Kelly and Derek Jameson and Larry Grayson not appear as guests on my shows? Not a bad little name-drop. Of course, although I appeared beside them, swapped jokes and was treated as an equal, I was never in their class. I never had their earning power, nor, as it turned out, their staying power. But was it not enough for a boy from a Gloucestershire village? Eventually I was rumbled all right, but never once did I guess it would be through ill-health. I did not see it coming.

I was in Portsmouth, in April 1986, on the deck of an aircraft carrier, when I first noticed it. I was making a 'corporate video' – a promotion film which is never transmitted, but shown internally to some group or other, the NAAFI in this case. I still drank in those days but, as I was working, was as dry as the nearby docks. Nor did it seem likely that the vast craft was swaying much. I had to walk and talk at the same time, explaining the benefits of the NAAFI to the shipmates. I felt slightly uncomfortable. We often joked at home about how I was incapable of doing two things at once, but this I had mastered over the years – it was a professional requirement. I thought no more of it, putting it down to the height above sea level, perhaps, or something in the NAAFI food. In the next couple of months, however, I was now and again aware of a certain imbalance. I was aware, too, that I could not hear very clearly the words of the pop songs my daughter Ellie played – and I could not just attribute it to lack of interest.

After a few stumbles, I became increasingly aware of a problem. I was between lodgings at the time, and staying in a flat near Kensington Church Street belonging to Annie Howells, a senior producer in the radio department in which I was working, who was abroad with her husband Nick. My car was off the road because of the crash, so I had to travel in to Broadcasting House – BH as we always called it – by tube. One July morning, I was standing in a crowded carriage, when I felt myself falling. I reached in desperation for the nearest support, which happened to be a more than ample bosom. Whether or not the lady enjoyed the experience she did not say, but she smiled and treated it as a mere accident.

Some days later, a more dangerous accident occurred. I was nearing the top of an escalator. I was carrying a laden briefcase at the time, and took my hand off the rail to shift my balance. To my alarm, I started to topple backwards and was arrested only by the man behind. He, too, started to fall back, and so on down the line until about thirty people had fallen backwards like dominoes. Had it not been so dangerous, it would have been laughable. Luckily no-one was hurt, and we managed to right ourselves before having to step off the moving stair. But it was enough.

I decided to see my doctor. I was not too perturbed, although I was worried by these sudden spells. I put it down to some infection of the inner ear – perfectly curable. As it happened, I drove home from London and called in on him on the way. As usual, the feeling of glorious escape swept over me as I crossed the Severn Bridge. I drove along the Wye Valley, one of the most attractive routes in England. The sun danced on the river, the trees absorbed the windless warmth, the rock faces glowed in pleasure. I thought once again of how Wordsworth had recollected this scene in tranquillity and, in so doing, had immortalized it. It happened that Dr Calland's surgery was that day in Tintern. The little waiting room looked out on to the abbey, and the abbey looked back, for all the world as if with a message of goodwill from the monks of the Middle Ages. It did not seem possible that anything could desecrate so lovely a scene.

Tony Calland is a spruce young doctor, well scrubbed and shinily suited. He is said to be something of a heart-throb among the maidenhood thereabouts. But he is nobody's fool, and we have learnt to respect his judgement over the years. He peered into my ears, and then mysteriously asked me to stand on one leg. I thought it was a joke, until I discovered that I had some difficulty doing what he asked. He suggested that perhaps I was not hearing the words of Ellie's pop songs because my ears needed washing out. But he did not really think that was my problem. I ought to see a neurologist, and he knew the very man in Bristol.

It was preparing for a warm July day when I drove across the Clifton Downs at 8.30 in the morning to see Dr Campbell. It was the first and only time in my life that I agreed to see a doctor 'privately', but if Dr Calland was right, this was a matter which could seriously affect my livelihood and, for my family's sake, I needed to clear the matter up as soon as possible. I started the ritual which was to become familiar: I tried to stand on one leg; I tried running my heel down my shin; I followed the doctor's finger with my eyes; I tried to catch and touch his finger tips as he moved them about. I could perform all the actions, but with difficulty. Something was clearly wrong, but it never occurred to me that it could not be put right. The doctor hummed and hawed. He did not look too worried either – but then that is what doctors are paid to look like. He said he would write to Dr Calland.

Looking back, it seems inconceivable that I should have treated it all so cavalierly. My mood matched the weather – fine and sunny, with the outlook bright. I simply was not watching for the storm clouds on the horizon. At home, things were beginning to go well after the trauma of the move and the house-building. What had been half a dozen sheep were now considerably more, and we were all beginning to take pleasure in getting to know them – Ada, Ariadne and co for the first year, Bernadette, Beatrice and co for the second – and in the variations of type and colour they produced – from chocolate brown, through honey, to white. Jo was beginning to learn to spin. The relaxed feeding of the wool through the spinning machine was a therapy for us all, and with words like 'carding' and 'teasing' we learnt a new vocabulary.

In our second summer at Harthill, we were finding new pleasures. The wood was an overgrown fairyland, full of surprises – an extraordinary mixture of uncultivated plants and trees, with what had once been cultivated. Rhododendrons painted splashes of purple among the beech, oak and fir. We found new paths and old streams, with stone bridges. Jo found a patch of Solomons' seal which she adopted as her own, and we agreed with the Forestry Commission to a Preservation Order being put on the magnificent avenue of Wellingtonia which had once graced an elegant drive. We could not have been luckier in finding albeit a somewhat primitive cottage, but a home set in a wonderland' we shared with badgers, foxes, rabbits, hares and owls, to mention but a few.

That weekend, I manned the public address system at Tutshill Primary School's summer fête. It, too, was an amalgam – a combination, like so many, of an old village stone schoolhouse with makeshift prefabricated classrooms added as populations expanded. The result was a good mix, and Ellie had settled in nicely. The fact that the opening speech was to be given by Alan Bartlett, Headteacher of Wyedean, the comprehensive to which Ellie would be going, only complemented the feeling of normality and hope for the future; and the fact that his wife Fiona had worked in the Wardrobe when I had been at Dundee Rep only added to the feeling of complacent security.

Things were picking up at work, too. The tense upset of the 'Lime Grove Six' affair was beginning to recede. The people who had employed me before were happy to go on doing so, and the fact that by this time the independent sector was beginning to expand, peopled by many ex-BBC producers, meant that whole new areas of employment were opening up. Like most freelancers I was prepared to do anything and everything. Someone I had known in Kensington House, John Bird, asked me to write and narrate a film with which Legal & General were to bid to be allowed to build a new shopping centre in Bromley. John was working for John Gau, who had been editor of *Nationwide* and then Head of Current Affairs, before leaving to start up Greyhound Productions. While I was recording the commentary, I was faintly aware that it was not as easy as it had been, but I put it down to overwork. Certainly I had no trouble with another job I picked up while I was there, doing a short voice over for a Channel 4 programme. This was the way it would be: one job would lead to another – and jobs were more forthcoming than I had feared. I could look forward to plenty of bread-and-butter work, and my voice would provide the jam, perhaps even earn my pension. How wrong, O Lord, how wrong.

I was also working a lot in radio, where television people often go to lick their wounds. Fortunately I had always worked in Broadcasting House, and it had been good to me. Once again, I was made to feel that it was not too displeased that I had time on my hands. Since 1981 I had been disappearing into the sound archives every third week or so to do my Monday morning programme of pickings from the past; I enjoyed deputizing for Margaret Howard on *Pick Of The Week* while she was on holiday; and I was doing an immensely enjoyable feature called *A Gentleman's Place*, about those somewhat anachronistic premises around St James's which manage to combine sinister power with the smell of leather and old shag.

I was also working for Schools Radio. It was Industry Year, and Schools planned six programmes to celebrate it. This involved a certain amount of industry on my part, both as writer and presenter, and also a certain amount of travel around the country to shows and exhibitions. At one of these, I was pleased to see that the other guests included a team from 771 Search and Rescue Squadron at RAF Culdrose, and I took some pleasure in introducing the producer, Sarah McNeil, to one of the best and bravest of the divers, Larry Slater. He had recently been awarded the George Medal for his part in rescuing Simon Le Bon's team, after they were trapped under water, when their power-boat overturned in the Atlantic during their attempt on the record for the fastest crossing. Good though he was, he had not appeared much in *Rescue Flight* because his language included an expletive every second word or so and, as we all know, BBC rules demand that expletives be deleted before 9 o'clock at night. During my nostalgic chat with the crews, it never occurred to me that I would never again be able to take part in such hazardous filming.

I had not worked for Schools since my days as an actor a quarter of a century before. I remember one play with particular pleasure, because included in the cast was a young man doing his first job – and by no means his last. He turned out to be one of the finest actors in Britain. When, all those years later, he was guest presenter of *Pick Of The Week*, he was good enough to include an extract from one of my very last broadcasts, *Horizon – In My Lifetime?* Martin Jarvis turned out to be a generous friend.

Summer 1986 was also the time of the Royal Wedding between Fergie and Prince Andrew, and there were to be special broadcasts marking the occasion. I am glad to say that my friends in television thought the event to be of greater significance than Peter Pagnamenta's pride, and it was felt that a quirky view was called for, amongst all the hype. I was never quite sure where the accepted mythology came from that I had an alternative view to contribute, but I was lucky enough to be asked to make two films. One was to be shown the night before the wedding, the other at the end of the wedding day. We had half a day (and a drive to Hampshire) in which to make the first, and a day while the whole country was otherwise occupied to make the second. The brief was brief: do a sort of 'Dummer prepares' piece (Dummer was the village where Fergie was born), and then do a 'Glyn's view' of the wedding day.

I had my usual cold fear in the gut. What would the films be about? As so often in television, we would have to make it up as we went along, 'busk it', as they say. Fortunately I had been to Dummer before, when the engagement was about to be announced. On that occasion I had managed to do a piece along the lines of, 'this is the village in which Fergie does not live, this is the school she did not attend, this is the pub she does not drink in, and here are the villagers she does not know!' It finished by even casting doubt on the certainty that the event would take place, and produced in evidence a huge banner headline from the *Daily Express* on another royal romance, which by luck I had kept. It read: 'CHARLES TO MARRY ASTRID, CERTAIN'. On such flimsy material is much television made. I had not wanted to make the film, on the grounds that there was not enough material, and yet by the skin of our teeth we survived. It was adjudged a great success, and Frank Bough was good enough to remark on air when it was over, 'Follow that!'

For the day before, I made a film on how the villagers of Dummer were in hiding from, and outnumbered by, the gentlepersons of the press, and on the day itself one on how the wedding was celebrated in an old-folks' home.

Television is taken for granted by the viewer – yet never was there a better example of how the industry flies by its own boot straps and gets through by the skin of its teeth. That evening's programme, an hour long, was to take the form of highlights of the day, plus a few extras (like my film). The whole thing was to be linked from an outside broadcast studio in the Mall by David Dimbleby and Selina Scott, but compiled in Lime Grove and recorded between 8 o'clock and 9.30 p.m. There was no script; David and Selina were told what the next insert (piece of film or video) would be, and asked to improvise a link into it; then the people in Lime Grove would run the insert and gradually the programme would be built up.

Meanwhile, I was having problems of my own. Despite promises, there were no machines available at 5.30 on which to edit the film – all machines and editors were in use. We did not start until 8 o'clock, and had less than an hour and a half in which to do a job which would normally have taken three hours. The quality suffered as a result. We arrived, sweating, in the compilation area, only to find they too were having problems. David and Selina had been talking to the nation since early morning, and were tired. The links were not always perfect, particularly Selina's, and had to be done again. For technical reasons, each time there was a retake the tape had to be run back to the beginning of the last insert and played again. Valuable time was being lost. The producer in Lime Grove had already lost his cool, and what he had to say about presenters was not exactly complimentary. He should try it.

Eventually, they reached the point of no return and the producer in Lime Grove announced that there was less time until transmission than it would take to finish the tape. A violent argument ensued, until the outside broadcast producer asked who was going to tell the Controller of BBC1 that there would be a large hole in prime time just when the whole nation was expecting to watch an important programme. This thought concentrated the mind wonderfully, and it was decided to broadcast the tape of what had been done so far and compile a second short tape of the rest (including my film) and hope not only that it was ready by the time the first tape ran out but that it could be timed to start so that viewers at home would not notice the join. Mercifully, this was done successfully and my labours had not been in vain. We sighed with relief when it was all over, and prepared to go to the party which had been arranged to toast the happy couple. Unfortunately, no one could remember where the party was, so after a fruitless drive around London four of us had to settle for a deserted Indian restaurant at midnight. We drank the toast anyway.

On 1 August I had my head examined. It was some weeks since I had last seen Dr Campbell, the neurologist in Bristol. He had written to Dr Calland and, when I thought about it, which was irresponsibly rarely, I was impatient. I did not know then that nothing anyone could do would impede the progress of the disease, nor that no prognosis as to pace was possible. Dr Calland had explained to me that the next stage was to look at the cerebellum and check it for any visible atrophy. I was lucky in that Frenchay Hospital, near Bristol, where Dr Campbell worked, was one of the best equipped hospitals in the country to examine my problem. For one thing it had a machine which could take a picture of my cerebellum, and a doctor who could administer the test and check the results. Both were available immediately. The cost would be three hundred pounds. If, however, I had not got three hundred pounds, or was not willing to pay it, then I might have to wait a couple of months for the examination. I thought about it. The situation was this, the dilemma of all ill people: if you had the money you could get quicker treatment; if you did not, you could not. I looked towards Dr Calland, who did not seem too perturbed that I should be willing to wait a couple of months. I thought about the situation: if I paid money, then both the machine and the doctor were available; yet if they were available, they were available – why could they not be available to an NHS patient? And if there were NHS patients on the list in front of me, why were they not being dealt with now by this available doctor, with his available machine? Furthermore, although I did not know it then, an early diagnosis would not have meant an early cure. There is no cure. Quite apart from anything else, I had no money apart from my income; I had spent it all on the house. I told Tony Calland that I would literally rather die than queue-jump. He did not argue. I suspect I know why.

The summer meandered on. It was not particularly hot, but in the beautiful Wye Valley the warm days seemed to make up for the wet ones. We had abandoned the idea of a family holiday – although I was working relatively frequently, there was no permanency or certainty about my income and, although I still did not believe it would seriously affect my work, there was still the matter of my health to clear up. Jo swore that a holiday to her was time alone with the sheep and the landscape, and so we arranged that, during a week when I would be away working, Ellie would go away too. We had discovered 'riding holidays', where girls were occupied with horses during the day and spent their evenings at discos and in swimming pools. Ellie was keen to try it, and I was never so proud of her than when she came back with two rosettes. My holiday was almost a return to my childhood. Every summer, the Gloucestershire Cricket Club play a 'Festival' at Cheltenham, on the College ground, and I was content to take that week off to go and watch the cricket. I was older now, and a member, so I was able to organize my time there as I pleased. Sitting in a deck-chair, with the warm evening sun casting long shadows and a golden glow across the Cotswold stone buildings, as men in white, Gloucestershire men, quietly pushed on to victory, was my idea of heaven. This is the idealized picture of Cheltenham Week that I carry round with my life membership card, although I am aware that it frequently rains, and Gloucestershire occasionally loses.

Although I was not aware of it, my world was beginning to contract. Bill Jones and Dave Hanington had been asked to run the flagship programme of the new South East region, which was to be based at Elstree in the old studios previously used by Associated Television. They planned a series for the new year called *On The Road*, in which three reporters would each do a film and then link the programme outdoors from one of the locations. The films were a variety of human and political interest stories, much as we used to do on *Nationwide*, and Bill and Dave felt that, in addition to two young reporters, John Diamond and Diane Kenton, the programme should have the ballast of what was fast becoming a 'grizzled veteran' – me! I looked forward to the venture, not knowing that it would bring me to my first real crisis.

Meanwhile, my energy quotient was normal and my work pattern as varied as usual. On 1 September I went back to see Dr Calland and received the news that my cerebellum was indeed shrunken. Still unperturbed, I drove across country to Brighton, where an old friend, Angela Hind, was helping me compile a special 'Gloucestershire Archive' which I was due to deliver live, with the aid of a tape recorder, to a local society. The following evening, after a day of listening to and cutting tapes, I drove to London, then took a train to York where I was interviewing the staff of the Gillygate Cooperative Bakery for the Schools series.

Such was the variety of life. It was only a few minutes before the train arrived that I felt my subconscious had noticed my name in the paper I was reading. After careful scrutiny, I discovered it in the birthdays column: 'Glyn Worsnip, broadcaster, 48.' I had completely forgotten that it was my birthday and, had I not read about it in the *Guardian*, might not have remembered it at all. And if I had not, I might have forgotten that 4 September was our twenty-first wedding anniversary. I pondered the fact that I would be spending it away, working, and reflected on how the fear of unemployment had so often got in the way of the important things in life.

In addition, the event for the first time prompted me to think seriously about the cerebellar syndrome. Did the fact that I had forgotten my own birthday mean that my memory (which had always been bad) was starting to be affected? Would my thinking brain atrophy too? How long would it take? My imagination temporarily ran riot, but once again pressure of work blotted out my fears and I was soon back to normal.

For no particular reason, I seemed to be making a speciality of commenting on the printed press. On the Thursday, I was back in London to do some pre-filming for *On The Road* on the subject of Robert Maxwell's new venture, the ill-fated *London Daily News*; on Friday I chaired the first of what was to become a popular series on Radio 2, *The Press Gang*; and the following week I wrote and presented my first *Stop Press* on Radio 4. *The Press Gang* and *Stop Press* were to become important features of my life, one a light-hearted quiz programme, the other a more serious look at press behaviour, both broadcast on the same day. I was beginning to find a niche. On 17 September, seven weeks after I had been X-rayed, I went to see Dr Campbell again. He confirmed that there was indeed shrinkage, and showed me pictures which made it clear that there was a large space around the cerebellum. I remember making some feeble joke about needing this information like a hole in the head. As to what it would all mean, he was less clear. He showed me once again how my balance was being affected. At this stage there was no noticeable deterioration in speech, or at least none that could not be corrected. Then he told me that he could make no predictions. No two cases were the same; there was no pattern. It might mean disablement, it might not. Then he used words which at last convinced me that I was in serious trouble if the disease (for that is what it was) ran its worst course. 'You might,' he said, 'be a zombie in five years; it might take twenty.'

I was aghast – as much at his use of language, as at the information. It was a slow and sober drive back to London, where that evening I was to meet Dave and Bill and plan out some more of the coming season for the South East. At least that would not be affected – or so I thought. Dr Campbell had said that beta-blockers were effective in some cases, and that I should try them. Tony Calland explained that they were pills which inhibited panic. As he put it, if you were in a room which was suddenly invaded by a pride of lions, and you had taken beta-blockers, you would be able to think clearly about how you might escape through the window and do it, rather than being trapped into rushing about like a mad thing and not achieving anything. I realized that I had been prescribed something which would not so much clear up the condition as fortify me against the knowledge that I had it. In the event, they did not work with me. I was not to escape the lions.

The microphone seemed twice as big as usual. Threatening. The voice distant and broken. The earphones clamped to my head were uncomfortable, and did nothing to hold me steady. 'Right, here we go. From the top. Retake.' It was the next day. I had been booked to do a commercial recording in the afternoon. Normally, it would have been as easy as falling off a log. Once I had checked the pronunciation of obscure jargon in the plastics, medical or machine tool business, or whatever it was. But today it would not flow. 'It's Flo's day off!' as we used to say in the theatre. I was not really frightened yet; just conscious that yesterday's news was not good news. Give me time, I'll recover. It reminds me of the sick joke Arthur English was later to tell me during an edition of *The Press Gang*. It concerns the patient who went to see the doctor. 'I've got good news and bad news,' said the doctor. The patient opted for the good news first. 'The good news,' said the doctor, 'is that I've discovered you have twenty-four hours to live.' The patient wondered what the bad news could be. 'The bad news,' said the doctor, 'is that I forgot to ring you yesterday.'

I finished the job, but it was not quite satisfactory. I had taken the precaution (as I was always tempted to do) of warning the production team that I was just recovering from flu and that the work might not be up to standard. They smiled, and in the end pronounced themselves satisfied. But I heard later that they had re-recorded the commentary with someone else. It was the last time I risked a commercial recording with people who did not know, and who could not be told. I had said goodbye to the pension.

Filming was different. For a start, there is the distraction of the picture and the actuality. The voice should always complement the pictures not, as in radio, be the be-all and end-all of the item. In commercial films, greater emphasis is placed on the voice because the subject itself is not so intrinsically interesting. I have never (though you might not believe it!) been of the school of reporter that thinks you should always be seen as well as heard. My view is that, if the subject is sufficiently interesting, you should not stand in front of it, particularly when, as on so many programmes nowadays, the film is short and sharp.

There are times, however, when the story needs explaining, or progressing, when only a piece to camera will do. I was successfully negotiating these, and having no problems at all with the interviews. Even when it came to recording commentary, I suppose the fact that I was among friends and more at ease, that there were no commercial pressures of time, made it all more pleasant and relaxed.

Certainly there was plenty to do, and I was rushing from one film location to the next, often making more than one film in a day. I was at that time a sort of unofficial arts correspondent for *Breakfast Time*, and I was vastly enjoying myself. Prior to the opening of *The Phantom Of The Opera*, I discovered that even Andrew Lloyd Webber sweats a lot, and that his wife, Sarah Brightman, never answers a question without her husband's permission; David Puttnam, Ray MacAnnally and Cherie Lunghi (such is the power of television) interrupted a smart launch (and lunch) to talk to me about their film *The Mission*; I was entertained to tea and cake in his Cotswold cottage by the veteran film producer Michael Powell; I joked with Spike Milligan when the Imperial War Museum staged an exhibition of his wartime memorabilia; and I wandered round his idyllic Hampshire home with Norman Thelwell, the man who made horses funny.

It was not all art. It was the height of the Jeffrey Archer affair, and I was despatched to the House of Lords to interview the wily old Lord Denning about great British scandals. Off camera he bumbled and burred; on camera he became as sharp as a knife, and one realised why his name figures so frequently in significant British case law.

At the same time, I was making a documentary about the iniquities of diplomatic immunity, in the wake of the shooting of WPC Fletcher outside the Libyan Embassy in St James's Square, and I became involved in a very minor scandal myself. I had interviewed the Foreign Office minister Tim Eggar, about the British Government's attitude towards escaping responsibility for crime by pleading diplomatic immunity. He had replied by committing an enormous gaffe involving the Syrian Ambassador. Somehow the story got out, and the Minister's mistake was plastered all over the press. The Foreign Office begged the BBC not to show the clip, and to re-shoot the interview. We agreed, on the grounds that we would rather have the facts than waffle. I had the pleasure (never intending to use the question) of starting the second interview by saying to the Minister, 'On Thursday you told us that this was Government policy. What's today's story?' The Minister had the grace to laugh, but it was all we could do to persuade the hatchet-faced minders (civil servants) that all was well and that we had no intention of using anything that would show the Government in a bad light. The whole thing was like a sequence from *Yes, Minister*. Afterwards, it was rumoured that Norman Tebbit, who at that time was not best pleased with the BBC, had declared that things would not be so bad if everyone behaved as responsibly as the makers of our programme. I thought my career was at an end – I had problems enough on my hands without receiving compliments from that quarter.

Life was a rich and colourful tapestry, and it seemed inconceivable that it would all be brought to an end. Yet I must have been worried. At lunches with friends I told the whole story, as if sharing it would make the problem go away. I think by this time I had subconsciously accepted that something serious was in the offing, although I saw no reason yet why it should radically affect my work. But perhaps I thought that by admitting it to people, I was beginning to prepare the ground for an eventual calamity. In a strange way, I was painting to them a blacker picture than I was prepared to paint to myself.

Before I began *On The Road* in the new year, I had one more radio programme to make. For twenty-five years, John Ebdon had been prowling the BBC archives. His voice was as rich and brown as the pipe-tobacco whose rich aroma he always left lingering among the shelves. His facetious patrician tones every third Monday morning, his sense of the absurd, his ear for a word mistakenly out of context, his famous cat Perseus, delighted much of middle-England as much as it infuriated a small minority. Some people saw him only as a poseur, but he is a complex man – emotional, an ex-actor and fighter pilot, a skin salesman in Africa, a sincere practising Christian as well as a hellenophile with a lifelong devotion to astronomy. He became Director of the London Planetarium. After twenty-five years broadcasting from the archives he was giving up. As the senior member of his humble successors (I had only served seven years), I felt that a silver anniversary tribute to this remarkable broadcaster was called for, and I am glad to say the then Controller of Radio 4, David Hatch, agreed. Angela Hind (who had produced John) was to be the producer, and the main interview was to be recorded at his immaculate Wembley flat. We got the preliminaries over first, which included John welcoming me to the flat with his inimitable catch-phrase 'How do you do?' then settled down to a superb lunch. John and his partner Mary are unashamed *gourmands* and careful hosts, and there was wine to match every course. This was a great pity because, since I was working, I had to eschew so much, but I was happy for John to drink if it made him feel more at ease. And, of course, *in vino veritas*. As I had expected, not a syllable was out of place and it was a very relaxed and revealing conversation. As the day wore on, it seemed churlish not to help finish the bottles of red wine and I, too, drank the afternoon away. As I had hoped, it was more a conversation than a formal interview. But it was the last time I remember wine being a help rather than a hindrance. It was the last time I allowed myself to 'drink on duty'. One of my real grievances about the cerebellar syndrome is that the merest touch of alcohol turns me and my speech incoherent. I become not drunk, but incapable, and an already slurred speech quickly becomes even more slurred. I have had to give up one of my favourite pastimes, and I am only glad that my last memory of drinking without any ill-effects involved such good company, and such fine wine.

After all that, I went on in the evening to a belated farewell party for David Lloyd, who had been so supportive during the 'Lime Grove Six' affair and who had now moved on to Channel 4. Looking around, there was a sea of well-remembered faces and, as someone at the party wistfully remarked, 'there are an awful lot of talented people NOT working for the Beeb any more.' But what I really remember the party for was the dancing. I was always an energetic (and sweaty) dancer, if never a very good one, and that evening I amused, and amazed, my friends with an exhibition of old style rock 'n' roll jiving. I cannot remember who saved the last dance for me, but last dance it certainly was. It was 18 November 1986, and I never danced again. Now that I think about it, it was some Tuesday.

The ground slid from under my feet. I could not coordinate speech and movement. The air around me became hazy with mist. It was four weeks later. We had started pre-filming for *On The Road*, and I was in a greenhouse demonstrating a new method of watering the desert which had been developed by some enterprising businessmen in Thame. The air around me was meant to go misty as I walked and talked, from fine drops of water escaping from the nozzles. And, if one's suit was to be preserved, it was advisable to do the take in one go. Bill Jones, who was directing, settled for a less than perfect take. He was both a perfectionist and tactful, but I could see he was not best pleased. It was the sort of trick I used to perform with ease. Winter was upon us and, although it was a fine December day, the cold was beginning to tell.

A week later I had a splendid day in Tunbridge Wells. It was just my sort of film, about Nick Berry (Wicksy from *East Enders*) appearing in pantomime in that strait-laced town. Nick was an engaging young man, with a hit record called *Every Loser Wins* which was mysteriously relevant to the story of Dick Whittington – but he was an Eastender in Tunbridge Wells. What did he make of them? What did they make of him? We settled for a draw – and a draw he certainly was. I interviewed his mum in a posh tea-shop; I interviewed Nick in the theatre. It was a long day, but we all had a lot of fun. I ran errands for the director (Dave Hanington on this occasion), and literally ran, looking for picturesque locations. But the work was mainly indoors, and that was beginning to make a difference.

As luck would have it, it was the worst winter in the south-east that anyone could remember. The snow was so bad that lunatics were driving the wrong way up the M2. While others were failing, I managed to get my car (and the production team) to the coast and the ferry to France for a film about the Channel Tunnel; I endured a nine-hour drive from Dover to London in blizzard conditions; I would film in three or four locations in one day; I would lunch in South Wales and dine in York. But, I was beginning to lean against the wall as I stumbled down the stairs at my digs. In the beautiful churchyard at Aldbury in Hertfordshire I tried to do a piece to camera and found I could not walk in a straight line. On Southend pier and at the new City airport, I kept having to do retakes on simple introductions for the programme. At the bus station café in Banbury I discovered that I could no longer offer anyone a cup of tea – half a cup, yes, at a cost of a few pence and a burnt hand. I was no longer steady enough to carry it. Bill Jones said it all when he told me that he was now pretending other things were wrong so that I would get another chance. And when it was so cold and snowy that we had to introduce the programme from outside the BBC studios at Ealing instead of at the intended location, my jaw seized up and I could not keep the slur from my speech.

An experienced film-editor looked at the piece in amazement. 'Is Glyn drunk?' he asked.

'No,' said Bill. 'He has a problem.'

CHAPTER 7

Crisis

It was a busy week. You do not go into the National for a rest. I was tested, prodded and scanned. I learnt a whole new vocabulary: biopsy, electroencephalographic, somato-sensory-evoked potentials, autonomic. My hair was filthy with gum from electrodes attached to my head while they measured the electrical activity in my brain. I had speech therapy, occupational therapy, physiotherapy and intelligence tests. To my astonishment, my memory for words and for faces was one hundred per cent; I hesitated only over Rasputin and Karl Marx. I visited what was known as the 'torture chamber', where tests on sight, hearing and balance involved my head being fixed in an almost medieval clamp while only my eyes moved. I tried to keep my balance while a pink gingham cloth moved around me. It was like having had one too many in a bistro. They put me on a tilting bed and measured my blood pressure lying down, standing up and at all angles in between. I blew down tubes until I almost fainted. They poured hot water into my ears, then cold. I thought my head would burst. And after all that, a doctor confessed that he was only asking me back because the tests were more relevant to his ongoing research than to improving my condition. Which seemed likely to be cerebellar ataxia – as if I did not already know. If the truth be told, very little was known about cerebellar ataxia. There was an hereditary version, but I did not appear to have it. I was a 'primary' case. I began to get a glimmering of the frustration and alarm felt by the many other people with diseases where there was little hope of recovery.

Perhaps not surprisingly, for the first time in my life I accepted sleeping pills. They created a hangover effect in the morning, thus ensuring that I dozed through that hateful time around six, when noisy people ply everyone with unwanted cups of tea. The pills also made me disinclined to pay attention during doctors' rounds, which may or may not have been a bad thing.

I was something of a celebrity on the ward – not because I appeared on radio and television – but for two reasons. First, because of the people who came to see me, and second because I was seen to be reading a book. When Sue Cook came in, I could see some patients who had difficulty moving other parts, doing extraordinary things with their eyebrows. They said nothing at the time, but afterwards there was much questioning. I was even asked if I *really* knew Sue Cook. I caught myself saying that, if I did not, it seemed improbable that she would visit me.

The second reason for the interest was that I had a copy of the still banned *Spycatcher*. I had conducted an interview on the subject for the Radio 4 programme *Stop Press*, which I then presented, after illegally quoting from it. It has always been my view that a broadcaster's duty is to defend press freedom, break down barriers and extend the state of the art. No-one objected to my quoting publicly from the book – although whether this was because no-one minded, or because no-one listened, I have never gathered. At any rate, there were only two interesting pages in it – about the so-called plot to discredit Harold Wilson – and the rest was mind-bendingly boring. Once I had started reading it, however, amid so much vicarious scrutiny, I felt compelled to endure it from cover to cover. The most pleasure I got was being able to lend it to a Ministry of Defence mandarin who was temporarily in the ward, and who foresaw that reading it would garner him more than a point or two at the tennis club.

The past six months had been a hard-working and enjoyable time. I will not say it was the last time I enjoyed making films, because as it happened there was one more period the next year, but it was the last time I enjoyed film-making unrestricted by ill-health and disability. I was ill all right, and I knew it, but it was the last time I could get away with it without OTHER PEOPLE knowing. I was sufficiently mobile and spruce of speech so that at the very least any slowness or sloppiness could be put down to encroaching middle age. I was prepared for remarks like, 'Glyn is not what he was,' although happily, if they were said, I did not hear them. Active travel was still a problem. At the end of March 1987 and the hectic *On The Road* season, I embarked on one of my favourite types of filming. It was a half-hour documentary about flying called *Goodbye London Aerodrome!* The subject was RAF Hendon, which was closing down, but whose story encompassed much of the history of aviation and provided plenty of opportunity for elderly reminiscence and aged film archive material. It was directed by an old friend from *On The Road* and *Nationwide* days whom, in deference to the women's movement, I had nicknamed 'Person-person', he being called Chapman. We worked well together, he being efficient and tidy, me being inclined to go off into flights of fanciful imagination and language. He also knew of my problem.

The Queen Mother, who did not, was due to take the salute on the day, and there was to be a nostalgic fly-past of historic aircraft, which was to be the climax of the day and the film. We filmed all over the country, and there were no problems with my mobility. We filmed air aces from both World Wars and found a photograph, taken in 1911, of a pilot sitting in one of those aeroplanes which appear to be made of balsa-wood and string. Amazingly, the pilot was still alive, and now nearly 100 years old.

When we filmed at his Knightsbridge home, the film-crew were startled to be told that they might make tea below stairs while the director and I were served tea in bone-china with the Wing Commander and his wife. They went without demur! It is one of the perennial pleasures of filming to meet so many people with different values and differing lifestyles.

The Queen Mum, as usual, endeared herself to everyone, and so it was more the pity that it was a dim day with constant rain and a cloud base of below 500 ft. There would be no fly-past. It was a bitter blow, but in the end we managed to save both the day and the film by commandeering a lonely RAF helicopter and performing the fly-past ourselves. I hung out of the side door to commentate as we flew over Hendon, with no other ill-effects than a lost voice and a sore throat. What with the wind and the engine noise, I could not hear myself speak. Fortunately, the microphone could. In a short time I would neither be able to clamber aboard nor to commentate.

Good summer though it was, with few obvious difficulties, there had been one or two warning signs. I had started to keep an occasional diary, on tape. One entry ran:

Friday 13 (sic) March 1987. Today I started to slobber. I tried to tell myself that it was because of a hole in my mouth, where a tooth had recently been removed. But I suspected it wasn't. I suspected it was muscle control, or lack of it. I wondered how long it would be before the condition was permanent.

It was during a piece to camera for *Goodbye London Aerodrome!* We were out at Hendon one evening filming an anniversary 'upside down dinner' to commemorate the first loop the loop. I was resplendent that evening in a dinner jacket, and had no hanky handy. I muttered about the tooth, and carried on.

All the crew were required to work in DJs, but one extra electrician who had been drafted in too late had not been warned and had to stand outside the window throughout. This was the kind of impractical pomposity we were constantly up against. Somehow it would not have seemed so ridiculous had it not been for the fact that, of all the many RAF officers mustered, not one was capable of flying an aeroplane – even the right way up.

Over the May Day Bank Holiday I had another shock. They broadcast *Anything You Can Do*, a light-hearted look at the battle of the sexes, which Bel Mooney and I had presented for Bill Stewart, the producer of *The Price Is Right*. It was an elaborate piece, which included complicated tests of skill – could a woman service a car engine, could a man be a successful agony aunt? It proved nothing but it was good fun, there were richly contrasting guests (Claire Rayner, Derek Jameson, the President of MENSA), and it contained the first televised male beauty contest.

I was aghast when I saw it. Not at the sight of young men parading in bathing slips, but at the sheer dexterity of the programme. It had been made a year earlier and taken a long time in the editing. I looked five years younger. I realized that I would never again be able to run up and down rostra like some electrified Robert Kilroy Silk, interviewing people. I would never again be sure of reading autocue or improvising as fluently. I would never again be sure I could readily record for several long hours after two full days of rehearsal. Already the disease had begun its 'progressive' course.

In the summer I had to do a sponsored horse-ride for some good cause of Ellie's. It did not require speed and it was a gorgeous drowsy day. We meandered about in the hills above Tintern and the horse munched at passing delicacies. But it was steep, and I was constantly having to push aside overhanging branches. It was idyllic; I clung on and, though I said nothing, knew it would be my last ride.

I was working no harder then I had ever worked, but it was too hard. The agonizing thing about cerebellar ataxia is that you feel better and forget your problems if you work, but work begins to take its toll. It is, as they say, a 'Catch 22' situation.

In June, I had finally rung Dick Smith, the *Breakfast Time* doctor. Within a week, he had discovered Anita Harding. Within another week, I had asked my doctor to write and within a month I had seen her and fixed the spell in hospital for the last week in August. I could not complain about the speed with which the NHS was working – but why had I not acted earlier? I now realize that I could not have stopped the disease, or even slowed it down, if I had grasped the nettle, but I did not know it then, and at the time cursed myself.

Meanwhile, with the tests still ahead of me, I was working apace. Rachel Atwell, a big and beautiful girl (I had once watched her being unsuccessfully propositioned by a rich and arrogant businessman on the steps of the Imperial Hotel, Blackpool while she was directing an interview with Clive Jenkins), was now editor of *London Plus*, the nightly regional news show. She asked me if I would make some 'feature' films for the programme – nice human interest stories with a beginning a middle and an end, quite unlike the short news stories that are so boringly and inexplicably popular with fashionable BBC moguls. I readily agreed, glad to fall back into the old *Nationwide* mould.

The effect was astonishing. I was clearly regarded as some grand old man of film-making. What seemed to me workaday stuff, was greeted by the young presenters and reporters as some new concept in film-making. I found, to my surprise, that the office turned and watched my films, as some sort of treat, or a wonder to be marvelled at. I need hardly say that I was much flattered by this, and I threw myself wholeheartedly into filmic story-telling. Only John Stapleton, now mercifully restored to the BBC, was of the old guard. He knew all about that kind of film-making, not least because he had done it himself, in happier days.

It was a curious couple of months. I looked at my grey hairs and realized that, to many people, I was a veteran. They say that television is a young person's game. That may be, but standards must be maintained if the BBC is to survive the commercial attack from the vulgar, the rich and those who would appeal to the lowest common denominator. Sadly, the signs are that it is giving way to pressure. Analysis, investigation and short features are unfashionable. It is felt that all you need to know can be told in short and oft-repeated headlines. As Jo has often said, even of the radio, 'I can recite the effing news by the end of the day.' Where there is analysis, it is regarded as a highbrow activity, to be broadcast at unsocial hours. At Frank Bough's farewell from *Breakfast Time*, he lamented the fact that the BBC no longer felt it important to interest 'Fred and Freda' in current affairs. He was absolutely right. Popular current affairs programmes have disappeared from the schedules: *Nationwide* has gone; *Breakfast Time* has donned a suit and tie.

In June and July 1987 I was doing my bit for popular culture on *London Plus*. I made a film about keeping the legendary Vickers Viscount flying. For this I flew from Southampton to Guernsey and back (filming all the way), and then drove to Southend in the evening. I also made up and filmed a piece to camera in flight. With none of these projects were there any problems either of tiredness or of incapacity. My hopes were inordinately raised. I began to wonder (and so did Jo) whether the original diagnosis had been correct. Or whether, at worst, I would remain on a plateau with difficulties only in unusual conditions, such as extreme cold – whether, in short, any problem could be contained.

I made picture-stories out of natives of the Indonesian jungle who had come to build a rice-barn in Piccadilly; a houseful of puppets in Ilford; the 'Holy Show' – a group of cavorting priests and nuns; a recreation of the old Brooklands racetrack, with ERAs and John Cobb's Railton Special; and the world champion backwards runner. For this I devised an elaborate ending. The theory was that, if one person did it, the whole world would follow suit. The final shot had to show the passing pedestrians and vehicles all speeding backwards. This necessitated my doing everything in reverse, so as to appear to be going forwards when the film was reversed. I had to cross a road, avoid a bollard and end up looking surprised at seeing the world go by in reverse. It was a complicated manoeuvre which, if it came off, would make the film. Of course here (as so often) my acting came in useful. The question was, could I manage it physically? It was successful, even at the end of a long hard day. 'One-take' Worsnip had struck again, just as the light started to fade – in more ways than one. The situation seemed now to be that the physical imbalance, which I had noticed first, had stabilized, and the verbal disability was still disguisable.

It was working for *Breakfast Time*, on those hot July nights, that helped me to define where the line lay between ability and disbility.

For *Breakfast Time* we were required to work all day and then all night. On the night of 6 June was held the Berkeley Square Ball, one of the social events of the year, and *Breakfast Time* wanted a witty report ready first thing in the morning. When making a Radio 4 feature called *Phantoms of the Railways* that same month, we had wound up looking for a hotel in Hull after midnight. I noticed that I was a touch impatient. Well, they do say, 'In Hull, Hell and Halifax . . .' but it was not my usual style and later, when we came to record some commentary outdoors, late in the evening, in the increasing cold, I noticed that I was not my old fluent self. My body seemed to be telling me that I now performed less well when tired. But then, I was forty-eight – was it not just old age, rather than cerebellar ataxia? I clung to that thought.

The same thing happened on the night of the Berkeley Square Ball. I was working with an old friend who knew her onions,

Gill Ballin. It was an amusing occasion and there was plenty of material to laugh both at and with. 'Bubbles' Rothermere was there, looking like a large and gooey meringue, and she consented to hold court in the organisers' tent. There were enough old friends from the glitterati prepared to contribute loose ends of conversation if asked – Ned Sherrin, who was very rude about the type of people who attended the Ball (almost exclusively second-hand car salesmen, he thought), Lionel Blair and Andrew Neil, now the Editor of the *Sunday Times*, whom I had known since *Nationwide* days. We waited an hour to film the arrival of a royal guest. Personally, I was more intrigued by a line of disconsolate and under-employed nurses, but was told we could not ignore the guest of honour. By the early hours of the morning I was becoming distinctly tetchy again, feeling we had enough material and that we should go back to base in order to start putting it together. In the event, I wrote the script between 3 and 4 o'clock, recorded the commentary and edited the videotape until five minutes before transmission. By the end, I had had enough.

The same pattern emerged in another film I made for *Breakfast Time*, about the Kirov Opera, who were visiting Britain. Again, the director was Gill Ballin, so I did not have the kind of anxieties that arose when I was harnessed to totally inexperienced youngsters. And this time shooting was over by midnight. Joan Bakewell happened to be at the dress rehearsal too, as Arts Correspondent of *Newsnight*. Television may be a young person's business, but Joan is one whom age does not wither. She is as attractive now as when she was dubbed, 'the thinking-man's crumpet' in the 1960s. I was never much of a thinker, but Joan was always one of my favourites. She was always kind to me and, although not a close friend, was one of those in television who sent me a concerned and distressed note when I went public with my illness. We often met and exchanged jokes while covering artistic events in our differing ways. I remember whispering to her that this opera appeared to be about a group of bad-tempered German aristocrats, who were haunted by a man in a red woolly pullover. In fact this was only the conductor/director making last minute adjustments. Joan laughed, and suggested I use the line in my report.

I had always found all-night editing good fun, and still did. There is an artistic thrill to be got from seeing how a point can best be made in the shortest possible time, and whether by word or picture. (On *Breakfast Time* the time was always short, even in the days when they made funny, absorbing, human interest stories.) But I was finding the long haul harder and harder going. Things started to look ominous at the end of July. On Thurday 30 July I spent the day filming near Chester. It was a moving story, which two years later became even more of a *cause célèbre* when my old boss Desmond Wilcox made a long documentary about it in *The Visit*. It concerned a little girl called Katy, who suffered from a phobia of light. She could not endure more than the light of a 40-watt bulb indoors, and could not risk going outdoors at all. It was a touching and tragic story and, in the hateful way of television, was one of my better films. They ran it at over six minutes and (even more unheard of), cancelled another item to fit it in.

We got back from Chester at about 5 o'clock in the afternoon but, in the irritating way in which television treats its workers, there were no machines or operators available until after midnight, so we started then. People do not realize it, but it takes six or seven hours to write, record and edit five or six minutes of material, and many a cup of coffee or chocolate is consumed from the nearby machine, which mercifully is free of charge at night. By 3 o'clock in the morning, I was ready to record some commentary.

The opening words are etched on my mind. They were: 'Nobody asks what Katy did at school. Katy doesn't go to school. Nobody asks, "Can Katy come out to play?" Katy can't.' To my horror, I could not say them. I must have tried half a dozen times, before we managed to cobble together a half-way acceptable version. It was put down to over-tiredness. (We had already done a day's shooting in Chester, and I had been up all night two days previously with the Kirov Opera film.) But however tired, I had never before failed to get my tongue around words which I myself had written. I knew it was more than tiredness. It was a sobering moment.

It was the same with movement. I was at the stage where, in optimum conditions, nothing was noticeable. But throw in tiredness, or stress, or alcohol, or extreme cold, and the effects of the disease *were* noticeable. By now, too, the tabloid press had been on to my agent asking if the rumours were true that I had multiple sclerosis. When I heard that, I realized it was the beginning of the end. I would have to say something soon. An awareness of restricted movement which had begun on the deck of an aircraft was certified on the deck of a rusting college barge. I did a series of films in and around Oxford with my old friend and talented director Bill Jones, who was helping *London Plus* out. One was about the restoration of Oxford college barges, of which there were only three or four left. One of them we found tied up in a reedy backwater off the River Cherwell. To my astonishment, it belonged to my own college, St John's, and on it I had drunk champagne thirty years earlier. I was able to do a nostalgic piece to camera from the same spot, saying how young and spruce and full of hope we had both been then. 'But look at us now!' It was an affecting moment. Later, when I tried to walk across the deck, I knew at last that I would never walk in a straight line again. Later still, when I tried to record some commentary at Radio Oxford, I fluffed and excused myself, and fluffed again. Luckily, only Bill and I were present. We both knew that my speech would never be the same. It was a difficult session, and it was only because Bill was a friend, and knew the problem, that he made no comment. But I could see the pain in his eyes.

But I dared not stop. In my new freelance status, I felt I had to accept any work I could get. The money had to come from somewhere, now that I had no regular contract. I had nothing put by. The irony was that even I had already begun to realize that what David Dimbleby had once said to me was true: 'There IS a world out there,' and I was talented enough to take advantage of it.

Towards the end of September I began making half-hour documentaries for *Friday Report* (a Panorama-style programme) on such cheerful subjects as football violence and 'Buddies' (people who befriend AIDS victims). On radio I was the scourge of the tabloids with *The Press Gang* and *Stop Press*, and I was still making films for *London Plus*. I remember one in particular, where I accompanied some old soldiers back to Dunkirk.

The sight of Chelsea pensioners on the lonely French beaches, with the distant sound of The Last Post echoing behind them, was very affecting. It absolutely poured with rain as we gathered round the war memorial, but the old men were unflinching. I had to borrow a pair of jeans from the 'sparks' – electricians – to get back to England in, and they were at least six inches too short, but no one seemed to mind. On the return journey by hovercraft, I typed a script balancing the typewriter on my knee, with people being sick all around me. As usual I was with an inexperienced director, a secretary, a production assistant, a man from the newsroom, or a temporary attachee from the sound suite. The were all keen and talented, but they needed permanent help from the older hands. *London Plus* only had one official film-director, Gaby Koppel, with whom I had made the film about running backwards, and she was fired at the end of the season. It seemed to us that the new regime at the BBC either thought films simply came out of the air, or counted on extra effort from the more experienced – or, worse, just did not care if the product was not up to standard. All this added strain to an already stressful situation. Long hours of extra supervision, under pressure in busy cutting rooms, no doubt added to my problems. But I had always thrived on work and it never occurred to me to stop. Even when a director was inexperienced enough to ask me where the studio was, I did not realize I was doing too much. It was amazing, and perhaps irresponsible, how I managed to put my condition out of my mind.

Occasionally, I was stopped short, but generally I ignored the problem. When I visited the Labour Party conference in Brighton, to record some interviews for *Stop Press*, it was the first time for many years that I had not been a permanent part of the conference team. I was greeted by old pals in the newsroom like a late lamented friend. My 'Diaries' for *Nationwide* and *Breakfast Time* had been popular, among both observers and politicians, and many were glad to see me and harked back to the old days. Yet I knew in my heart of hearts that, even were I still under contract, I could never have borne the strain of many weeks of little or no sleep and the pressure of seeking out material, and always with a new angle.

* * *

The first great crisis came two days later, at the beginning of October. It was the last *Stop Press* of the current season. Emily Buchanan, producer of the programme, was out of the room when I finished the script, so I popped next door to Ann Sloman, Head of the Special Current Affairs Department, which produced *Stop Press*. What date were we returning? Should I mention it as I said goodbye? Ann, who was not easily thrown, looked me in the eye and told me that it was safer not to mention it at all; that Michael Green, Controller of Radio 4, had not yet decided whether he wanted a new series; that no date had been fixed.

I left the room in a sweat. Emily had told me for certain that the programme was returning in December. When she came back, I taxed her. I could see the implications of this deceit. Emily is a blusher, and her face went as red as her hair. She eventually confessed that Ann had been worried about my condition, that the readings had not been as fluent as they had been, and that there had been enquiries as to my health in the BBC Duty Log. But no decision had been taken, and none would be before we all had a chance to talk about it. It was a lie. I had been fired, though no-one said so at the time. It did not make it easy to record that final programme.

I spent the next fortnight filming 'Buddies' for *Friday Report*. I had reached the stage now where I would not start any project without taking the director into my confidence about the disease. I was protecting myself, I suppose, as much as them, in case anything should go wrong. I was lucky in that my directors and producers were all either old friends or sympathetic. Clare Patterson, who directed 'Buddies', thought that we could overcome any problems while the film was being edited, and was more than helpful at a stage where my confidence was very low.

In this way, I was taken out of myself. Furthermore, 'Buddies' entailed filming in Brighton, and I was glad of the sea air and the break. It gave me a chance to visit my old friend from Oxford and *That's Life!*, Norma. I had lived with her (in the nicest possible way) after the death of her husband, the American film-music composer Bernard Herrmann, and it was only when her son Daniel was on the way that I had moved out. She now lived in Brighton with Daniel's father Roger, a somewhat conservative Police Superintendent who enjoyed a mutual josh about politics, or any other controversial topic. On this occasion, in a restaurant, I teased him about the size and richness of the pudding he ordered, saying it was real 'heart attack' material. As so often, it was quite the wrong thing to say, for Roger went out to the car and, as far as we could tell, promptly had a heart attack. I spent an anxious night at the hospital, comforting Danny, and was glad to be there and of use. It made me realize how common medical disasters are, and how many people are affected. I am happy to say that Roger is now fully recovered, and that the seizure was found not to be a heart attack, but a result of overwork.

The experience also made me realize how hard-pressed are the hospitals, in which I was destined to spend so much time. There were patients in beds in the corridors waiting for places, and I overheard staff pleading with nearby hospitals: 'But you *promised* me a female bed!' Norma and I agreed that you only had to visit a hospital to see exactly how safe the NHS was in the Government's hands.

I have been lucky in my landlords and landladies. After leaving Norma, I shared my colleague Kevin Cosgrove's flat. One pleasure there was that, returning late at night, one would often stumble over a floorful of First Division footballers. Subsequently and for several years, I rented an attic from Kate Knowles. She then worked for Thames TV, but had been my researcher on *Pigeonhole*. Her japey friends kept me high during low moments. During *On The Road* and *Weekend*, I lodged with producer Dave Hanington and his wife Caroline, who had worked with me on *The Paras*.

Finally, when burgeoning family once more forced a move, I stayed with my old friend Sally Hardcastle, daughter of William. Callers imagined that because we shared an answerphone we shared everything else. Such was not the case. Sally has been a good friend to both me and Jo.

During my time on *Friday Report*, *The Press Gang* had started again. I cannot explain it, but throughout my period of illness, that programme buoyed me up and gave me something to look forward to. It was recorded at the Paris Theatre in Regent Street. On the face of it, it should have been the hardest thing to do. There were no retakes, and there was a live audience, who were devoted and kind. Perhaps the wit of Henry Kelly and Lance Percival, the acerbity of Denise Coffey and Frances Edmonds, the comic skills of Arthur English and Don Maclean, the absurdity of Gyles Brandreth and Mollie Parkin, the zany charm of Irene Handl and Christopher Biggins, and the skills of dozens of other guests over the years, was just the fillip I needed, but somehow I got away with it when, alone at the microphone, I was failing.

In October, in between times, I was composing three films about diabetes for Portobello Productions, the name adopted by Katya Krausova (with whom I used to share an office) and her husband Eric Abraham, formerly a *Panorama* producer. This involved sitting at a Steenbeck, a machine which plays both sound and picture and allows you to juggle the film around in ever-differing orders. The latest Steenbeck even greets you with a 'good morning'. The film had already been shot, but not written or structured. I was to record the commentaries, but the films were to be linked from a studio and Katya wondered if I had any ideas for a presenter. Philip Schofield seemed like a good idea, although I knew he was enormously busy. I also knew, from the time he was a guest on *The Press Gang*, that he was personable, fresh and wonderfully appealing to children of all ages. He was just the sort of person we needed, and I am glad to say that he agreed. There was, for me, just a bittersweet tinge of regret when I contrasted his hope and energy at the start of a long career, with the disappointment in me as I was brought to the end of mine. But the work itself was enormous fun, and it occurred to me that work of this sort would be ideal in future days. It is strange how secure and cosy you feel while a short job you enjoy lasts.

In the event, it was a bad day when I went to the recording studio. Although everyone was very understanding and tolerant, allowing me to persevere until I got it right, they must have been able to hear the strain in the voice. At all events, Katya later told me that they had reluctantly re-recorded my commentary, using Valerie Singleton. Val was an old friend, and was concerned that I might be upset. I was, but only with myself. I was having to face up to the fact that I was coming to the end of the line.

On the same day that I recorded that commentary, I went down to Walthamstow to make some recordings for a radio feature I was making for BBC Birmingham, on Working Men's Clubs. Walthamstow has the oldest Working Men's Club in Britain: a single room containing two snooker tables and little else beside its memories and the tick of the clock. It was a hut between buildings, reached by pushing aside washing and discarded toys, but nevertheless a warm and friendly place, a haven of calm and certainty and, to my astonishment, completely teetotal. Over a cup (cost 5p), I was much cheered, after a journey full of fear about my speech and speculation as to whether it would hold up for the interviews – particularly as they were to take place late in the evening. I will not say it was first class, but the quaint relaxing atmosphere helped to make it passable. The next day, we travelled up to Gateshead and reported on Stormont Main, one of the biggest and best of clubs, but full of blaring sound, beer and bingo. The interviews were successful, but my speech was a disaster. At one point, when I stuck the microphone in front of an interviewee and asked my first question, the reply was chilling. He asked simply, 'You've had a few, haven't you?' I was aware that some of my colleagues had thought much the same for some time, but had been more restrained about saying so. Here was a blunt accusation. I had deliberately drunk nothing but tonic all evening, but my speech was out of control, and the cat out of the bag.

The next morning, I confessed all to a perplexed young producer who must have been wondering by now why the first class presenter he had been promised was proving less than second rate. He was very understanding, said that he had heard rumours and that we could postpone finishing the job, but that he would have to tell his boss, the Head of BBC Radio in the Midlands, Jock Gallagher. I drove home full of trepidation, to find a letter from Ann Sloman.

It was exactly a month since the last *Stop Press* had been broadcast. No conversation had ever been held. Ann contrived to be both gushing and impersonal, in the way only certain executives can manage. She said that I was the best presenter and wittiest writer that *Stop Press* had ever had; but that I was not to be used any more. She spoke of defending the quality of her programme. I could not really complain – I had always been rather po-faced about the importance of excellence – although in view of some of the more recent imports to broadcasting from Fleet Street made by Ann's superiors, it seemed ironic that anyone should still defend the principle that *how* you say a thing is more important than *what* you say.

Jock Gallagher rang me the next morning and was incredibly supportive. He said there was no problem about delaying the programme. He said that even the disease was not the end of the world, and that I would be welcome in Birmingham anytime as a writer or producer. I was very cheered by that, although those around me were aware that I was by now clinically depressed. I had been in tears; showing bad temper; failing to deal understandingly with Elinor; quarrelling with Jo. At the end of October I went to my local GP, Tony Calland and, for the first time in my life, found myself on 'happy' pills. His choice of pills to prescribe was limited, as standard Librium and Valium produced just the sort of effects he was trying to avoid.

After that, events developed quite quickly. I travelled back to London and, at her request, went round to visit my friend Caroline Millington and her 'fella', the reporter Mike Robinson. Caroline was then Deputy Head of Current Affairs Magazine Programmes – always known as CAMP. (It says a lot about the imagination and humour of today's BBC, that it has now been changed to MP.) Caroline said that she had discussed it with senior colleagues, who were keen, and why did I not 'come out' on air?

I had already thought about this possibility and discussed it with close friends, incuding Jane Drabble, by then editor of *Everyman*, who felt there was a programme to be made about the spiritual questions raised by this calamity! In the end, it was agreed that radio would be a more intimate and less self-indulgent medium, and Caroline promised to find the best producer available. She kept that promise, and the next day I met Sharon Banoff for a quiet drink.

I suppose I was trying to prove to myself that all was still salvageable. Immediately before I met Sharon, I had been interviewing again for the Working Men's Clubs programme. The victim was George Tremlett, an affable man, historian of the Clubs and a senior member of the Conservative Party. He had always stimulated good copy for me at party conferences, by insisting on sharing a platform with Ken Livingstone in defence of the GLC.

In the morning, I had recorded the commentary for 'Buddies'. It was a full half-hour film. The day had not started well, when I had gone to the company's studio in Barnes instead of their West End location. I was late and I was fearful. To my amazement, helped by calmness from Claire and the sound recordist, all went well. It may be that my long-delayed decision to 'come out' had eased my mind. At any rate, I was in good spirits by the time I met Sharon.

She listened sympathetically to my story, and at the end said she would like to produce it. She made it clear, however, that if I wanted to do a documentary on cerebellar ataxia, rather than a personal story on how it affected me, then she was not interested. Otherwise, she would put off what she was busy doing and begin at once. At the end of February 1988 she was co-producing a new series called *Soundtrack* – films for radio – and she would rearrange the order to make this the first one, since I would want to get it over with as soon as possible. As usual, I wavered. But not for long. I knew at once that we would get on, although she was not exactly laid-back, and a woman who did things by instinct. I was very concerned lest the programme be too self-indulgent; she assured me it would not be.

By the time we emerged, two glasses of orange juice later, the decision was made. I was sweating with trepidation – but there would be a programme.

CHAPTER 8

A Lone Voice

Radio was, and still is, good to me. As an actor, I had appeared in innumerable schools broadcasts, in Saturday Night Theatre and in *The Dales*. For seven years I had been broadcasting regularly on Monday morning from the archives. I had been made a 'regular' by Brian Cook, who later became Controller of Radio City in Liverpool. Of all my broadcasting, the Monday morning spot was perhaps the best fun. Not only was there the pleasure of listening to old recordings and the great names of the past, but there was an opportunity to write almost anything one liked.

The programme had a biggish audience (in radio terms) because it followed the *Today* programme, and because people listened to it in their cars on the way to work. They either loved it or loathed it. I once had a fan letter from Neil Kinnock saying what a good way it was to start Monday morning and asking me how I got away with it. On the other hand, I got a letter from a regular BBC correspondent who said he always turned the radio off immediately if it was my turn on the programme, but he would like to take issue with something I had said last week . . .

It was a humorous programme, but to my astonishment sometimes also managed to be controversial. Once, during the Falklands conflict, I had made a programme called *Don't Mention The War*. Brian and I had felt there were so many programmes about the issue that we would eschew it. We made a programme out of twenty or so discs chosen entirely at random, and to our amazement every one of them contained something which could be taken as referring to the war. Most relevant was a dramatized version of how the news of the Battle of Trafalgar was brought to London. In view of the furore over the transmission of news from the Falklands which was raging at the time, this proved especially pertinent. Needless to say, that week's programme had a piece on the impossibility of avoiding any mention of the war. But on the morning of transmission, Brian and I agreed that we should remove the broadcast from the schedules in deference to the relatives of those aboard HMS *Sheffield*, which had just been attacked.

On another occasion, I was doing a parody of the great Wynford Vaughan-Thomas in a programme called *The Country-side In Winter*. Several people remarked on the authentic sound effects we had used, including the snow and the howling wind. Little did they know that it had been recorded under car head-lights on a cold winter's night on a mountainside in Wales. I had been filming *The Paras* at the time, and Brian had had to come down to Wales with the records. I had written the script in my spare time, and we had had to record it some way away on the mountainside in order to find somewhere relatively quiet. My hands were so cold I dropped the script several times, but we eventually finished it and returned thankfully to base.

I had also, increasingly, made documentaries and features, from Birmingham, Bristol and from London, in addition to short features for *Bookshelf* and *The Week's Antiques* and regularly deputising for Margaret Howard on *Pick Of The Week*. I had been a panellist on Radio 2's *The Law Game* and *On The Air*, and made *A Good Read* with Edna Healey, as well as guesting on *The John Dunne Show*, *The Pete Murray Show*, *Start The Week* and *Around Midnight*. I once ran from the *Archive* studio to the *Start The Week* studio, as a stunt, with just a two-minute news bulletin in between. If television was going to be bloody-minded, radio would keep me busy.

We listened to *A Lone Voice*, Sharon and I, with Caroline Millington, in her office. I was not sure that I would be up to listening with a bigger crowd, and reflected that it was the first time in my professional life that I had actually wanted a small audience. I had already heard it, of course, at home with Jo and Ellie and, with no restraints, had broken down uncontrollably.

The programme was prepared in secret, in the winter of 1987–88, mainly in Sharon's flat which was off Goodge St, conveniently near Broadcasting House. There were two reasons for the secrecy. First, I did not want to have to explain my illness over and over again and second, the purely professional one that the programme was the first of a new series, and we felt it would have more impact if it were kept as a surprise. We were fortunate in that the Peter Wright *Spycatcher* scandal was still occupying people's minds, and it was assumed that we were making a programme about spies.

At that time, my speech was good enough to pass muster in public, so we had no worries on that score. Nevertheless, I had spent some months wondering when, where, and how much to reveal to colleagues and the public. My feelings about coming clean on the radio were mixed. On the one hand, it would be a relief to have it off my chest; on the other, I felt that I would be committing professional hara kiri on air. It would be a spectacular way to go, but go I must. Or so I felt.

We began by recalling some moments from my recent radio broadcasts, and how I had been working away quite happily on the archive programme (then produced by Helen Fry) when I first began to notice a lack of balance – a trend not encouraged at the BBC.

I was not keen to start an industry out of my own illness, but I had agreed to keep my diary on broadcast-quality equipment in case we should need to use it. In the event, we used a good deal of it and I had to concede that Sharon's judgement about making it a personal document was better than mine.

I decided to keep the diary on tape, partly because I was a professional broadcaster and used to carrying around portable recording equipment, and partly because by then my ability to write by hand was so bad as to make it well-nigh impossible; and added difficulties, such as stress or tiredness, or even alcohol, made it worse. Having to struggle to write the cheque after a visit to my local wine-bar was one of the ways I knew the disease was getting a grip. There were the usual witty remarks about 'one too many', but the sad fact was that even then two was one too many, and perhaps even one. A glass of wine would make me incapable, but not drunk.

At the time of the broadcast in February 1988, surrounded by pieces of tape and fragments of my recent life and conversations, it was embarrassing for someone who had so often reported on other people's calamities, to be reporting on my own, but that was how I had chosen to do it. And not before time.

I described how I first noticed the symptoms and how I first heard from the doctor that it was no ordinary problem. Because I had been carrying the tape recorder with me, I was able to record the authentic sounds of the various technicians and therapists at work, when I went to the National Hospital for my check ups. There were regular 'autonomic' tests, where my blood pressure was checked in various postures; body and brain were scanned and scoured; blood, heart, muscle, nerves, strength and memory were tested, even my intelligence – and especially my patience. Also, my lungs. A tube was inserted into my mouth and I was required to blow over a count of ten. The effort made an absurd noise, but I passed the test all right. The disease had not got too firm a grip yet.

Nevertheless, after nearly fifty years of healthy insouciance, climbing mountains and hanging from helicoptors, I had got my come-uppance. I did not enjoy watching fellow patients go shaking, creeping and wheeling past my hospital bed. Was this the future? I did not know then that they were suffering from a variety of diseases. I did not particularly enjoy hearing a Consultant Neurologist in London confirming that what I had first heard in Bristol, but had for so long pretended *must* be happening to someone else, was truly happening to me.

Dr Anita Harding knows as much as anyone about how the cerebellum works. Yet even she admits that little is known. What was observable was that a 'premature death' had occurred in my nervous system, chiefly confined to those parts which controlled balance and speech. They call it cerebellar syndrome. How many people have it is not known exactly, and I learnt that there was no specialist group funding or supporting research. There was no known cause, and no cure. Hence there was very little in the way of treatment. 'But,' said Dr Harding, 'I think there is slightly more than nothing that we can do.' Hence the tests. Yet, with all this lack of knowledge, how could she be sure of an accurate diagnosis? Her reply was confident.

She might not know the cause, but she could weigh up the symptoms and what she found when she examined me. Like the doctor in Bristol, she looked at my eyes, she got me to touch fingers and noses, to hop on one leg and saw how I coordinated – or did not coordinate – arms and legs by performing simple tests. I found myself, for example, with the occupational therapist, putting kidney beans into pots, and as a result of all these tests Dr Harding concluded that the 'story' was right, that I had a degenerative disease which was getting worse. Sometimes, these so-called 'progressive' diseases stopped for a while, but more often they developed at a uniform, slow pace. So what was the end-product? How would I end up?

'Well, you are likely to find that your walking becomes more difficult, as you know it already has. You are also likely to find that the clumsiness in your arms gets worse. (Carrying a cup of tea, for example, is an absolute disaster area.) You have to concentrate more – and that makes you more tired.'

'What's the best and the worst that I can expect?'

'The best you can expect is that it will stay as it is. The worst is that it will worsen slowly but to an extent, for example, that you could lose the ability to walk.'

'You mean a wheelchair?'

'Yes, that's right.'

A wheelchair might well be a problem for a television reporter. But not necessarily for radio. After all, listeners need never know, or care, whether the person speaking to them had cerebellar disease. If it were not for one thing more – the speech.

In *A Lone Voice* we gave an example of how a radio show was made. Just before Christmas, the producer of *Going Places*, Irene Mallis, had asked me to make a documentary on 'warm-up men'. I had explained my problem but, being a good friend, she had been prepared to do the extra work. The documentary had gone well and the interviews fine. Then we came to the recording. Here I stuttered and stumbled a good deal, and a lot of extra editing work was required. The result was all right, but the process difficult. In *A Lone Voice*, we used a recording of how that programme had been made to make clear to listeners what had been involved. Producers are used to consigning presenter's fluffs to the waste-paper basket, they cobble and contrive – all art is artifice after all – but not on that scale. A presenter with cerebellar ataxia is, as they say, 'a whole new ball game'. The voice deepens, becomes less flexible, cannot cope with consonants too close together. Despite the patience of colleagues over the previous year, the condition had become harder and harder to disguise. And sometimes – let's face it, the listeners are not daft – impossible.

'Is Glyn Worsnip unwell or something? He doesn't sound his normal self.'

'What was wrong with Glyn Worsnip this evening? His enunciation was definitely slurred at times.'

Those two calls to the BBC Duty Office cost me a favourite series, *Stop Press*; but they forced me to face, at last, the probability that my condition would eventually cost me my career. Many, many have had to do the same. To wonder whether, and when, to explain to workmates, how and whether to 'come clean'. The broadcast, a personal one – self-indulgent even – was my way of doing it. But I hope it spoke for many who have endured the loneliness and anxiety of facing up to a crippling disease. In case I was tempted to gloss over certain thoughts, I decided to share the diary which had helped me admit to myself what I was now admitting to the listeners. Here are some of those thoughts.

6 November 1987: Today I went home and, having been asked to be chairman of my local comprehensive school's annual quiz, I felt rather dubious, rather frightened that I might let myself down by not being able to speak the words clearly. However, the evening went off quite successfully and Jo said that really they would not have noticed that there was anything wrong with me. Always I have the problem that *I* know there's something wrong – I can hear it in the voice, I can hear it in the sounds I make, and so can my fellow broadcasters. But as yet, even after nearly two years now, this thing has been going on, I can still get away with it. We've got through to the coffee break, and they haven't rumbled us yet. But the sad fact is that people are beginning to rumble something at any rate, and they are beginning to ask questions. The other day, for example, a journalist rang my agent, Jeanne Griffiths, and asked whether it was true that I had multiple sclerosis.

24 November: Elinor's eleventh birthday. The whole problem of how to explain this thing to an eleven-year-old has been difficult. On balance, we decided that openness was the only answer. She has been very reassuring. For some time now, I've been wondering how I'm going to make up to her for the long absences that my work has meant, although there are times when I know that my inability to do things and my irritation, particularly with myself, do stop her short a little.

Today I went up to London for my first speech therapy at the National Hospital. I was not surprised to learn that I was attempting everything too fast but Margaret, the therapist, was convinced that there were tricks which I could apply to speech which would make things easier for myself and also make things sound more natural, or at least passably natural. I must think consciously about breathing and slowing down, for example.

Time is a thing I think about a lot, because within speech it is very important – the amount of time it takes to get from one sound to another. And in life, as in speech, time is proving my great enemy.

1 December: Today I contacted the first cerebellar sufferer that I've managed to find. Despite her bravery and good humour, she is already in a wheelchair, although it is only four years since she was diagnosed. She is also very slurred of speech. She used to be a shorthand typist, but now it takes her two hours, I gather, to type one page, on one finger.

2 December: Already the round of Christmas parties has begun. I went to one today. It was full of people I knew, and they were all full of chat, and plans, and telling each other what they had been doing. All this jollity made me rather depressed. A friend asked me to come over and talk to Laurie Lee, who was there. Laurie Lee of course is one of my heroes, and I really wanted to do that. But I suddenly got rather down about keeping my end up in the conversation and in the finish I did not go over. I felt rather rude, but I was not up to it somehow, and left early to go home.

3 December: They repeated my *Through My Window* programme today on Radio 4. It's a very personal thing, sitting looking through your own window and talking about what you see and the thoughts it prompts:

'And so it is lovely, it is idyllic. People say, "Oh, how wonderful that must be, oh how beautiful." But what they don't realize is how much work goes into simply living in the country.'

It reminded me that working, for example with chainsaws and other mechanical instruments around the fields and the garden, you have to do things quickly and efficiently, and that speed and efficiency have now gone – or will have to be paid for. But where is the money going to come from?

'I think you are going to have to do a bit more, but it will require some effort.'

This was Jo, at her most brisk and efficient.

'That's fine at the moment, but what happens if – when – it gets to the wheelchair stage? I'll just have to sit there, I suppose, and wait for you.'

Another of those endless conversations with Jo, full of both laughter and tears, going over again what we must and must not do, could and could not, should and should not.

'I do love this place,' she said, 'but I think the difficulties are too great.'

'Yes,' I replied, 'but, I mean, I'm not going to waste away. For a start, my body is not going to go, it's just the sense of balance and the speech, so it shouldn't be too bad.'

I had not realized then just how far the balance and the speech *would* go. Or what an effect fatigue would have. Jo, as usual, was right.

'We don't know, do we? We're just going to be pragmatic, and play it by ear as we go along.'

We paused to listen to the wind. We were set on a hilltop right in the teeth of the south-westerly gale. Jo reiterated one of the reasons we had come here: 'I love that sound. Just love it. We will just have to grope our way along –'

'Some of us literally!'

We laughed a bittersweet laugh.

'– we must just learn to deal with problems as they arise. I want us all to continue to enjoy life.'

4 December: Another Christmas party today. At one point I was asked to dance. 'Have a bop' were the words used. I could not, of course, because I cannot dance now. I started to think, too, about the subject of flirting, which one tends to do at these kinds of parties. Flirting I think is something you do with the knowledge behind you that you *could* go through with it if you wanted to, and it is that thought that gives the whole thing its fun, and its impetus. Somehow the thought that I am now 'damaged goods' does not encourage me to flirt with exciting young people – or even people of my own age! It is coming to something if you cannot even flirt at a Christmas party.

Caroline Panton, the first cerebellar sufferer that I've ever met in person, is forty-ish, separated. She has suffered since she was eighteen.

'Really men don't altogether want to know, largely perhaps because they're not quite sure. The answer is, well, just to avoid it anyway. I tend to stick to friends that I know well. I cannot go out among strangers – at least, I could but I feel a little apprehensive and embarrassed.'

I asked whether she felt her condition was more obvious than it really is.

'Yes, I think I do feel it, more than it shows, because I know myself how unsteady I am, and what I mean to do compared with what I actually do. It does sort people out, I mean who is a friend, and who is not. I still cannot get used to it. I mean, after all these years you would think I would have, but no, I still cannot swallow this thorn in the flesh. It's really a case of, why is it me? I just cannot understand the situation, really – and yet one has to live with it, one just has to go on.'

'Have you at any time managed to get any fun out of it? Or laugh at it, or laugh at yourself? Or is it all . . . awful?'

'Sorry Glyn, no. No laughs, not really. I find the children have a good laugh and I do perhaps smile with them, but I'm not really laughing. They may laugh because Mummy fell down while trying to play football, but I wouldn't have liked other people to have been looking. Really. . . No, I think you've just got to ride through it, somehow or other.'

8 December: Had supper tonight with my friend Jane, who seemed astonished that I was still driving and was, I suppose, worried about it. Until now, one of the few places in which I have felt safe has been sitting behind a driving wheel, where I am comfortable and secure and in charge.

Dr Harding at the National says that I have not got to worry about it at all yet, that if she ever felt that I did have to, then she would let me know. The DVLC at Swansea would write to her asking about my situation, and then probably give me a more limited span licence, to be re-assessed on, say, a three-yearly basis.

I asked how I should define it if somebody asked me what the matter was. Was it a disease? A disablement? Dr Harding was positive. I had cerebellar ataxia. I could say that some of the symptoms I had were similar to those of multiple sclerosis, which they are, and then people would know what I was on about, rather than looking frightened and pushing off!

9 December: Went to have a chat today with Bob Monkhouse about warm-up men and 'being funny', and we discussed how strange it seems that all the words with which I have real problems enter particularly into my sphere of work – words like 'word processor', 'facility', 'editor'. Or is it just my imagination? I took the problem to the speech therapist and she confirmed it. For example, I could say 'auditor' much easier than I could say 'editor', because the 'au' sound is much longer than the short 'e' sound.

10 December: Coming to work today, I was on a bit of a down. The crowds are building for Christmas, shopping in Oxford Street, and working my way through them I bumped into so many people that in the end I just thought, 'What the hell, let's get into a wheelchair and have done with it.' This is me at my lowest, I know, but today the thought occurred how very detached I feel from everything that's going on around me. Sometimes people clearly cannot see what an effort it is for me to stand, to walk, or to talk. I suppose I look fairly normal, but it's as if that normality is just an outer shell carrying on a performance, and that inside there is another and more real me battering at the shell and looking out, wondering why people cannot see that I'm not there any more, that I'm completely different, that I'm locked inside, that really I want to give up.

But how can I give up? There is work, income, family. It's impossible.

26 December: Two days at home with Jo and Ellie, two days of jollity with visitors. There is a tremendous requirement to be jolly which Christmas imposes, and I suppose it's more of an effort nowadays. My brother's family came and were all very cheerful. The usual words of, 'How are you?', 'How are you getting on?' but although they asked concernedly, I felt there was no real desire to talk about it – it would get in the way of Christmas festivities, and that's probably very right and proper.

1 January 1988!: I spent New Year's Eve alone, or rather almost alone. Ellie was upstairs in bed. It is very difficult to get a baby-sitter on New Year's Eve, and so Jo went to visit some friends on her own. It gave me time for thought all right – all those awful, nagging thoughts about what the New Year will bring. I've got some work, but will I go on getting work? And, more importantly, how long can I expect people to go putting in extra time out of loyalty to me?

An old friend rang from London this afternoon. She had just heard the 'warm-up men' programme. She said that she could definitely hear that I was finding it harder, so ... that's it, really. It's all up, and I really am going to have to find something else to do.

I have found another cerebellar sufferer: Mike Drew from Nuneaton. I went to visit him on 5 January. He'd had the same experience.

'Yes, in 1978 I was advised to give up my job as a travelling representative of an insurance company and take a more sedentary job, and I now fly a desk.'

It was a good day, visiting Mike. He has the hereditary version of the disease; his father had it too. Mike is about my age, perhaps a little younger. He has had to make changes, of course, but is working happily.

'I felt people were looking at me, and as a representative you do need to be sharp and on the ball. I don't think I'm not that, it's just that I, er ... once heard the remark that I appeared to be drunk, which was totally untrue. I don't feel I have to tell everybody. It's funny the way this has worked out, but I generally only tell those of an equal professional standing, or above. I have never felt the need to tell juniors. But I don't mind who knows. It's nothing to be ashamed of.'

I asked what effect it had had on his family. Presumably with the hereditary, or 'familial' version, he had a worry about his children?

'I took the view, when the children were quite small, that it would do no good to have them diagnosed. To have a label hanging round their necks saying they had a cerebellar problem, would only make people look at them in an odd sort of a way.'

I asked how he faced up to it, himself.

'I don't think you can waste time feeling sorry for yourself. People don't want to know about your bad news; they only want to know about your good news, so get on with life. If it means a change of occupation, you will have to change. Find something you can do, and do well. Use your contacts now, and get yourself fitted up with a job you *can* do. The thing to do is realize that it's not the end of the world, that there are people about worse off than you, who cannot even do the things you can do. I mean, there are plenty of people who cannot carry a pint of beer.'

He had a wonderfully 'common sense' approach to the problem, and did me a power of good, really. I needed a jolt to stop me feeling sorry for myself. It was a good meeting.

12 January: I've got the first live *The Press Gang* of the new series coming up on Radio 2 tomorrow. There is a certain amount of worry about that, but maybe with the help of the speech therapist things won't be as bad as I might suppose. On the good days, I sometimes wonder what the fuss is all about. I feel that with a little dextrous editing, with a little harder work on my part, things will be perfectly all right.

17 January: We had the *That's Life!* reunion today. All the old presenters came back, and there was much talk and excitement about what people had been doing; memories of the good times – and the disastrous times. There were times in the rehearsal when we had to cross some steps and rostra, and I really did worry that, when it came to the real show, I would stumble and fall and make an idiot of myself. It didn't happen, but I must have looked pretty wobbly, and it was nice that Esther and Kieran, my old friends, who both know, were very understanding and very discreet in shifting things around to make it easier for me. There was a moment in the show when we were all lined up and the audience told what amazing things we had achieved in the years since we had left the programme. There were times when I wanted to shriek, 'It's all a fraud, there's going to be no more of it!' I really must get away from what is, I think, becoming almost an obsession with how things are different and how I cannot do any more. There must be lots of good things I can do.

26 January: It happened today. I woke up, and just did not want to get out of bed; I really wanted to lie there for good. It had been a good week, but this morning was slightly different. Last night I had spoken to Jo and, because she has been so supportive, she has determined to get a training and a job, in order to make life easier for us. There is a very suitable course in Bristol, but all the places for September are taken. She optimistically told me that she was just hoping a young student who wanted to see the world might drop out, leaving an empty place. I wondered whether this illness was a blessing in disguise?

'I think maybe it is. I must say I hadn't envisaged working full-time; I had thought that maybe one or two days a week would be interesting and fun, and worthwhile.'

But what about the sheep?

'It's just that instead of a lot of sheep and a little teaching, there'll be a lot of teaching and a few sheep.'

We laughed. I got the impression that, in its curious way, this was a whole new exciting challenge.

'It is. I cannot pretend that it isn't a blow, to have this happen to you. It is. But the thought of starting a whole new challenge and project for myself is very exciting.'

'It means that I'd be home a lot more.'

'Yes, but it also means that I wouldn't!'

We laughed again. There seemed nothing else to do.

Jo again: 'What it really means is that one is not going to get bogged down in the tragedy of it all.'

28 January: It's almost an insult, because they are so professional, but today again the nagging thought came to me that even the friendliest of producers must just wish I would stop and go away. I suppose I must ask – perhaps Andy Wilson from *The Press Gang*.

'I think you just stop when it doesn't work any more. When *you* think it doesn't work, or when we think it doesn't work. At the moment it's working OK. In fact, in many ways your voice is better than it was some time ago, perhaps because of the techniques you're using. It's when the programme might become difficult to listen to, or embarrassing to listen to.'

But had he got time and energy and so on to help me overcome it?

'Yes. That's no problem, apart from the odd slur that has to be specifically adjusted.'

But was there any question of people putting up with me for old time's sake?

'No, not at all, no. You're a *nawfully* nice chap, and if it came to the worst we'd all feel extremely sad about it, but no, I mean the programme has to come first, because the listener has to come first.'

Andy was very commonsensical and reassuring, in his droll Scottish way. But when he tried to book me, he was advised not to by the BBC Contracts Department. Did he not know, they asked, that Glyn Worsnip was terminally ill? They were even now getting together all the money the BBC owed me, so that I would have it before I popped off. He said he was quite aware of exactly what was the matter with me, and would like to book me anyway!

But it was a sobering moment. I rang Controller 4 (Michael Green) and said that rumours of my forthcoming death had been exaggerated. He apologized on behalf of the Contracts Department, and promised to put them straight. Nevertheless, a few days later I received a large cheque with all the outstanding money. It was the only occasion on which I can ever remember the BBC paying on time.

5 February: It has been a good week. It has not been a bad week at all. And I wonder, suddenly, if that's the reason why there's been no diary this week? When it's good it's all right, but when it's bad I want to talk about it? Maybe. Maybe.

6 February: Today was a good day. We went pony-hunting. We must be crazy, I suppose, even to think of buying a pony in these circumstances, but Elinor has been so good and has got so much to put up with that I think it's now or never, really. She was very excited at the thought. The prospects today were, she explained:

'Tango, and he's fourteen hands. He's a dun, with a black mane and tail. And the second one, he's called Sundial and he's bay, also with a black mane and tail, and he's got a white blaze on his face. That should be pretty. I think I like Sundial best.'

I smiled. It would be the more expensive one!

7 February: Talked on the phone today to my colleague Ray Moore, from Radio 2. I said how appalled I was at his news. He has cancer of the throat, and has given up broadcasting. He has made a clean break. Ray and I used to do those voices that come on between television programmes, promoting other programmes. We used to sit in a little booth. It was live, and confident, and carefree. I can remember some of them now:

'Tomorrow night at 9.30, *Sportsnight With Coleman*. Yes, the big fight between Mohammed Ali and Georges Chuvalo. That's *Sportsnight With Coleman*, tomorrow night at 9.30, here on BBC 1.'

Yes, we didn't care much in those days. We did it without thinking. It was just part of what we were able to do.

9 February: Moods change very quickly. Good morning. Went swimming with Elinor, and it was good fun. Later, there was a moody moment. There's an old Bing Crosby song which has words with a simple magic: 'Where the blue of the night, meets the gold of the day.' I thought of that when I was standing out on the hillside this evening. It was late dusk, and Jo was out feeding and checking the sheep, and it wasn't the blue of the night and the gold of the day, it was really the reverse. The trees were all different shades of intense black, or blue, or dark green, and the branches were etched against the sky over the top of the Welsh hills, and the few odd clouds about made patterns against the brilliance of the sky – orange and yellow and red. An intense feeling of guilt came over me. It's *my* fault if we lose it, it's my fault that we got it in the first place and, having arrived here at a place which Jo, of all the places we've been, loves so much, we're going to have to lose it. There are two kinds of people, I suppose. There are those who spend all the money they've got, and there are those who keep some back for a rainy day. I did the former and I gambled, and I lost. Because it's raining now, all right. Hard.

Jo and I resumed our conversation. She was adamant:

'I don't believe it's all for a cause, at all. It's very random. So all you can do is battle on.'

'Yes. A place like this demands mending fences, whenever you come home. In more ways than one ... It is a danger, this getting maudlin. Be positive. That's the watchword.'

'I think you just get on with it.'

'It comes to the same thing.'

20 February: On Thursday when I went up for *The Press Gang*, the general opinion seemed to be that three days at home had done me good. Certainly, although I thought at one time during the day that I was going to be very tired by the time we did it, when it came to it I was on as good a form as ever, and I really did smile.

That was part of the diary. It didn't tell everything, of course, but it conveyed some of the flavour. When *A Lone Voice* was broadcast, it seemed to catch a nerve in the listeners. There was a tremendous reaction. I heard from old school, college and university chums I had not seen in thirty years. I heard from a mass of disabled people of one sort and another, expressing solidarity. I heard from hundreds of people expressing confidence in various forms of alternative medicine, some of which I have tried. My general conclusion is that, although all these things do you good, none of them actually cures cerebellar ataxia. There was a deluge of explanations as to the cause; from the presence of nearby lay lines to overhead electric cables; from toxin in the sheep feed to mercury fillings in the teeth. Several hundred cerebellar ataxia sufferers came out of the woodwork, usually with the same cry: 'I didn't know there was anyone else who had cerebellar ataxia.' We joined up with the Friedreich's Ataxia Group, which does fine work for those (mainly children) who suffer from that particular form of the disease. There are beginning to be small support groups dotted around the country. The BBC gave me a week's secretarial help to cope with the mail. A year and a half later, I have still not replied to them all – people I know personally in particular. I hope that, through this book, I will be able to apologize to them and say how much I appreciated their writing. The most heartwarming thing was to discover how many friends I had, through radio and television, who I did not even know about. People who did not know me personally did not have to write, but they did, in their thousands. According to the *Observer*, the programme received the highest 'Reaction Index' (listener interest) of the year, and there are those who say that it produced more mail than any previous programme on Radio 4. People wrote to say that they had stopped what they were doing to listen; they did not go into the supermarket; they parked in lay-bys; they stopped the ironing; and some did not go to work at all.

Throughout all this, my producer Sharon Banoff trod the delicate tightrope between personal exploitation and professional exigency – and did it beautifully. It was a professional piece of work, and hers is the credit.

I appeared on innumerable programmes and chat shows to talk about the illness, from *The Treatment* on ITV to *Wogan* on BBC1. (Some people would do *anything* to appear on *Wogan*!) Luckily, my old friend Sue Lawley was hosting the show that evening, so it was much less frightening than it might have been – not that Terry is frightening, but it was relaxing to talk to someone I had shared a desk with many times. I was never so popular as when I was ill. It is a curious thing, but as soon as people heard that I had difficulty in speaking, I was inundated with invitations to speak about it!

The newspapers, which are not always so careful, were kind to me on the whole – from the *Times*'s short paragraph headed 'Worsnip Stricken', to *Today* which did an excellent three-page spread that did much to explain cerebellar ataxia to an uncomprehending readership. That particular paper had someone on my remote Gloucestershire doorstep within hours of the news breaking in the London *Evening Standard*. Jo did not much care for being cast in a brave little wifely heroine's role, which she felt was not suitable, but, that apart, we could not complain about the newspapers, which did a fair job of putting rare brain disease 'on the map'.

Naturally enough, BBC bureaucracy had the last word. John Stanley, the BBC Press Officer who had handled things so well for me, was reprimanded by his boss, who pointed at the newspaper hoardings outside in Portland Place. 'Look what it says down there,' he complained. '"TV Star Has Rare Brain Disease." TV star this, TV star that. Don't you know this is a *radio* programme?'

It was easily the most successful broadcast of my life. And I wish I had never made it.

CHAPTER 9

Year of Grace

The smile lasted for about a year. I ended up like the Cheshire Cat. I felt there was nothing left but the smile, as one bodily function after another disappeared. While I was making *A Lone Voice* I worked hard on other things, still feeling that I must keep going as long as possible, still hardly believing that I would ever have to stop. It was a year in which I was to learn a lot more about disability, both from my own experience and from other people.

The work was varied. The year began with the making of a film for *Friday Report* on the series of disasters that had occurred over the past few years: the Bradford football stadium fire, the Zeebrugge disaster and the King's Cross Underground fire. The film examined how the disaster funds were handled, and in the course of making it I learnt a good deal about calamity and how people handled it. Despite the appalling physical pain that those involved had suffered, I learnt that the psychological pain was almost as bad. It did not seem to matter how the pain was caused, the suffering was as acute. I thanked a God I did not believe in for sparing me too much physical pain.

But the pieces to camera were agony; not so much in the doing, as in the preparation. They were easy enough to write, but then I had to see if I could *say* what I had written and, if not, change it. I worried for days in advance. My fear was that I would let myself and my producer down by not getting the right nuance or tone into the voice. It is, of course, possible to make films without the reporter ever appearing, but in this case the material demanded some information and a few comments and links from the reporter. I was still seeing the speech therapist, but I was learning that what was acceptable to her was not 'broadcast quality' as I understood it and had practised for years. I remember discussing a 'piece to camera' which I had to do at King's Cross station. The fear was not so much about what I was saying, as whether I could say it, particularly as we had drawn a big crowd, as filming often does, and I had to keep up the banter with those whose sitting rooms I had so often occupied. I discovered a curious fact: that I performed better 'off the cuff' and with an audience, than I did with a prepared piece. I had less time to worry about it. My fears at King's Cross were more psychological than actual, though nonetheless debilitating, despite all the help that a sympathetic producer, Clare Patterson, could give me. Nevertheless, I got by and the piece was acceptable if not brilliant, although, as I said to Margaret Brent my speech therapist, I ought to be able to perform in front of an audience by now. After all, I had had a fair amount of practice.

The trend was confirmed by *The Press Gang*, which came back in the new year. This, too, had a live audience, and much of it was improvised. There were greater problems editing the beginning and the end, where I had a prepared script to read, than in the middle, where I tended to make it up as I went along. I was beginning to be more fearful in advance than I was once we had started, and whereas at the beginning I had worked right up until the taxi came to take me to the Paris Theatre, now I was taking a rest before the show.

On the advice of the National Hospital, in I went for more tests at Southmead Hospital in Bristol. A nurse there recognized me, and asked if I was still working. I assured her that I was, but the incident only served to remind me of how low my profile was these days. My spirits dropped even lower.

I worked at home, and I worked in London and Birmingham. I had taken up where I had left off with my feature on Working Men's Clubs, and was confident enough to face recording the commentary. I also went out again on the road. Thanks to old friends from Lime Grove, Vincent Hanna and Virginia Ashcombe, who, like so many, were now working in the private sector, I was commissioned to do the interviewing and the script (but not the commentary) for a film which put the National Union of Teachers' case against Mr Baker's education proposals. Over the last few years, more and more talented people had left the Grove, their skills unappreciated, and had formed various independent companies. I used to think that the loss of a BBC contract was a disaster, but now I was beginning to believe that there was life outside the Grove and that I would not have too many difficulties finding employment. It was only ironic that this realization should have coincided with my illness becoming more serious, with the consequent reduction in efficiency.

After the broadcast of *A Lone Voice* on 2 March, I had a new lease of working life. I has feared that the programme would signal the end of my broadcasting. Such was not the case.

It is true that my income was diminishing, but that did not matter as long as I was kept busy. Much of my work was 'regional' rather than 'network', so that viewers outside London and the south-east thought I was doing less than I was. Thanks to Colin Stanbridge, Head of South East Region television, and Peter Lowe, one of his senior producers with whom I had worked on *Breakfast Time*, I was kept busy – in the winter on *Friday Report* and in the summer on the south-east's version of *The Holiday Programme*, *Weekend*. Both these men, along with my old friends Tony Chapman, Patti Steeples and Clare Patterson, were well aware of my difficulties, and I was flattered that they were prepared to have me on their programmes despite them. They were ready to put in extra time and effort to have an old salt working with them, and I am grateful to them for that. They seemed to agree with the listener who had said after *A Lone Voice*: 'After all, what's a slur between friends?'

The income and the profile may have been declining, but elsewhere things were burgeoning – namely Jo, Ellie, and the sheep. Jo was now more than ever determined to become a teacher. Her grasp of what was to happen was much more realistic than mine. Her degree from Exeter University was in modern languages, but these days you cannot even teach infants or juniors unless you also have a teaching diploma. She cast around and found that Bristol Polytechnic had the best and most suitable course, with very high standards. As usual, she felt that only the best would do, and Bristol was just about accessible, being about fifty minutes drive from our home, on the other side of the Severn Bridge. She was too late in applying by a fraction, but was first on the waiting list. In her day a pass in a science, usually biology, had been sufficient qualification, but nowadays you are required to have a Maths O'level or equivalent. She set about it at once. With the help of a retired teacher, she swotted for the new GCSE. It was a year's course and she had four months. It was also the lambing season, and very cold. She was up all hours, not for the last time, and often made do with two hours sleep, or even one. She was beside herself with tiredness. The flock increased from just under thirty to over sixty – some ripped untimely from their mothers' wombs, some brought back to life from hypothermia with the aid of a syringe and the family aga. While all this was going on, she devoted some stolen hours to maths, and passed.

With this over, the anxiety grew as to whether or not there would be a place on the course. Partly to avoid unwelcome publicity, and partly to establish herself as a person and a teacher in her own right, she had changed her name. Eventually she gave up hope, as with two days to go she had heard nothing. Suddenly there was a phone call. Would she like to start on Monday? Would she ever?! Quite how and by whom her last-minute inclusion on the course had been approved, we shall never know. Certainly, despite her best endeavours, her identity was rumbled by some of the tutors and students. A family picture appeared in glorious technicolor in the *Sunday Times* magazine's 'A Life In The Day Of' series. That it should appear just as the course was about to start was the purest coincidence, but it was enough to blow her cover.

The course changed the lifestyle in our household completely. For the first time in Ellie's experience, not only was her father away, but so was her mother. Jo had to leave before the bus left on the ten mile journey to our local comprehensive, where Ellie was in her first year. Mummy was no longer always at home when she came back in the afternoon. Ellie was not exactly a 'latch-key kid', but she spent a good deal of time being farmed out to other families until her mother came back after six. Meals were later, homework was delayed, mother was exhausted with driving and, fearing that failure was inevitable at fifty, worked long into the night. Daddy was, as usual, gadding about in London or elsewhere, and at weekends, because of his illness, was disinclined to do much at all, even if he were able. It was not a recipe for successful family life. Tempers were lost, resentments incurred, battles fought. The *joie* had gone out of the *vivre*, and I was blinder than the others. I put off discussions about how unsuitable it was to live on a steep hillside, all slopes and steps, and how we needed to think about moving; I did not think that the disease was progressing as fast as it was; I did not foresee my income drying up completely; I did not foresee Jo not getting a job; I did not foresee how disabling would be the depression that accompanies disability. All the disabled people that I met, or was about to meet, were remarkable in their tolerance and their achievement; I did not foresee that not everyone was like them; I did not foresee how debilitating disability could be.

Sometime in 1987, I had met Jeff Milland of HTV West. He had proposed a new series called *Pilgrimages*, in which I should report on six visits to different communities throughout the world. Gradually, not to my enormous pleasure, the plan had changed so that six different reporters would make pilgrimages of their own choice. By now I was not sure that I was up to that even, and had explained the problem to Jeff, but he was reassuring and went away to think about it. In the end he decided that, in the circumstances, I was just the right person to make a pilgrimage, although in case of ill-health it would be easier to manage if we remained in this country.

Accordingly, I chose to visit the Anglican friars tucked away at Hilfield in Dorset, who not only provided food and lodging for wayfarers and looked after the permanently disabled, but took in short-stay guests who were going through a bad patch. After the nine-day wonder of the extensive press coverage and the innumerable guest appearances on chat shows (I was even paired with Eddie Edwards for the British Forces' Network in Germany, presumably on the grounds that we were both overcoming the odds!), I was in need of a rest, and Hilfield was very welcoming. I went there several days in advance of the film crew, so as to form my impressions in peace.

What I discovered was a group of carers who made no spiritual demands of their guests, merely allowed them space, and who made no claims for themselves about rectitude. They were, in fact, simply people with as many faults as anyone else, who, because of their faith, had opened their hearts and minds to their fellow human beings; but they only appeared when needed. My theme, in describing their life, was that just as they had given up so much and changed their lives completely, so my life had to change. I could not accept their faith (although I went to many of their services and talked to their 'guardian', Brother Bernard, as long and hard as I could), but crossing their path undoubtedly taught me a great deal.

Brother Bernard was an encouraging soul. Tall, silver-haired and handsome, he could just as easily have been an old Etonian Guards Officer. His uncomplicated vigour and steadfastness were inspiring, whether or not you accepted his faith, and his readiness to accept that being a member of an Order gave you no claim whatever to perfection of any sort, reassuring. There was much to learn – especially how important it is to learn to *accept* love freely given, that some people enjoy giving and that there are an awful lot of things in life which, with no great difficulty, it is possible to give up. My problem, ultimately, was that although I myself might be willing to give them up, I was not sure that I could give them up on behalf of other people (my family). But the whole experience was a reinforcement of something a wise correspondent had written to me: 'Remember always that you are one hundred per cent of your new self, not seventy per cent of what you were.'

We were back at Hilfield over Easter, when the friars celebrate the Passion with a service that lasts from darkness until light. They light a bonfire during the darkness, and do not emerge from their chapel until the embers are almost out. It is a refreshing experience, this celebration of change, no matter what your faith is (or is not) and the great lesson, for me at least, was that there is always the hope – and for some, the certainty – of renewal.

A curious incident emerged while I was at Hilfield. One of the friars, Brother Raphael, produced a photograph of me that he had cut out of the *Radio Times* some months back, at about the time of the onset of my disease. He had no idea who I was until I was introduced at Hilfield, but had had an overwhelming sense that I needed care and, with the photo always to hand in his room, had been praying for its anonymous subject ever since.

I have always been dubious about 'signs', preferring to see them as random coincidences. There are times, however, when one's incredulity is stretched to the utmost. One such time was shortly after we moved from The White House in Clearwell to Harthill Cottage. The couple who bought The White House were a charming pair called Nancy and Peter Granger. Peter was a sound engineer with the well-known pop group *Dire Straits*. He was often away from home, but whenever he went he would always send Nancy a dozen pink roses.

Shortly after their arrival in Clearwell, they had a baby, and shortly after that Peter was mown down by a youthful, unlicenced car driver in the middle of the local town, Coleford. He managed to toss the baby to Nancy but, a few tragic days later, he died of head injuries. The morning after he died, Nancy looked out of the bedroom window across at a bright yellow rambling rose we had planted some years before. In the middle of it were a dozen beautifully flowering roses – all of them pink. Nancy was so astonished that she went across to a kindly neighbour and gardening expert, who agreed that it was indeed amazing. It was, of, course, possible that it was a throwback to the flower's ancient stock – but why on that morning? Coincidence?

On 10 April two events occurred. One I had been looking forward to, one was a surprise. The first was the arrival of Ellie's first pony. We had been too cautious about our previous choice, Sundial. By the time we had organized a vet's report and asked friends about the drawbacks, he had gone. This time we were luckier and Fudge, a gentle dun, joined the family. Ellie was delighted, and so was I. I had thought for some time that she needed a friend and companion, what with her being an only child, us living in so remote a spot and her luck having turned so bad.

Although the National Hospital had opened a fund in my name, the proceeds to go to cerebellar research, some listeners had sent cheques which they insisted go only towards a pony. This put me in a quandary but, seeing unemployment lurking and having learnt from the friars to accept gifts in the spirit in which they are given, I confess to having done as I was asked and allowing the donation to go towards the pony.

I was so preoccupied with Fudge that I perhaps did not pay careful enough attention to what I was doing. At all events, that evening I discovered most painfully that my condition now called for the utmost care. Jo was out dealing with the sheep, and I prepared some potatoes for dinner. For some reason, Ellie liked my roast potatoes (despite my general failure to learn to cook) and as I was very pleased with her and for her, I thought I would get some under way. I prepared some hot fat and tried to pull it from the oven. I lost my grip and my balance, and the boiling fat poured all over my right hand, dropping the skin to the floor like a wet dishcloth.

Jo returned seconds after I had done it and leapt into action. Within twenty minutes a doctor had arrived and I was on my way to the local burns unit at St Lawrence's Hospital, Chepstow. For several days I carried a plastic bag full of puss and blood on my right hand, and thereafter the wound was bandaged and I was required to hold my hand upright. I had to visit the unit every two days at first, and so stay at home. That was no hardship, but it did mean cancelling several jobs I had contracted to do and a number of interviews for possible writing jobs.

Eventually, it was decided that a skin-graft was essential, and here I experienced one of those medical mysteries of which there should be more. For some time, I had occasionally been seeing someone in Brighton who practised alternative medicine, including acupuncture and radionics. The latter is a system whereby the healer 'tunes in' to the patient, wherever they are, by means of a black box. I never really understood how it works, but it seemed at the least to do no harm and a friend swore by it, so I thought I would give it a try. Just before my skin-graft, my friend told the doctor in Brighton that I had burnt myself badly, and so he immediately 'tuned in'. Back in Chepstow, knowing that a general anaesthetic did my condition no good, they tried a local one. It did not work. They tried again. Even after two I could still feel the fingers in my hand. They eventually resorted to a general anaesthetic, and I went to sleep expectantly. When I awoke, the doctor told me that they had not performed the operation after all. Apparently the wound had healed so well in the twenty-four hours since it had last been seen, that they had decided there was no need for a skin-graft after all. I shall never know whether or not it was the effect of the radionics, but there certainly had been a remarkable change. Still, as one of the nurses remarked afterwards, they could have found that out if they had simply removed the bandages before giving me all those anaesthetics.

After it was over, I spent a lot of time wondering whether I had just been clumsy, or whether it was part of the disease. At any rate, I was not allowed to make roast potatoes again. It was one more way in which I was no longer able to contribute, and I felt the loss the more acutely since my condition was now having an effect on people other than myself.

The feeling of relief that the whole subject of my problem was now out in the open continued to stimulate my working life. At that time, I could still just about do a walking piece to camera. I made several films for the ever-loyal *Weekend* programme, and when I found myself interviewing the Mayor of Rye on a narrow ledge on the church tower, high above the town, I felt that there was still something I could do – providing there was no deterioration. But I was clinging on to hope as desperately as I was clinging on to the battlements. I could not do it now.

The disadvantage of the *Weekend* programme was that, obviously, it meant working at weekends, but I did not shirk from it. I filled in odd Saturdays going to meetings of the Muscular Dystrophy Group, or the Friedreich's Ataxia Group, both of which honoured me with a Vice-Presidency or a place on their committee. I was back in the old routine of doing too much. It was a curious time. I still had the absurd belief that, even though I was treating every job as if it were my last, I had only to adapt and life would be very much as it had been before. I, and the world, knew that I was maimed, but I had not reckoned on the disease's progression. It seems impossible now, but it was so. Wherever I went, people came up and said what a good radio programme it had been, wished me well. I was buoyed up with the success of having admitted failure.

The reason I had plenty to do, I concluded, was that I was a medical 'case'. I had become our medical correspondent. There was a role for a disabled reporter. All would be well. I deceived myself and, with the help of speech therapy, others. I was also getting jobs I had not expected. I found myself deputising once more for Margaret Howard on *Pick Of The Week* – I even pinched her catchphrase, 'Hello again'. That week they had played the old pop song 'Life goes on', which seemed an appropriate choice. A sympathetic producer, Nigel Acheson, had sworn it could be done and, if not with the elan and elasticity of yore, done it was. I got a larger than usual fan-mail, welcoming me back.

True to his word about my condition not being the end of the world, Jock Gallagher asked me to write a large brochure for the return of *The Radio Show*, which he was directing. I spent all the spare time I had between radio and television doing this, for it included a short history of the BBC, which was great fun, as well as involving a fair amount of reading.

Throughout May and June 1988 I busied myself with this, with *Weekend*, more interviews and a new venture called *People*, introduced by Derek Jameson. This series was made up of short films in different 'strands' – generally about odd people in odd situations. It was much like the old *Nationwide* without the studio interviews, and proved very popular, not least because of Derek, who had made such a hit on early morning Radio 2. In fact, it had higher viewing figures than *Wogan*, which by all the BBC's most recent precedents, made it almost a certainty for being taken off.

The producer, an eminently civilized man called Peter Bazalgette, asked me if I would be prepared to make a series of films about people who had overcome serious disabilities. At first I had been disinclined to accept, being wary about being labelled, but in the end I thought, 'What the hell? Why not? It's work, it's useful and it's entertaining.' It was also to teach me a lot about suffering.

First there was Frankie. Frankie D'Agostino had had several cancers and eventually he died. He was seven, and completely bald from treatment. He was also blind. His spirit was enormous. At the time when I filmed him for *People* he was being given a special day in London, including staying at the Savoy, driving in a Rolls Royce, shopping at Harrods and driving their coach and horses. But for Frankie the main event was recording a pop-song with Brenda Cochrane, a Scottish singer who had taken to him. Frankie was particularly fond of singing and had a rare ability to memorize words and tunes, which he used to keep himself happy during his short and painful life. He was devotedly looked after by his parents and came from a loving family, but had a happy knack of taking to new friends with an affectionate ease. Meeting him was a pleasure, and he was an inspiration in the way he coped. But I caught myself thinking that Frankie was not burdened with any responsibilities and not used to any other life, and I was ashamed.

As a particularly disorganized person, I was also taught a lesson in rigorous discipline by an ex-Cambridge student called Jeremy Cuss. His father was a Shepherds Bush jeweller whom I had met several times. He had written to me with great sympathy when my condition was announced, explaining about his son, and I was glad to share his problem on film. Jeremy had developed severe amnesia. He could not remember anything that had happened five minutes beforehand, and sometimes forgot what he was saying in the middle of his sentence. The film was about the methods he used to overcome his problems – the use of the alarm on his watch, messages to himself telling him what to do next, what meals he had, who to ring and when and so on.

Perhaps the most sensational of the films concerned Heather Clark. She was a remarkable, and remarkably pretty, young woman who had suffered as a result of thalidomide. She had no arms and no legs, yet she lived a relatively normal life, with a companion and helper. She worked in her father's office and drove a specially adapted car. The film was about her attempting a free-fall parachute jump while strapped to another jumper and, what was more, doing it for another charity. I shall never forget her shouting, 'hello everybody!' from about a thousand feet up, after what she admitted was a terrifying experience. She very nearly did not make the jump. There was complete cloud cover until late into the day, but it brightened just in time. We could not see the first part of the jump because it took place above the remaining clouds, but she and her companion landed almost on the camera, and to a mighty cheer. Heather was a happy soul, and it was no surprise afterwards when she announced that she planned to get married.

It made, of course, a smashing film and, not for the first time, I wondered if it was exploitative. But Heather's personality was so bubbly, and her handicap so great, that it cannot have been a bad thing to introduce her to as many people as possible.

All the filming for *People* certainly renewed my spirits, and when my friend and colleague Viv Black asked me to fit in another radio series, I was in buoyant mood. Viv worked for the Archive Features Department where I had made so many programmes, and I think she felt that it was no longer making as much use of me as it could, given the friendly response of listeners to *A Lone Voice*.

I had stopped doing my Monday morning archive programme, firstly because the whole series had been cancelled during the last quarter of 1986 and secondly because, when Controller 4 had decided he wanted it back in 1987, Helen Fry, the Chief Producer, had told me that I was not being asked because such excellent scripts demanded great flexibility and expertise in the speech. I was to be replaced by Andy Kershaw. I was bitterly disappointed.

I think something of this was in Viv's mind when she asked me to do *Questions From The Past*, a selection of great moments from the *Any Questions* programmes of a quarter of a century ago. The programme was less political then and the speakers wittier, but the selection revealed some accepted prejudices of the time (I recalled having heard some of the original broadcasts) which today make my blood boil.

Helen Fry retired from Archive Features and was succeeded by Anne Winder, one of whose first acts was to get rid of me and Viv Black – who was faced with either becoming a secretary again, or leaving the BBC (she did the latter) – and to revive the programme with Ludovic Kennedy. Ludo has been a friendly colleague in the past, but Viv and I could not help taking a certain amount of pleasure in hearing a good many of our selections broadcast again.

I had now been sacked three times from favourite radio programmes: *Stop Press*, the archive programme and *Questions From The Past*. Somebody was trying to tell me something I already knew – that my broadcasting days were over.

But not quite.

Sarah England of Television South West had seen me being interviewed about my condition by Rene Wyndham on her late-night series *Postscripts*, and invited me to do an entirely unrelated half-hour documentary for her; Peter Lowe asked me to do another on Conductive Education for *Friday Report*; Claire Walmesley and Robin Brightwell asked me to do a *Horizon* about medical research, and *The Press Gang* (now produced by the amiable Dirk Maggs) asked me to do another series.

Ernie Wise and I flew up to Glasgow on 2 September 1988. We were both guests of *The Garden Party* in Glasgow, me because it was my fiftieth birthday. I was interviewed about 'coping' and highlights of my career were recalled. I was feeling in a good mood because Ernie had made me laugh, and I told a good Roy Hudd story from my theatrical chat show of the previous year, *On Stage*. This concerned the landlady who provided nothing but baked beans every night. Finally, as they were returning weary from their panto first night on Christmas Eve, Roy swore to his friend that if it were baked beans again he would throw it at the landlady. It was, but while stirring them moodily around he encountered a small sausage buried in the middle. He called her back. 'Here, you've made a mistake!' 'Yes,' she replied lugubriously, 'Happy Christmas!'

Afterwards I wished I had told the story that Michael Horden had told me about the elderly Scottish actor, Finlay Currie. Finlay went on working well into his nineties, and at this time he and Michael were in a play together. One morning, a very attractive young actress walked on to the stage. Finlay grasped at Michael's sleeve. 'Oooh, to be seventy again!' he breathed.

The interview went well, and the physical movement was still just about all right. The following Monday, I drove down to start filming for Television South West. The subject was Joseph of Arimathea, and the film traced the origins of the legend that he came to England, possibly with the young Jesus. It was beautifully set, chiefly at Glastonbury and in Cornwall. It was a pleasure to drive and walk around the countryside, and I did not dream that when I returned to make another series of programmes for TSW, only a month later, I would have to be driven and would be walking with a stick.

I was also able to fit in a concert for the Muscular Dystrophy Group at the Chichester Flower Festival. The Cathedral was beautifully decorated and it was a pleasure to do the compering job, particularly as Sir Richard Attenborough had been so complimentary about me at the MD Group's AGM, at which I had met so many inspiring people who were already in wheel-chairs. The concert was a success as well as a pleasure, and I think made a fair amount of money for the Group. I did not know it, but it was the last time I would do such a job.

I also consulted the list I had compiled of the fellow cerebellar ataxia sufferers who had formed a branch of the Friedreich's Ataxia Group. There was a sufferer in Fareham and I managed to visit him. This, too, was a last. I had hoped to call in on several people as I drove past their homes, but did not realize that driving fast and far would soon be denied to me.

Meanwhile, I worked on the *Friday Report* film, took some advice from the Hungarian instructors and learned from the spokesperson for the physiotherapists that their profession was undervalued, underpaid and overworked. That was my own experience too, and I determined to get as much value as possible from my none-too-frequent visits to the physiotherapist at the National Hospital.

As luck would have it, the annual AGM of the Friedreich's Ataxia Group was in Birmingham, where I was filming, so I was able to stay with my director friend Bill Jones again, which was always a pleasure. I chaired a question-and-answer session, made easier by the fact that I was among friends, and on 20 October I gave a lecture at my local library. Speech was now a little halting, although I was continuing with speech therapy under Dr Karen Brian (Margaret Brent having been elevated to motherhood) and it was enormously helpful. I tried to put into practice simple lessons on breathing, posture and pace, and it was remarkable how much it helped. As with *The Press Gang*, I wrote out a little card of key-word instructions and kept it in front of me as we proceeded. I took very little pleasure from the fact that I was the only working reporter who was undergoing speech therapy, and none whatever from the fact that I was reduced to taking instruction on how to speak. This may have had a psychological effect on my performance; it certainly did nothing for my self-esteem.

By the end of October the situation I had been dreading occurred. I started not to enjoy driving, especially over long distances. By the time I next went down to Plymouth, where I was making a series about cancer (our medical correspondent strikes again!), I decided to leave the car at Bristol and take the train.

It was an invigorating series, despite the title *Coping With Cancer*, and I learned a good deal. I did not know, for example, that ninety per cent of cancers are treatable. That is not to say that ninety per cent of patients are cured, because a large number fall into the ten per cent that are incurable. But advances have been made and cancer is no longer the bogey-word that it used to be. I had the pleasure of meeting Dr Sheila Cassidy, who had been so badly tortured in Chile and who was now concerned with the hospice movement. I learned a lot about coping, although not for the first time I caught myself wishing that the details of my own condition were clearer, more black and white, treatable or non-treatable. I even began to envy those with cancer for knowing what lay in front of them. I did not, and I did not like it.

As well as making the programmes on *Coping With Cancer*, I was pretty busy up until Christmas. I was juggling times and dates and producers. Once again, I had more than I could sensibly handle. I conducted some interviews for *Phantoms Of The Railways* near Peterborough and I wrote a television film about people who had to work on Christmas Day. The previous year, more than twenty crews had given up their Christmas to shoot it, and it was a fascinating story. From the lonely gypsy selling pegs to the farming family; from those who provide all the dinners to the men on the oil rigs (production never ceases); and of course the men and women who make and transmit all the radio and television programmes that everyone on holiday and at home takes for granted. Noel Edmonds was to do the commentary, and after he had recorded it I realized that there was another challenge ahead of me: I must learn to write for other people. I knew that everyone had his or her own style, but I had not realized just how idiosyncratic that could be. Afterwards, Noel said that there were certain things in the commentary that he could hear me saying, but could not give the same flavour himself. Things had had to be changed here and there. It was a valuable experience. The film was originally called *Christmas Day In The Workhouse*, a brilliant and evocative title, but some executive with even less imagination than sense changed it, and it ended up as *So This Is Christmas*. So this was part of the frustration of working for a big bureaucratic organization such as the BBC. Executives who have had nothing to do with the making of a programme, have to justify their existence by changing something. Anything will do. It is part of a battle which producers and reporters find themselves fighting all too often.

Mercifully, it was not true of the last and most important programme I made that year. This was a *Horizon* documentary on research, particularly into brain disease. It was a close-knit team, with the Editor of *Horizon*, Robin Brightwell, always on hand for advice and guidance. The producer was Claire Walmesley and, early on, when we had been mulling the project over, she had introduced me to her assistant, Kate Womersley. The combination of Walmesley, Womersley and Worsnip was too good to miss. Kate was big, efficient, played second row for Richmond Ladies and was an England trialist at rugby. I decided I had better do it.

CHAPTER 10

Horizon

At the National Hospital I found I was not, as I had thought, alone. There are many rare brain diseases and, according to my specialist Dr Harding, although individually they are rare and do not perhaps affect huge numbers of people in terms of being an enormous health hazard, the sufferers together constitute a large body of disabled people. These diseases often affect people who are at the peak of their professional lives, and people with families. At the National they deal with a range of conditions of brain, nerve, muscle and the distortion of the messages that run between them. By constant monitoring, experimenting with and researching into the patients' senses, actions and reactions, the doctors investigate, eliminate and eventually incriminate certain abnormalities. To the patient the equipment which is often skilfully developed seems primitive at first sight and alarming, and, as I have said, the barrage of tests is something of an assault course. But the brain is, so to speak, a grey area, about which, despite centuries of research, much is yet to be discovered. Will it happen in my lifetime? Some neurological diseases, such as Parkinson's, and strokes, although still perplexing are common enough; others are not. What is more, there are hundreds of variants. Patients of these are often told there is no known cause, no known cure.

The sense of loneliness, of separation from the medical mainstream, is by no means confined to those of us who live in remote areas away from centres of skill and learning. It is shared by many who feel that their particular condition is unfashionable, that doctors and the public cannot or will not pay them enough attention. 'Will patients like us continue to be the ones to miss out on research, or is there a "breakthrough" just around the corner?' is what they want to know.

And so do I. What we – and by that I mean me and the hundreds of people who have written to me – want to know is: what research is going on, and by whom? How is it organized and who pays for it? Does it filter through the National Health Service to us ordinary patients? What *is* the state of medical research in Britain today?

As luck would have it, these were questions the long-running BBC television programme *Horizon* wanted answered, and in September 1988 producer Claire Walmesley proposed that I ask them. As both a patient and a reporter, I was thought to be a good choice, and as for myself, I was glad of the opportunity to work on a major project. The programme was broadcast at the end of February 1989.

We used the National Hospital as a starting point, and spread outwards from there. It was obvious from the beginning that there are not enough patients with, and not enough doctors concerned with, neurological diseases, to form an effective lobby. That is why there is a danger that money for neurological research will be one of the easier targets for cuts.

Attached to the National Hospital is the Institute of Neurology. Part academic, part clinical, its reputation for research is second to none, and yet the Dean of the Institute, Dr David Landon told me:

'We are chronically short of funds, and this has happened progressively over a number of years. It is particularly frustrating because there is so much to do at the present time. Nonetheless, there is a lot coming in from the medical charities, and this is very helpful to us.'

Dr Landon's particular interest is in the structure of nerve tissue and muscle. He looks at them through a fifteen-year-old microscope, but increasingly his time is spent looking for money. It costs the interest on a million pounds to set up a professor, a researcher and a secretary. Dr Landon's research is funded partly by university money, which is declining, partly by Medical Research Council (or Government) money, which is also declining, and partly by charity money, which is increasing. But would more money mean more cures automatically for diseases like mine? Dr Landon was not sure:

'I think it would be a mistake to say automatically. But undoubtedly some more money would mean a greater chance for finding, not necessarily cures, but methods of alleviating a wide range of diseases, and would certainly make more accessible the existing treatments that we have at the moment for diseases we do know about.'

Charity money and the public's desire to help research is invariably boosted temporarily by publicity about personalities who have been stricken – Terry Thomas, David Niven, Jacqueline du Pré – and, of course, children, who add enormously to the appeal – like David, who has the most virulent form of muscular dystrophy, duchenne. Muscular dystrophy has earned itself a very high profile among the charities, although there are only about 15,000 sufferers in Britain. David's mother faced up to it robustly:

'I'm a teacher. I know nothing about medicine, basically, but when things were obviously not right with David I did read, and I became familiar with the name duchenne. I knew it was the worst possible. The symptoms are progressive muscle death from the feet up through the body until it finally reaches the heart. David will now go slowly downhill, progressively. That is the prediction, but at the moment he has just started school. The consultant said, "Don't give up hope. I've known other diseases cured within a lifetime and I believe this one can be as well," and I've clung on to that. I came home, looked up muscular dystrophy in the phone book, said, "I'm here, what can I do?" and it's taken over my life ever since.'

Jill Brownbill has raised thousands of pounds for muscular dystrophy. She is a teacher at Haberdasher's Aske's Hatcham Girls' School, Young people will support a good cause, and in many colourful ways. I have myself contributed in small ways over the years, little dreaming that I would ever have a personal interest in charity money, and have watched the MD Group grow. There are some well-known personalities associated with the Group, not least Sir Richard Attenborough, who is very active in publicizing its work. On the afternoon I was at Hatcham, he was presented with a huge cheque on the stage, the proceeds from a fancy-dress disco run by the pupils. His comments were trenchant, emphasizing the importance of the research and how finding a cure would mean saving thousands of lives.

The charity of which we cerebellar ataxia patients have formed a sub-branch is Friedreich's Ataxia Group. Friedreich's ataxia also begins in childhood and condemns patients to a wheelchair by early adulthood, but there are only 1,500 sufferers in Britain. Fund-raising events deal in tens, not thousands, of pounds. Nevertheless, the Group supports one small research team, led by Dr Sue Chamberlain at St Mary's Hospital, Paddington. But she is uncertain about the future:

'Diseases like Friedreich's ataxia have never really attracted the money from the Medical Research Council or the Wellcome Foundation. They affect too few people, to their mind. They have their list of priorities, and obviously cancer and things like that come first, so the rarer disorders tend to be neglected. It's not totally their "fault", because often there aren't many researchers interested in investigating these disorders. The larger disorders, such as cystic fibrosis which affects quite a lot of people, represent quite a financial burden to the NHS; but for Friedreich's the support group is very much a family organization. The patients have pushed and the researchers have responded by identifying the offending gene.'

And, of course, the numbers with cerebellar ataxia are even smaller: our support group is only about a hundred strong. But if they depend only on charity, are these smaller groups in danger of going to the wall? And thus will groups like Dr Chamberlain's also be in danger of folding?

'Well, it's always conceivable that if they cannot continue to raise the money, then the research *will* fold. It's as simple as that. It's really the charities in this country that are entirely funding this type of research, and if they fall down, so do we.'

At least with Friedreich's ataxia there *is* a group. Where there is none, people feel very alone, with a disease that nobody has heard of, to which the public will not donate money, and in which researchers are not interested. If the present trend is for the Government to rely increasingly on charity, where does that leave them? Even if they galvanize themselves, as we have, is 'research by coffee morning' a satisfactory way of going about it?

The Association of Medical Research Charities is more positive. They believe that it is through the charity sector that the public have the ability to express their opinion as to what the priorities are. They think that the increasing number of small charities, focusing on specific diseases, does actually indicate where there is a public perception of a need for research that is not being met in full by public funding.

Dr Dai Rees of the Government-backed Medical Research Council is more sceptical:

'The charities may be well-off this year, but their prosperity next year depends on how much the collecting boxes bring in, how the public feels about a particular disease; and so I think, quite rightly, that charities are more cautious about making long-term investments.'

Diseases such as mine, with no cure in sight, demand long-term investment. But Alistair Dennis of the Association of Medical Research Charities does not accept the point.

'I don't think that it's a very fair comment to make, given that the increase in funding provided by the charitable sector has been substantial and sustained over a long period, whereas, as a matter of fact, the money being put by the Government into research is, if anything, static or marginally in decline.'

In recent years, research funding has been radically reshaped. In the early 1980s, charities gave £73 million and the Medical Research Council £110 million. By 1988, the MRC was contributing only £132 million (excluding a special £14 million grant for AIDS), but the charities gave £138 million. The MRC has turned down many projects which it admits are highly rated. Given its doubts about charity's uncertainties, I asked for a straight answer about whether or not the MRC would fund research into obscure diseases like mine. Dr Rees told me:

'We try to strike the best balance we can between different types of medical research. It has to be recognized that there are many different projects we can take up, of great importance, which can be seen to be directly relevant to medical problems. The evaluation process depends very much on our perception, or our judgement, of the appropriate balance of activities, not only between that which is with the patient at the bedside versus that which is in the laboratory with molecules in the test tube, but also that which is relevant to mental disease versus infectious disease versus cancer, and so on. We cannot take a single proposal and make a judgement *in vacuo*, as it were. We have to start with a view of what is the balance of activity that we ought to be supporting.'

The third begetter of research is the international drug industry. Merck, Sharp and Dohme's purpose-built £24 million laboratories are among several that have sprung up in the English countryside. Among their tasks is to watch the effect of a new drug, MK801, on brain tissue which has suffered stroke damage. The eventual aim is to use the drug quickly – say, within twenty-four hours – to block the effects of electrical activity, which presently spreads damage to surrounding areas. If these results can be extrapolated into the clinic, they would certainly be on to a very exciting line of treatment – and a very commercial one, because at the end of the day they are in the business of making new and saleable products for the company. But they also happen to be in an area where new products such as this would be of great benefit to patients and to society, because a stroke is a very common and disabling disease – and a very expensive one. But do the drug companies do anything for, as it were, the 'unfashionable' diseases? Dr Leslie Iverson of Merck, Sharp and Dohme told me:

'The great challenge to our scientific understanding is, I think, in the area of neuro-degenerative disease. We have very little understanding of what goes wrong in the brain, leading to the irreversible loss of brain cells. In many cases, we are treating the symptoms of damage that has already occurred. In the next century, we hope to have enough understanding to be able to treat the damage itself, and maybe prevent it from occurring or slow down its progress.'

The next century. Companies such as Merck, Sharp and Dohme aim to recruit the very best scientists, and offer far better pay and conditions to tempt them. In the universities, life on short-term contracts is far less attractive. The pay is about half and the security non-existent. As Dr Stuart Eggington of Birmingham University told me:

'It's the response to the challenge. That's why most people do research.'

It is a challenge that is increasingly formidable. Stuart can only get a mortgage because his wife works as a midwife. He has finished a two-year contract and a one-year contract, and is now on the luxury of a three-year contract. It takes anything up to three valuable months to put together a grant proposal, with no guarantee that, however good the science, it will be accepted.

Research is a serendipitous business. Occasionally, someone has a bright idea and follows it up; but in the present climate, this sort of fortuitous discovery is being stifled. So why do more researchers not join the brain drain? Dr Thelma Lovick was enthusiastic:

'Because when you *are* funded, it's fantastic. I mean, it's a very exciting business to be in. That's why I'm still here. It's as simple as that.'

A colleague agreed: 'You have got to take into account that we're all fairly ordinary people. We like to live in this country. Some of us have got families, husbands and/or wives who also have jobs. It's not always easy just to uproot yourself and take yourself where the opportunities are.'

Dr Leslie Iverson admits there is a differential between academic and industrial jobs:

'Unfortunately the differential is widening year by year, making it more difficult nowadays for scientists to switch between the two career structures, largely because the university system has fallen behind in its rewards. That's not a situation we regard with any great equanimity. We feel that the strength of the academic science base in Britain is crucial to our future success, and we don't like to see it going downhill.'

At Oxford University they agree. In 1986, Professor Denis Noble spearheaded the 'Save British Science' campaign:

'We have now got a major morale problem among the younger researchers. They are finding it very difficult to get what are called "project grants" – small grants to get started. We are having difficulty in attracting the young into science. I was chairman of the examiners in Physiological Sciences here a year or two ago, and none of our first class degree students wished to come into science. The biggest group here go off into various aspects of pushing money around. Now that's a very important part of our life, but it's not totally what we train scientists for.'

Yet, recently, Kenneth Baker awarded scientists £300 million over three years – what they had asked for. Was that not enough? Denis Noble was not sure. He wondered, first, exactly what that money was going to be used for – first class research, or structural reorganization? And second, is it going to be maintained over a period of years? Because this only inches us up towards being competitive with foreign countries. Sir James Black, who won a Nobel prize for inventing anti-ulcer drugs and beta-blockers, is a great believer in 'Friday afternoon research' – backing wild hunches.

'Maybe what we should have is some kind of National Research Bank, which you get money from not on the basis of your promises, but on the basis of your performance. I would like to see young researchers given initial funding without any kind of string at all. Your future funding would then be heavily determined by what you did with that first, unearmarked, subsidy.'

Another progressive idea is taking shape at the Institute of Molecular Medicine in Oxford. With mixed funding, it offers new opportunities in research both for basic scientists and for doctors in clinical practice. It has already started to attract young people who have, or undoubtedly would have, made their careers in the United States. It is a centre of excellence both for the patient and for the distinguished people working there. Professor Sir David Weatherall, its Director, thinks that dubbing it 'science for science's sake' would be dangerous:

'If you look at the history of penicillin, it didn't actually come from a chap sitting down saying, "How can we cure dangerous infections?" No, it was years of learning really quite fundamental things about bacteria, years of basic science which are not really directed towards that, and then a sudden fall-out. When you've had good basic science, the fall-outs follow.'

I wanted to know how certain it was, as things stand, that research would be conducted into obscure diseases.

'Well, you're raising a fundamental question here about how research should be organized within a community. It has been suggested that we ought to have a national policy for medical research – a committee that sits somewhere in London and says we will spend £X thousand on X disease, £Y thousand on Y disease and so on. I'm very sceptical about that actually. I think if you try to push research too hard in one direction, you may waste an awful lot of money. If you were to give me £5 million right now and say, "Do something about back-ache," I'd have difficulty spending it well, because the actual science and the questions that are ready for answering are not there.'

I confess I was not so concerned about back-ache. I asked what the situation would be if I were to give him some millions for brain/nerve/muscle-related diseases.

'It's very promising at the moment, because the science and molecular biology and cell biology are just starting to understand a little better how the normal brain and muscle functions. I think it's going to be enormously exciting, in advances over the next few years.'

Professor John Newsom-Davis runs a specialist clinic for myasthenia (weakness of muscles) in the Institute. He also pursues research. This enables him to identify the crucial questions, and what is achievable. Professor Newsom-Davis acknowledges that there is a gap between the number of patients he can see and the number of myasthenia patients throughout the country, but salutes the charities for the information they provide, the fact that they chivvy doctors into producing proper services and for the research money they provide, which helps supplement what the NHS provides. But occasionally research money is being used for beds, laundry, nursing. In this case, there is a danger of the Government relying on charity money and seeing no need to provide proper resources. It is a trend the charities are not happy with, and they perceive a danger of it spreading.'

I wondered, too, whether, if there was a breakthrough at the Institute, it would automatically filter down through the NHS – whether I could be sure the NHS could afford it. Sir David was emphatic:

'No, I think you could not be sure. I think that there's no limit to what you could spend on health, because as one gets better and better at preventative medicine, the population's age is rising astronomically.'

I have been lucky. At the time of the *Horizon* programme I was still relatively mobile. I may live in the country, but I worked a good deal in London. The speech may have been impaired, but I could still seek out answers. Many people, particularly those already confined to wheelchairs, depend solely on the knowledge of their local GP. And, as my own local GP explained:

'One of the big jobs of the GP is to pigeonhole the patient into the right slot, and to recognize their needs. If he or she is too overworked, then the patient is not necessarily going to get to the right specialist or the most appropriate therapist. One of the problems for the GP is that we are extremely well served with information. We have anything up to four different weekly publications, then there are the fortnightly publications, and on top of those the monthly publications; the difficulty is in finding the time to read them.'

And does he?

'Not often, no. I mean, it's not because you don't have the interest, but when you've got twenty patients sitting outside every Monday morning, and then another twenty in the afternoon, and visits in between, some teaching to do and committees to go to, you don't have a lot of time to pop off to the local major post-graduate centre, particularly from an area like this.'

So, treatment is patchy. It can depend on how much your GP knows; on whether researchers into your particular illness are interested, or funded; on how quickly research results reach the patient; on the ease with which the patient can reach the centres of excellence. Would I be better off if I went private? Dr Harding, back at the National Hospital, is firm:

'No. Probably the reverse, in fact. Quite a lot of new things that can be done are still being validated, are only available, in university departments and therefore not in private medicine.'

But is anything being done for brain disease, as is being done for cancer and heart patients?

'It's not always easy, one has to admit, to have really good ideas, particularly in diseases which affect parts of the nervous system which are not completely understood. I cannot, much as I would like to, take out your cerebellum and look at it, because you wouldn't like that very much. Without really understanding the cause, we cannot hope to have a go at sensible therapy.'

* * *

Giving up for the moment on curing, let us concentrate on coping. Here we join a mass market which includes people suffering from nothing more than old age. At Brunel University, using Hillingdon Hospital patients as test pilots, an entirely private enterprise bio-engineering department – complete with retail outlets – researches and tests marketable 'tools for living'. The department is headed by everyone's idea of an eccentric German professor, Heinz Wolff. He enthusiastically showed me an 'eating tool' with which a patient managed to clear his plate for the first time in several years. It seemed very simple. Why had it not been thought of before?

'Well, I used to have an acronym which I called URINE: Unexciting Research Into Necessary Equipment. People on the whole are not prepared to do unexciting research. They would much rather do research into artificial kidneys and artificial hearts – dramatic things – and it has really taken quite a long time for us to recognize that the degree of intellectual input required to make something simple is just as worthy of an MSc or PhD or some other higher degree as doing things with handfuls of computers and chips.'

Again the 'unfashionable' diseases miss out.

'If there are only ten of a product required in a year, then that product is unlikely to be commercially viable and the companies will, of course, realize the same. Now, here you may have identified one of the areas where the Government may have to step in, or alternatively where specialized charities have to step in.'

Mary Marlborough Lodge, near Oxford, is one of the few such centres funded by the NHS. It takes patients with specific problems, for two weeks, designs a solution and then puts it into practice. Dr George Cochrane is in charge:

'Anthony is unable to make any purposeful movements, except with his head. He cannot speak and he cannot use his arms, except when they move quite involuntarily and very powerfully, but with his head he has got fairly fine movements. Strapped to his head is a source of infra-red energy which beams out from this tiny emitter, and is picked up by the sensor in front of him. By his gyrations, he can go backwards and forwards, right and left. I think the idea arises from the recognition of need. For example, we utilize the ability Anthony has to use his head. This provides a chance to do things which we as doctors, nurses and therapists cannot do, so we work very closely with engineers. We are very lucky here in having the Oxford Orthopaedic Engineering Centre immediately adjacent to us, and so we work together. We can have the ideas here, then they can be refined and made possible there, and returned to us to be applied.'

If Dr Cochrane and his colleagues can give back to disabled people, to a greater or lesser extent, the chance to conduct their lives independently of the help of others, then that saving in monetary terms is tremendous – but how much more rewarding it is for the individual. Nobody wants to be dependent on other people; they want, above all else, to be able to conduct their own lives. In sum, said Dr Cochrane:

'Disability brings with it loss of opportunities, and that's what we want to give back.'

Because of financial cuts Mervyn, the researcher who made it possible for Caryl, who can only move her foot, to play chess, will have to find other work. So will nine of his colleagues at the nearby Oxford Orthopaedic Centre. It is like the old joke about the shopkeeper banging on the counter and saying, 'For the forty-seventh time today, there's no call for it!'

So what *is* needed? Even Dr Dai Rees, who works for the Government-funded Medical Research Council, admits:

'About an extra £40 million a year above the present level, which is £140 million a year, for a period of something like four years.'

Jill Brownbill, amateur fundraiser and mother of a child with muscular dystrophy, told me:

'What I'd really like is this: if we as a school can raise £10,000, I'd like the Government to match that pound for pound, or even double it. That would really make it worthwhile.'

And Dr Stuart Eggington, researcher, said:

'You have a momentum in research, and it can take ten, fifteen, twenty years to get up the momentum which will enable you, by serendipity or whatever, actually to make the breakthroughs which will cause an advance in therapy. You can turn that off overnight, but if you then suddenly decide to turn the funds back on, forget it. It doesn't work that way. You have to wait another ten or fifteen years to get up steam again.'

Having heard all these views and questioned all these experts, my conclusion was that there was slim chance of a breakthrough in brain disease research occurring in my lifetime. We have the ability to research. There are some innovative new opportunities. We are beginning to attract better talents back from abroad. Drug companies are investing in long-term research in the hope of long-term profits involving long-term diseases. There is more money going into research from charity; giving has become almost an epidemic. All this may produce spin-offs for everyone – but will it last? Those with 'unfashionable' diseases still depend on public money, which is declining, and on bureaucrats dedicated to cutting public expenditure. Changing the funding of research does not seem to have changed priorities.

We must all live in hope, of course, but it is clear to me now that the people who will really decide whether or not research into medical matters in this country goes ahead will never be at the sharp end, either as researchers or (though who can ever tell?) as patients.

CHAPTER 11

1989

I said at the outset that this was no fairy-tale, and it isn't. There are no heroes or heroines. Jo is not the 'stand by your man' figure depicted by the newspapers. She has, unquestionably, stood by me, working, worrying, wearing herself out, trapped by the demands and limitations imposed on her, but it is understandable that occasionally she has felt the need to put her own needs first in the effort to survive. She needs space around her and coping with me has not proved easy; no wonder she sometimes has to go off for long walks on her own to think, or let off steam.

Elinor has not always been the 'comfort' that many correspondents assume she must be. Like the girl with the curl in the middle of her forehead, she has veered from being very difficult to most loving. Certainly at times she has saved us from ourselves. At Christmas she presented us both with a stocking; she must have spent days seeking out little gifts – a tangerine, a walnut, a book, a drawing – and the pleasure the gift generated was immense. Not for the first time, I was in tears. But on other occasions the tears have been tears of rage, of frustration: twelve is a difficult enough age in any case, but my illness has made her pre-teenage years even more difficult. Life has radically changed, and while it is not his fault, Daddy's illness is the cause. No wonder she chats so frequently and devotedly about the big love in her life, her pony. No wonder she loves to spend the night away at a friend's house. She is an only child, in a lonely spot. She needs to have someone to talk to.

Ellie's occasional resentment has been perhaps the hardest thing to take. Yet when I kiss her goodnight after 'story' – the nightly story is still a family ritual – I see her at her most vulnerable, and I know I would do anything for her.

I return to the theme. I, too, am not as depicted. I am close to being 'rumbled'. I am not an heroic figure making the best of a downhill battle. True, I have kept up a certain face in public. I have played my part in putting cerebellar ataxia and other rare brain diseases 'on the map'; I have doggedly gone on broadcasting longer than I should, taking advantage of a genuine sympathy vote. I have accepted, and delighted in, the praise at my survival, much as I used to accept the praise for good work. But I lose my temper, I cry, I flounce, I feel sorry for myself at inappropriate moments, I despair. And the sad fact is that the people who least deserve these exhibitions – the family – bear the brunt of them. The sad fact is that we are all at our worst, and lowest, in the privacy of our own homes.

I feel that all three of us seem to reserve our darkest moments for the other two. Only at home can the mask slip, can we be ourselves, and when all three masks slip at the same time, some ugly faces are revealed. It is choosing the moment to let the mask slip that is the hardest thing. Or rather, the knowledge that the mask is about to slip at a thoroughly inopportune moment.

I am all too conscious of how I am capable of doing things at one moment, and incapable at some other time. When I am well rested, I can help in the kitchen, albeit more slowly than was once the case. I may even break a plate. On other occasions, perhaps having returned from London, I need just to sit, whatever the time of day, whatever needs to be done. It is a fact of disablement, things are no longer the same and it is too late for recrimination. It is particularly hard for Ellie to understand; if he can do the washing up one day, why not the next? Disabled people everywhere will know what I mean by the frustration and disappointment of being thought to be taking advantage of one's disablement in order to avoid responsibility.

Jo has one specific characteristic which was difficult enough to live with before, but which disability has made particularly disheartening. She is a perfectionist. She has extraordinary patience with painstaking jobs. She is more competent than I, has more of an eye for detail, more willingness to persevere. In other words, she is less compromising. So when, for example, there are two jobs to be done, such as the washing-up and preparing the clothes for the machine, she will argue that she might as well do both, since she does both quicker and more efficiently than I. True. And, of course, I am disabled and therefore need the rest. Generally true. She can be rocking with tiredness and eager to start her school-work when both jobs are done. But my contention that if I do the washing up, albeit more slowly, while she prepares the clothes, both jobs will be completed sooner than if she did one after the other, is rejected. So she gets down to her school-work later and more tired than she would otherwise have been. What I gain in energy is dissipated in frustration. It seems hard for those who care for us to understand how important it is to allow us to do what we can, when we can and, knowing what extra work we cause, be able to make our contribution.

1989 began badly. At the end of the first week, I went up to London for my regular check-up with Anita Harding. I seemed to be stable, but when they repeated the autonomic tests – checking my blood pressure sitting, lying, standing and moving – I was aware that there had been a decline. What had been merely an amusing sound effect at the time of *A Lone Voice* – blowing noisily into a tube – was more difficult. This time, instead of lasting out, I passed out. It was momentary, but noticeable. When I was asked if I had been aware of losing consciousness, I replied that I 'may have lost concentration for a moment'! I think I genuinely believed it at the time, but it was a euphemism nonetheless. That evening, I stayed with Jane and Tony Chapman, a haven of civilization, but my pleasure was soured by the knowledge that my condition had 'progressed'.

On Saturday I drove to Harthill, and on Sunday I turned round and drove back to my sister-in-law's at Horsham in Sussex. Or at least I drove part of the way, handing over to Jo once we had got past London and on to the M25. If you can handle the M25 you can handle anything. We were both aware that long drives were beginning to tire me, and the time had come for Jo to help out. I was reluctant, because it meant admitting that another milestone had been passed. Jo and Ellie thought that my reluctance was a typical male-chauvinist desire to resist allowing a woman to drive my car. I wish it had been as simple at that. It was on a similar trip to Sussex that Jo had first driven the car. She had always had a spot of trouble with right and left, but nonetheless she handled the unfamiliar automatic well and we arrived safely.

This time we had come for Jo's mother's funeral. Rita had been nearly eighty. She was tired of travelling back and forth to Spain, but loyally accompanied her husband, who always had pressing business there. He claimed to be eighty-four (no-one was quite certain) and still insisted on driving right across the peninsula. Until recently he had driven across France too, avoiding the motorways. He was reluctant, it was said, to pay the tolls, so the journey was longer. This last time, with a sixth sense for danger, Jo had begged Rita not to go, but old habits die hard and Rita felt that Ted could not look after himself. In the end she went, although this time they were accompanied by Jo's younger sister, Geraldine (a trained nurse) and her husband John. It was fortunate. At San Sebastian disaster struck. Rita had a massive stroke which left her almost wholly paralysed and unable to move or speak. Eventually (for some reason Geraldine did not tell her sisters what had happened for over a fortnight), she was flown back and cared for in a local hospital near Littlehampton. It was obvious that she was aware of what was going on around her, but clearly unable to communicate except by smile and a slow nod. At first, Ted was convinced she would come home where she would be better off, but after a failed attempt she was moved to a nursing home where she was well looked after. During several weeks there was no improvement, and visiting was difficult not only because of Jo's demanding course, but because we were so far away. No amount of fatigue would prevent Jo travelling at weekends, and on the first occasion when Ellie and I went with her it was obvious that the visit gave brief but intense pleasure. Ellie was remarkable. On the face of it, an afternoon spent visiting a dying eighty-year-old was not an attractive prospect for a lively twelve-year-old. But Ellie was superb. She seemed to know precisely what to say, and when. She held Rita's hand throughout and, adopting a gentle, almost maternal tone, was rewarded with some seraphic smiles. I was enormously proud of her.

Rita had clearly decided she would die, and was a ghost of

her former buxom self. She was refusing to take proper food, and I saw writ large in her something of that feeling that I sometimes experience – of a healthy mind screaming with frustration at being trapped in an inadequate body. I thought back to the stroke patient in my ward at the National Hospital, and how wrong I had been to see him as just an inert presence. There was a wealth of observation and thought and reaction there, confined as it was. I thought back, too, to the laboratories of the large American drug company in Essex, and how I should not in the least mind them making huge profits if only their research had already produced an inhibitor which could be used on the stroke victims who occupy so many of our hospital beds, and who must so resent being turned into little more than cabbages. What was certain was that no breakthrough would be achieved in Rita's lifetime. I thought, too, of Jo, of how she was prevented from visiting more often, of how much effort she made, and for what little return.

Within a week or two, Rita gave up the ghost. It was a beautifully British funeral. Rain spattered and wind blew at the graveside just enough to allow the priest's words occasionally to waft away from those gathered together. It was a church chosen at random. Although he had been warned, the priest constantly referred to 'Margaret' (because that was what it said on the certificate), whereas everyone knew her as Rita. Whatever quarrels there had been in the past were forgotten, when a perplexed old man cried at a graveside already awash with rain. Daughter Geraldine had worked her fingers to the bone to make sure the catering was done 'properly' (she did the Duchesse potatoes twice to make sure they were right). Children (even those who were twenty) were banished to the kitchen during the reception, making way for a group of Ted's elderly relations who had barely known Rita, and cared less. The English contingent was as tight as their waistcoats, the Irish (Rita's relations) extrovert and voluble. We all repeated many times what a lovely service it had been, and how suitable the reception.

My illness impinged even on this. There is a much-vaunted theory that grief can be discarded after a while, like a woolly pullover. I know that it depends; that what with looking after me and Ellie, what with coping with the animals, what with the all-pervasive teacher-training course, Jo has not had time to work out her grief for a stricken and dead mother, and I grieve for her in turn.

I was beginning to work too hard again. Even after the funeral I drove up to London, leaving Jo and Ellie to be driven to the station for the long journey home. I put in a full day on *Horizon*, then split the next between *Horizon* and *The Year in Question*, a quiz for radio between the quality papers chaired by Simon Bates. As part of my new persona, I was researching and setting some questions. That day I also did an interview for the *Radio Times* of the 'Worsnip Works On' variety and, discovering that I had mistakenly earmarked Friday for a recording in Birmingham, spent the evening taking a train to the second city, to be ready next morning. As usual, I was to be staying at Bill Jones's house in Moseley.

By this time, I was apologizing in advance to studio managers and sound-recordists about my condition, with many jokes about 'drawing the short straw' and 'initiative tests', and probably embarrassed myself and them doing it. I could not seem to get it into my head that they were already aware of my difficulties, and pleased to see me working and to be able to help out. I was, as usual, too conscious of what I had been, too reluctant to acknowledge what I now was. I was recording the second in an occasional series for the ever-supportive team at Birmingham, *The Phantoms Of The Railways*, and I often thought about how much more fluent I had been when I had recorded the previous one. I was worrying over whether the second could successfully be played with the first as part of the same series. I need not have. Both were repeated together in June 1989.

I did not go home that weekend. I had to write the *Horizon* script, and the fact is that I am too easily distracted at home. Looking back, I see that, compared with Jo, I always had the easy option. I would simply announce that I was up to my ears in work, and stay in London. No matter how much work she has, she has to go on thinking in advance about meals, sheep dipping and worming when required, making trips to collect pony-nuts, responding to Ellie's ups and downs. I may have worked hard, but I have had the best of it. I did it my way.

* * *

On Monday the editor of *Horizon*, Robin Brightwell, who confessed to having worked me as hard and treated me like any
other reporter, listened to the script. At this stage, the system is
that you read the script as the pictures are shown, timing the
words to fit the appropriate gaps in the 'sync' (the sound in the
film that you are meant to hear). The film-editor dips the sound
at the relevant moment, and the commentator speaks. I realized
that the commentary would be a disjointed, badly timed affair,
confusing to the viewer, if I read it, so for the first time in my
life, I had someone else – in this case Claire – read my script for
me. I realized that I was still writing for my own speech patterns
(not as they were now, but as they had been). Particular
emphases and idiosyncrasies of stress and timing had been
crafted for my voice, and I was reminded that I would have to
learn to write for other people, making any intentions as to how
the script should be interpreted clear from the writing itself. It
was a painful realization. I felt that my personality was gradually
being taken away from me.

Some of it was restored the next day when we started to
record the commentary. Claire had thoughtfully put aside two
days for the job. In the event only one was needed, but it was a
pretty tired and bad-tempered reporter who emerged, sweating,
from the commentary box at the end of a long afternoon. What
in the old days would have taken one hour had taken six, and I
was starting to be obsessive about my own inadequacy.

The next two days I spent researching *The Year In Question*,
during the course of which I found a new fear to add to the list.
A good deal of the research involved listening to records, and I
realized that my hand was no longer steady enough to lower the
needle onto the disc at the right point without a dangerous
graunching sound. Fortunately the more modern players allow
you to poise the needle over the required spot and then lower it
by means of a lever, thus avoiding trouble, and there were
enough of these modern machines in the archives listening
rooms. But it meant that any research would in future have to
take place on BBC premises if the archives were not quickly to
be depleted.

I also had my photograph taken for the *Radio Times* interview.
I was shocked at the result. I had always, as they say, 'taken a

nice photograph' but now the result was a gaunt, scrawny, grey figure who looked more like Dracula's mother than something you would want to see on television. I was due to start *The Press Gang* the next week and, among the worries, I thanked God (or whoever was currently standing in for him) that it was radio. I was reminded of Cliff Morgan telling me once of how his mother greeted him with the words, 'Hello, Cliff. I never see you nowadays but you're on the wireless.'

I did not go home that weekend either. The Saturday was taken up with a Freidreich's Ataxia Group committee meeting, and the Sunday with the final 'dub' of the *Horizon*. This is the process whereby the tapes are mixed together and the commentary, music and effects skilfully blended so that everything is heard at the right moment. Thankfully, the sound-mixer on duty was Brian Watkins, with whom I had dubbed many a film, under much greater pressure, for *Nationwide*. He was kind enough and patient enough to take a lot of trouble, adding to the good work of the film-editor, Chris Woolley, in making me sound as good as possible.

There followed a week of worrying – not about the *Horizon*, but about the new series of *The Press Gang* which would start on the Friday. Was this going to be the showdown, where I discovered I could go on no longer and gave up while actually broadcasting? Friends had been telling me that my speech was holding up and that I was no worse than during the last series; and it may have been true. What was unquestionably truer was that the nagging and possibly unnecessary self-doubt, yes call it fear, was greater this time than ever before. Circumstances could not have been much better. I was among friends – the small production team were willing me to keep going and prepared to put extra effort into the editing to help me. The panellists, particularly the regulars, Don Maclean and Denise Coffey, were prepared to talk their heads off to give me as little to do as possible, and the live audience was full of hardy perennials who knew about my problem and did not mind. Somehow, I got through it. When the producer, Dirk Maggs, had told me I would, I had not believed him. No one could have convinced me that I could successfully negotiate nearly forty minutes of banter and repartee, much of it improvised, yet the fact was that the adrenalin flowed in sufficient quantities to make sure that it happened. I just wished that as much was known about the substance missing from my brain as about the behaviour of adrenalin.

After *The Press Gang* I finally went home. It was the end of October, and this was to be my last weekend in phase one of the illness.

On the Saturday I went to see Dr Calland. I had been having digestion troubles for some time and, added to that, I was going to the loo about 500 times a night. It was agreed that I should try a different and less potent anti-depressant, although the dosage of Prothiden that I had been taking was hardly calculated to blow my mind. The effect of the change appeared to be catastrophic, although, as it turned out, it was entirely coincidental. Within twenty-four hours of the change, not only had the urinary and digestive problems increased, but I was feeling giddy much of the time, and definitely faint after certain movements.

On the Monday I was working at home, and called the doctor. He was away. Another member of the partnership advised me to go back on to Prothiden and report back at the weekend. On the Tuesday I spent the day at HTV West, where we were at last making the final adjustments to the *Pilgrimages* film which we had shot a year earlier with the friars at Hilfield Priory. We had the unpleasant task, all too common in television, of cutting a film from the length at which it worked best, to the length which the powers that be were grudgingly willing to allot it. Since the start of the project, the ITV companies had become embroiled in the cost-cutting exercise demanded by the leaderene, and this meant not only that jobs, but quality, were being sacrificed. Reducing a documentary from forty minutes to twenty-five was a heart-rending business, particularly when the subject matter was so compelling. The pile of film left on the cutting room floor only added to the sum of good quality material that is being sacrificed in favour of game-shows and other televisual nonsense. While we were having lunch, I noticed that the canteen was full of Australians, glamour girls and men with haircuts as unlikely and shiny as their suits. I gathered that HTV West was, to all intents and purposes, being used as a facilities house to produce yet more glossy dross.

I picked at my lunch, and sat very still while we edited the first half of the film. I was getting frightened that the faintness would affect my driving. I need not have worried. It had worn off by the time I drove to Bristol Parkway Station, where I picked up an evening train to London.

But at my digs in Sally Hardcastle's house during the next couple of days I seemed to spend most of my nights tottering to the loo and holding on to the wall while the bathroom disappeared before my very eyes.

On the Friday I had to do *The Press Gang* again. I could barely get up the stairs to the temporary communal dressing room. (The Paris Theatre, not before time, was being redecorated.) The place looked like a building site, and I was amazed that there was any audience at all, unless they had wandered in by mistake or else were looking for jobs as brickies. The previous week, the disc-jockey Adrian Love had very kindly come down to the Paris to stand by in case I could not manage, and this time it was Gyles Brandreth. The plan was that if I packed up half-way through the show they would take over, and by the magic of radio would record the first half 'wild' (i.e. on their own, without audience or panel) and it would be edited in afterwards. Dirk Maggs was a very skilled editor, and there seemed no lengths to which he would not go, in his carefree way, to keep me on the show. I have a lot to thank him for. As it turned out, none of this was required, but it was a damned close-run thing. Thanks to Dirk's dispensation, I went straight to my chair and delivered my customary 'warm-up' from there, rather than standing at the microphone down stage, and once again got through to the end without too many slurs.

But the strain was beginning to tell. Over the weekend Dr Calland was off duty again. I debated whether to go to another doctor, but decided that it was better to remain with the one who knew the case, and to see him on Monday. I saw him all right, but not quite as I had planned. On the Saturday I slept late, and once again had a debate with myself about whether or when to get up. Somehow the thought of struggling into my clothes, having to sit on the bed to get my trousers and socks on, just seemed too much. Then there was wondering whether or not to shave, and if so having to decide whether it should be a good wet shave, with the danger of cutting myself, or a bad electric shave, with less chance of mishap. Ridiculous decisions like this were beginning to assume a significance out of all proportion to their importance, and I was starting to realize how easy it would be to 'let oneself go', and how important it was to keep up appearances. I caught myself wondering whether Ellie had instinctively felt some of this. She had once or twice asked me if I intended combing my hair or replacing a food-stained garment, and it seemed more than possible that she was determined her dad should not be seen by her friends to be going down the Swanee. Jo and Ellie were both out that afternoon, and did not see me sitting in front of a rugby match on the television hardly daring to move. Even the homely tones of Bill McClaren did not raise their customary feeling of well-being. I went to bed early, having spent some time at my computer. A year had gone by, and I still had not replied to all the people who had kindly written. I could not bring myself to let on that I found all movement distressing, and I pretended to enjoy the food which Jo spent so much energy providing. I was beginning not to be able to sleep, out of sheer worry about the fact that Jo was still downstairs working through the night. My view was that she would be better for a rest, her view was that if she was to succeed on her course, there was no alternative but to work through until it was done. It was to remain a bone of contention between us, and it was heightened by the lurking suspicion that I resented the amount of stress it created in me. Jo saw it as an interference with her liberty, a denial of her own right to choose, an attempt by me to maintain a male-dominant position of ruling the roost. Those days were long-since gone.

As if to emphasize it, as if to emphasize my new weakness, my new dependence, Jo's strength and determination, I passed out cold on Sunday night. It was one of the pleasures of our country existence that we were only allowed to drink water from one tap, and that was the one in the kitchen. At some impossible hour, unable as usual to sleep, I stumbled downstairs, partly to get a drink, partly to see if Jo was still awake and could be persuaded to go to bed. I never made it. On the bottom step I felt the world disappearing from me. I turned to grasp the doorpost for support, thinking that it would pass. Instead I passed out. I hit the tiled floor and badly bruised my hip. This time I was completely unconscious and Jo, unable to get me upstairs to my bed, managed to position me on the sofa we kept in the kitchen. Shortly afterwards, I negotiated the stairs and went back to bed for what was left of the night. But Jo had seen for herself what I had been flippantly and dismissively describing, and had not been at all amused.

Tony Calland was immediately in touch with the National, asking whether the symptoms described were likely to be cerebellar-related. His view was that I should be hospitalized immediately, but the question was, where? If the symptoms were coincidental, then I could be in a local hospital; if they were consistent with a 'progression' of cerebellar ataxia, then I would be better off in a hospital that specialized in neurology. It was a feature of Tony Calland's work that he was always prepared to ask, always, unlike many other doctors, prepared to admit that he did not know. I shall always be grateful for that.

Anita Harding's view was that it could be coincidental, but that the symptoms were consistent with a progression and that it made sense to be under the umbrella of the National. By chance, there was one bed free. Was I fit enough to get to London? Jo took the morning off and drove me to Bristol Parkway where I got the train. I swore I would take it easy, not move too quickly and order a car to get me from Paddington to Queen Square.

At the station I bought a copy of *Private Eye* to read on the train. On the cover was a picture of a perspiring and overweight Minister of Health, Kenneth Clark, smiling and saying, by means of a bubble, 'Don't worry, we'll have you stitched up in no time!' I did not know what NHS workers at the National thought about Mr Clark's proposals for their service, but I had heard what I took to be my conservative country doctor on the subject, and knew what he thought about them.

The welcome at the National was as friendly as always. It was February 1989, eighteen months since I had last been there as an in-patient, but it was particularly nice to see some friendly faces on the ward. Nora, the Day Sister, and Ify, the night Staff Nurse from Nigeria, were both very cheery and both old friends; and, decorations complete, we were back on a ward which was big and light and had a fine view over the Queen Square gardens. A talkative Yugoslav called Boris, who spent most of his time either hobbling on crutches to the stairwell for a smoke, or seeking out patients in need of information on almost any topic, told me that this was the Italian quarter in London and that the handsome church opposite, whose flag proclaimed it to be St George's, was much frequented by the Mafia. I did not know that.

It may be irresponsible, but one of the side-effects of being in hospital is a curious abandonment of worry. For some reason (and there seems no good one), you feel insulated against the cares of the world. I seemed to say to myself, 'Since I am in hospital I don't have to worry about my tax affairs, about where an income is going to come from, about how and when we are going to move, about what the family will do.' It is a deceptive feeling, because all those anxieties do surface and whirl about your head during the long hours of sweaty semi-comatose dozing, but while you are awake there is too much to do. I have remarked before on how the National is no place to go for a rest. They cannot cure you, but, by heaven, they do not let you get away without doing plenty of research.

Small things take on an immense significance in your free waking hours. It is probably a way of avoiding the big decisions. For example, it suddenly became very important to know which colours of nurses' uniforms signified what: deep navy for matrons (or are they called something else now, like Principal Nursing Officer?); dark blue for Sisters; grey for State Enrolled Nurses; light green for medicare workers; white (or some other colour) for agency nurses.

At first I began the long round of form-filling. Actually, someone else fills in the forms; my job was to regurgitate information about myself which I have provided on many previous occasions. After that I was seen by two young doctors in succession who managed, curiously enough, to ask questions which occasionally varied both from the last lot and from each other's. Much later, one doctor came back and, pleading tiredness, said that he had forgotten to ask one essential question, and would I mind? I did not mind in the least. I minded more that it was only Monday, and already he had been working for thirteen hours. I thought of Mr Clark and the reluctance of certain others (including consultants) to limit the amount that junior doctors work. But then I am only a patient. I probably haven't got my financial priorities right.

With little to do on the first day, my thoughts turned to other, less fortunate, aspects of being on a hospital ward. The food, for example, which is not always as attractive when it arrives as you hoped when you ordered it. But then if you are off your food anyway, what does it matter? I seemed to get by on a diet of soup and ice-cream, both of which were perfectly adequate. But I thought it would be churlish not to order the pancakes which had been thoughtfully listed for the next day, Shrove Tuesday. A small touch, but someone had clearly been thinking.

Then there are always the noises: the crying in pain from other parts of the ward; the voices on the telephone in the corridor, trying to explain to bewildered spouses and loved-ones about unwelcome diagnoses, particularly of incomprehensible brain diseases; the anger of those for whom nothing can be done and who naturally enough, blame it on the doctors and nurses. There are also the less human sounds like the intrusive tinned music from so-called 'personal' cassette recorders and transistor sets, and the blaring television. I try to savour the irony of a television person not enjoying television, but on the whole I do not enjoy the sound of persistent machine-gun fire while I'm trying to sleep. If television is essential in wards (and I cannot say I was not sometimes glad of its company), then an earphone system as used with in-flight movies must be devised so that any patient can opt in, rather than no patient being able to opt out. The late-night movie (which was on but, not surprisingly perhaps, not being watched) was all about operating on dead bodies, which I thought in rather poor taste. However, it is one of the things I have noticed since becoming disabled, that patients take more delight in 'sick' jokes than their carers and friends do, rather as Irish, or Polish or Jewish people often relish jokes against themselves. Certainly a matter-of-fact approach by hospital staff, who are dealing with sickness all the time, does help anaesthetize patients against their own personal griefs, but I sometimes wonder why staff are so surprisingly insensitive to noise-nuisance.

If you are lucky enough to be offered the one available bed, you should not cavil, but I certainly had not realized I was joining the world snoring championships (although, as my consultant said, this was only the heats). The two men nearest me in the ward were only enthusiastic amateurs compared with a third, who was a regular champion. Indeed, he was being operated on for just that. His snoring was a result of him stopping breathing during sleep and was dangerous. However sympathetic, I did find it hard to nod off, although I finally managed it at about 10.30. It was short-lived. I woke again with a start at two o'clock in the morning and could not get back to sleep. I wandered the corridors in the dim clerestoral light and sat outside to avoid the noise. The only sounds were the dim tinker of the night-staff at work, and the occasional moan of protest from the wards. It was curiously restful. Eventually, at about 4.30, I went back and tried again and this time dropped off at about 5.30 – only to be woken again at 6.15 by a zealous nurse with a cup of tea I did not want.

After that I decided that the best time for sleep was during the doctors' rounds, for they not only took an age to reach you, but I remembered that the visit consisted largely of a discussion amongst themselves. I eventually woke up to find my consultant at the end of the bed with her merry band of persons, including an occupational therapist (you could tell by the trousers) and a registrar (you could tell by the suit). The consultant glanced down at the *Private Eye*, which I had left suitably prominent, looked at the picture of the Minister and muttered quietly, 'Ah yes, the thinking man's lager lout.' Sycophantic laughter followed. Various tests and medicines were prescribed and the group passed on.

At lunchtime I dressed carefully and, with permission, wandered out to a shop for some essential supplies – toothpaste, razor blades and batteries. I intended to do some research work for *The Year In Question* while I was in, and the batteries were needed for the desk-top computer which had become a permanent companion. It was a sort of electronic filofax, essential now that my handwriting had deteriorated so badly that I could no longer jot down notes.

On the way back I was struggling, although I had been in hospital for less than a day. I was beginning to realize that I was plumbing the depths of a long-built-up tiredness, depths I did not know I had, I was extremely glad to be back on my bed, and spent the rest of the day in a combination of fitful sleep interspersed with interviews of various sorts.

Towards the end of the afternoon, the man opposite came back to the ward, having waited all day only to be told he was not to be operated on after all – an event described bluntly by the Sister as a 'cock up'. It meant that he would be back in his bed that night, and snoring! It seemed like a good time to get some sleep.

I had been intending to go down to Plymouth that week in order to be interviewed by Rene Wyndham on my experiences of making the series about cancer, but now I had to cancel. Again it was a new experience, and not a pleasant one. I had already postponed the *Working Men's Clubs* item, but I have never cancelled before. Worse, I had to cancel my appearance in that week's *The Press Gang*. I talked with the producer, Dirk Maggs, about this, and he was more than supportive. My fear was that I had opted out in the middle of a series, without saying why, or goodbye. We agreed that the best plan would be to return in a week or two, finish the series and then make a clean break, handing over the programme to someone else. In the meantime, Gyles Brandreth would take my place. The programme would go on. Dirk was wonderfully consolatory, and used the time-honoured phrase used by broadcasters when things go wrong: 'It's only radio!'

Relief that everything was arranged was tinged with insecurity. Would the show be better without me? Did it matter? Would the listeners care tuppence? Would there not be a general relief that a man with a speech defect was no longer in the chair? I listened on the radio to the cheering that greeted the announcement that Gyles was to be chairman, and I do not think I was ever so low. Would I ever get back? During the day I could forget about it. My worst fears were reserved for the bleakness of the night. The escalator seemed to be dragging me slowly downwards.

The neurological tests could be conducted *in situ*, and I could be generally monitored to see if the drugs were working. For specific problems, however, I was farmed out. For gastric problems I went to the Middlesex, for waterworks and sexual dysfunction I went to Barts. I was provided with an ambulance (at what cost?) and for a chaperon (I was still occasionally feeling dizzy) I was provided with the ward's prettiest staff nurse. She was there for experience, and was discreet enough, but I could not help wondering what would happen if, by some miracle, I regained my bodily functions during the course of the tests. The gastric examination was simple enough. I was given something to knock me out, then an endoscope was inserted and I was checked for ulcers, cancer and the like. I was clear. My problems appeared to concern muscular malfunctions of various sorts, brought on by the cerebellar ataxia. It was the same with the waterworks and the sexual dysfunction. But in order to check this I had to be wired to some complicated computer equipment while various leads were attached to unmentionable parts and electric shocks administered. It was almost as if they were trying to jump-start me. It did not work, and once again the condition was confirmed as being cerebellar related.

Modern science is a wonderful thing. I learnt that a new technique has been developed whereby patients can make love after injecting themselves (at suitable times and in suitable places) with a special drug. But only once a fortnight. It seemed a very clinical way of going about things. 'Excuse me a moment while I just . . .'

All roads led in the same direction – cerebellar-related. After a fortnight in which I underwent some of the same tests as before and a few new ones, and tried various drugs, I was relatively stable and ready to go into the outside world. I dreaded the thought. It meant facing up to all those decisions again, making all that effort. It meant putting on that grin which reassures other people that you are suffering from an illness, bravely borne, and that they can smile at you, say what a brave fellow you are, and above all, not *do* anything. Some of my friends do not fall into that category. They know who they are. They have provided transport, a place to stay, carried the cup. They have not disappeared into offices in which they had no business rather than meet me in the corridor. They have helped share the burden. They have acknowledged that there, but for the grace of God . . .

I cannot help feeling that, while in the National, I contributed to research. While Sally and Sue and my brother Patrick were visiting, an Australian doctor doing research into the behaviour of eyes in neurological diseases came up and proudly showed the assembled audience how I appeared to be confirming his thesis. Another doctor was very excited that my movement, which was closely photographed, appeared to disprove conclusively an assertion made by German researchers. And when Anita Harding was lecturing young doctors about ataxia I was wheeled on (literally) as a star exhibit, and one who could still speak well enough to describe the symptoms and their effects. And a very good house it was – for a matinée. But nobody found a cure.

It seemed I had very low blood-pressure (which was why I had been passing out) and I was constantly monitored. I learnt to live with the look of surprise in the nurses' faces as they saw the difference between the pressure while lying down and the pressure when I stood upright. I learnt to live, too, with one method of overcoming this difference. This was to keep the head permanently higher than the rest of the body by always lying with the bed at an angle, preferably of fifteen degrees. This was easy enough to do in hospital – you simply wind a handle – but more difficult to achieve at home. When I asked a doctor how it was to be done, he paused for a moment and then suggested telephone directories. There is a simple answer to everything. I do not know whether you have ever tried lying on a bed propped up at an angle of fifteen degrees, but there are further difficulties. As time goes by, you slide down the bed and the benefit derived from the better blood pressure is dissipated by the energy spent kicking yourself back up towards the pillows. There is a simple NHS answer to this too – flannelette. Apparently, the rougher the sheets, the less you slide. Silk sheets are out, not that you are likely to find those in hospital. Of course you can prop yourself up on a luxurious heap of pillows, but a simpler answer, which I have achieved both at home and in London, is to unscrew the legs at the bottom of the bed but not at the top.

One good thing about an angled bed is that you can see what is going on in the ward more easily. Across the room from me was Donald, who at one time seemed barely able to move at all.

At others he could totter across the ward at great speed. He would occupy long hours at a stretch (presumably when he was not feeling mobile) in drawing a picture in pastels, achieving his effects by smoothing in the pastel with his finger. He had learnt patience, which is, I have discovered, lesson number one if you are disabled. You must resign yourself to long periods when you would otherwise be hopping on a bus, or popping round to visit people in a car, or playing tennis, or simply walking, but when your body does not permit these things you are forced to remain where you are. Sometimes Donald would sit and stare, sometimes, especially at night, he would spend hours over one movement, occasionally standing on the bed and appearing to be wanting to walk up the wall. You learn very quickly not to offer help in a hospital ward. People have their own ways of achieving salvation, and who could say that I would not be doing the same shortly?

I marvelled at his patience, and in conversation learnt that he was an MSA patient. This turned out to be 'multi-system atrophy', where not only is the cerebellum distorted, but the nerves and the muscles are affected too. I was saddened by this news, and sadder still when I was told that I, too, had MSA.

Epilogue

Train journeys are bad. People want to talk. They have read about me. They are very sorry. I do not want to know, yet at the same time I know that behaving normally does me good – 'gets you out of yourself', as they say. I look out of the window. I look into people's back yards. They reveal a range of activities. Always activity. Here they keep pigeons; there they eat out a lot, at the barbecue. Here they have children with a range of forgotten toys; there they have not, and the lawn is immaculate. Here they care about gardening; there they do not. Each reminds me of things I can no longer do: sing, whistle, dance, push a wheelbarrow, fly a kite, take a walk. I see an old church in the middle of a field. I know I could never explore it. A game of football or cricket makes me realize I will never run again.

I turn away. I ask myself for the umpteenth time why I never had an ordinary job. I see adverts on the back of the newspaper of the man sitting opposite: 'Wanted: Driver'. How uncomplicated – but I cannot drive any distance; 'Wanted: Barman' – but I cannot carry a pint of beer. I watch the ticket-collector coming down the carriage. Why did I not have a job like that – nine to five, unstressful, regular shifts? He writes me out a ticket – but I cannot write any more. There are few things I can do any more. Walking more than a few yards is impossible. Even talking is a strain.

She broke the news gently, sitting at my bedside. MSA, a logical progression from CA. No need to bother me with the possibility before it happened. With CA you tend to go downhill at the same rate as you started; I had surprised them with how long I had held up. But the condition, although it may have been progressing, was easier to conceal then. With MSA it is not.

I started cancelling things. A quiz I was going to do for Phil Bainbridge's benefit at Gloucestershire County Cricket Club had already gone by the board. So had three episodes of *The Press Gang*. I decided to finish the season and then retire gracefully. The gang urged me to stay, but I had to go. The strain was too great. After the final edition, Denise Coffey came over and kissed me. I hobbled forward. I thanked my producers, Andy Wilson and Dirk Maggs. I cracked my old gag: 'Yes, he really is called Dirk Maggs. But then if you're called Glyn Worsnip you shouldn't laugh . . .' I thanked the gang, especially the regulars, Henry Kelly, Gyles Brandreth, Denise Coffey, Don Maclean, Molly Parkin, Claire Rayner and many others. But most of all I thanked the audience and the listeners. I had known about my cerebellar ataxia ever since the programme began, three years ago. They had known for a year – and not minded. They had all been real pals, and I would miss them. I turned from the microphone, choked.

I had already written to David Hatch, the Managing Director of BBC Radio, saying I wanted to give up live broadcasting. This had been interpreted as *all* broadcasting. I had not meant that. Perhaps I should have. But there was one more thing to do. Jill Marshall, who had written kindly after *A Lone Voice*, had already asked me to do a *Down Your Way* and was determined to go through with it. I sought permission from Michael Green, Controller of Radio 4. He agreed.

Just before Easter 1989 I drove to London. It took four hours and all the stuffing out of me. It used to take two. My friend and landlady Sally Hardcastle was good enough to drive me back. It was the last time I went to London by car.

Thereafter, I drove first the forty minutes to Bristol, then finally just the seven miles to Lydney, and thence went to London by train, changing at Newport. The canteen staff there got used to me hobbling in, asking for a small tea in a large cup, and tottering with it to a table.

Back at Radio 4, there were some internal wranglings and some of my work had been rejected. This hurt more, perhaps, than it should have done, and I uncharitably felt that the stick had been kicked from under a crippled man.

I did my *Down Your Way*. It was about the Forest of Dean. Edna Healey was on the following week and also wanted to do the Forest, where she was born, but I pipped her at the post. Originally, I had wanted her to take part in my programme, and she apparently had wanted me to appear in hers! But in the end she agreed to choose another place. She is a very jolly soul. We had worked together on *A Good Read* on Radio 4, and it would have been nice to see her again.

I was very nervous, but both Jill and Pete Smith, the sound recordist, were very patient. We used a number of archive recordings, since the archives were very much down my way, if not up my street, and in the end it was not a bad programme. I was never more gratified than when Michael Green wrote to say he was glad I had done it. With such small things is a broadcaster made to feel secure and wanted.

Since then I have finished two films for the ever-loyal *Weekend*, and although they asked me to do a third, I have had to decline; getting to Margate and staying overnight is beyond me. During the summer I had enough strength to book, and to go and sit at, various gatherings. At *Horizon*'s twenty-fifth anniversary party, I had the unusual experience of having royalty led over to meet me – Mrs Duke Hussey brought the Duke of Kent over for a chat – and I struggled through giving the Hague Gulbenian lecture at the Muscular Dystrophy Group's AGM. But depression was beginning to get a grip, and I found it hard to make journeys of any sort. By the end of August I was in the National Hospital again, this time for several weeks.

It is like a drowning man coming up for air, knowing he will return to water, conscious that he can swim no longer – happy, almost, to go under. I am, of course, depressed. As my consultant said, 'If you weren't, you'd need your head examined.' It is odd that they claim to be able to cure depression, which is mental, but not cerebellar ataxia, which is not.

Jo is working non-stop. I can no longer cope, and she deals with all those brown envelopes. Now that I am home again, I offer nothing except grief, anxiety and superfluous or unwanted advice.

Jo has taken a part-time teaching job, having successfully passed her training, and also acts as a supply teacher. She knows that tiredness is catching up with her, but is carrying on personfully. I have had a week's convalescence in Brighton and, on a trip to the sea-front at Hove, took to a wheelchair for the first time. It was a traumatic experience – a gesture of resignation. I felt isolated and conspicuous, but soon realized I was neither. In Hove, half the population is in a wheelchair, so no-one but me thought it odd.

At home again, I am perhaps more depressed now than I was before. I am conscious of the burden I put on Jo and Ellie, conscious of having to sit, powerless, while everything is done for me, conscious of being conscious, but useless.

People, particularly doctors, have often asked me whether I ever feel like putting an end to it all. In the past I always replied with an emphatic 'no'. When I was misquoted in a certain tabloid newspaper as wanting to commit suicide, I had to write to many well-wishers assuring them that such was not the case. I only got one letter congratulating me on a sensible decision. Now I give a more considered response. At my worst moments, although I would not like to *do* it, I do just wish it could be done peacefully for me, that I could die quietly in my sleep and take the problem away with me. In my better moments I think no such thing.

One of the most depressing elements of all this is the realization of how society treats disabled people. We are the only class who are not encouraged to save. If we have no money, we are supported, at subsistence level, by public expenditure. If we have some savings, we must spend them until we are poor enough to qualify for support – again at subsistence level. Being disabled reduces you, and your family, to the lowest common denominator. In disability alone are all persons equal. Income support, mobility allowance, attendance allowance, invalid care allowance, sickness benefit all whirl together, none are quite what they say they are, none pay for what they say they will, but all are regarded as 'benefits'.

I have been trying to think what good things have come out of all this. Perhaps the publicity about rare brain diseases has made some people feel less alone. Perhaps the formation of a cerebellar branch of the Friedreich's Ataxia Group has given some comfort to a hundred or more souls. For me, the best thing is that I have found my first girlfriend, Pat Earey, again, after nearly thirty years. Our first meeting was a somewhat nervous affair, but then we were able to continue talking as if we had never left off, and she has said that she does not intend to lose touch. Maggie Keswick has also been restored to me. If depression is a prison then they are prison visitors, providing that little tent of blue.

I have found out who my real friends are. It is noticeable how, despite the gaps, the oldest friends have proved the staunchest. It is noticeable, too, how, with certain honourable exceptions, the letters of concern have come from the top of the market – Joan Bakewell, David Dimbleby, James Hogg, David Lomax, Jeremy Paxman, Richard Stilgoe, Alan Whicker, Martin Young – rather than from colleagues with whom one has worked closely and often.

I have found out that my wife is a friend indeed.

I have heard voices that echo across a gap of many years, and I have failed, although I have tried, to answer them all.

Offhand, I can think of few other blessings, try though I might.

I was famous once, and am again, this time for being ill. That is the truth of the matter. The trappings of the fame that goes with radio and television have proved a chimera indeed. The view from my window is as beautiful as ever it was, and is made more poignant by imminent loss. The sheep are gone; the house is on the market. I have been rumbled at last.

I have stopped running. Through standing still I have allowed the escalator to take me down to the very bottom. I find it hard to see a way of picking myself up again. Perhaps writing is the answer. I have had an offer from a newspaper; I have a commercial video to finish; I have been asked to research and write a new Archives programme. If only the depression would go away. I am used to running. Now the best I can do is stand still. Perhaps if I move to the side and reach for the up escalator, there is still a chance. If I grasp the handrail firmly, I will be carried upwards willy-nilly. It will not be as far or as fast, nor will it be so far to fall. But at least it will be up.

LONDON – THE FINAL DAYS

I finished UP THE DOWN ESCALATOR in the nick of time. It was the last work I did, apart from a column I now do (or dictate, after a fashion) thanks to the Manchester Evening News. My condition 'progressed' rapidly, and, apart from finishing the commercial film I had shot, I had to give up the work I had undertaken. I found the last chapters of the book hard to write. Not hard to think WHAT to write (my thinking brain, they say, is still what it was), but hard to get the words down. My friends Sally Hardcastle and Libby Spurrier (with both of whom I stayed), and Jo, looked after me. I finished the book at home, but it was nonetheless with a sigh of relief that I sent the completed manuscript to the publishers. I had written it 'off the top of my head', just as memory dictated, without pausing for research or recollection. Needless to say I received help from my editor, though I was amused to find that the proof-reader was too young to know whether some of the dates of major political events in my past were right or wrong!

Towards the end I was sitting at Sally's, when I knew I couldn't cope any more. I was booked in to the Hewlings-Jackson (Psychiatric) ward of the National Hospital where I stayed for several weeks. Then I went home.

THE OLD HOUSE

This was infinitely superior, but I started fainting again, and Jo found she couldn't pick me up. My doctor rang the National again, and again they very kindly took me in at once. This time I went back to Gower's ward. I stayed there, again for about a month, towards the end of which I realized that Jo was doing too much. She was having to sort out all my papers, find and fill in all the relevant forms, sell the house and a flock of rare-breed sheep at a time when she was getting no help at all from the government, hold a teaching job down, and find a home for me.

Eventually I went home for Christmas and the New Year with some sort of plan. Dr Anita Harding had explained that a colleague of hers, Dr David Stevens, ran an N.H.S. home in Gloucester called Ermin House into which he was prepared to accept me until Jo could sell the house. After that I would alternate between home and Home, so to speak. Jo gave up her teaching job and concentrated on the rest; even so it took a year to sell the old house and convert the new one.

ERMIN HOUSE

I had originally been brought down from the National by my friend Libby Spurrier, and though I walked (with some difficulty) from her car into Ermin House, I could not walk out again.

There have been some good moments. Visits by Jo, Ellie, and friends from London and elsewhere (including Brian Wenham); two trips to London (one to collect a joint prize from the Association of Science Writers for my HORIZON film about research into brain disease, once for the F.B.I. – Frank Bough Interview); complimentary reviews and letters about my book; Television South-West made a tribute/in memoriam film about me, in which Esther, Sue Lawley, Richard Stilgoe and Sue Cook said nice things about working with me, and Kieran Prendiville said (amongst other things) that I was not dead, Jo and Ellie were in it too, and so were my brothers. I was also enormously heartened by two things. One was when my very good friends David Goodland (he used to read the extracts when I presented STOP PRESS), and Sharon Banoff (she produced A LONE VOICE), arranged that my ex-colleagues buy me an electrically-driven trike/wheelchair, which has fantastically increased my mobility. The other thing was that, in order to help the family generally and in particular Jo, with the costs of conversion, four old friends from St John's (known in our family as the Four Just Men), Peter McManus, now an IBM executive, Brian Harrison, now an Oxford don, Ricky Shuttleworth, now a City solicitor, and Cormac Rigby, have, under the patronage of the President of the College, formed a Trust, which has been contributed to by kind contemporaries.

I have my downer moments. The nursing here at Ermin House is first rate. But I can't now stand or walk without support. I can only write and read a few words at a time. And though people say that my speech hasn't deteriorated much since I came here, I am conscious that I have to put more effort into maintaining the same standard. Perhaps my mental state has improved a little since I have been here. Generally I am tired of living, and scared of dying. 'Don't worry' said one nurse 'you'll probably be around to bother us in ten years' time.' 'I can't think what to do this afternoon' I replied, 'let alone in ten years' time.' I still hanker after the old broadcasting days. Many years ago I wrote and presented a programme on radio called THE CLICHE OF BROADCASTING. I concluded that the words most used were 'But first. . . .' In nursing they are 'All right?' I know they are well-meant, but I have taken to replying 'Of course I'm all right. That's why I'm here.'

THE NEW HOUSE

The new house is now nearing completion, and I have made several visits there, as well as a good stint over Christmas and the New Year. Jo has worked very hard; a shower and loo have been installed near my bed, which has been positioned alongside a window overlooking the garden, everything for me is on the ground floor and I am going again on Thursday. I look forward to spending most of the summer there.

Ermin House, Gloucester, Jan., 1991.

Index